OUR TOWN

OUR TOWN
Race, Housing, and the Soul of Suburbia

David L. Kirp, John P. Dwyer,
and Larry A. Rosenthal

RUTGERS UNIVERSITY PRESS
New Brunswick, New Jersey, and London

First paperback printing, 1997

Library of Congress Cataloging-in-Publication Data

Kirp, David L.
    Our town : race, housing, and the soul of suburbia /David L.
    Kirp, John P. Dwyer, Larry A. Rosenthal.
        p.   cm.
    Includes bibliographical references (p.   ) and index.
    ISBN 0-8135-2253-6 (cloth : alk. paper)—
    ISBN 0-8135-2456-3 (pbk.: alk. paper)
    1. Discrimination in housing—New Jersey—Mount Laurel (Township)
I. Dwyer, John P. II. Rosenthal, Larry A., 1959–   . III. Title.
HD7288.76.U52M685   1995
363.5'5'0973—dc20   95-19056
                                                                    CIP

British Cataloging-in-Publication Information available

Copyright © 1995 by David L. Kirp, John P. Dwyer, and Larry A. Rosenthal
Published by Rutgers University Press
Manufactured in the United States of America

To the memory of
Ethel Gertrude Robinson Lawrence

The annals of the civil-rights movement celebrate the deeds of the great and good, Thurgood Marshall and Ralph Abernathy, Andrew Young and John Lewis and Rosa Parks, Julian Bond and Fannie Lou Hamer and, of course, Martin Luther King Jr. Rightly so: without such heroes, there would be little in American race relations to celebrate. Though Ethel Lawrence is by comparison an unknown, because of what she accomplished in her own quiet, persistent way, she belongs on this honor roll.

For more than a quarter of a century, this South Jersey woman, great-great-great-granddaughter of slaves, prayed and pushed to open the suburbs for poor and black families. At the start, the needs of her own family were her inspiration. Soon enough, though, she became a community organizer, speaking out for her neighbors in the small town of Mount Laurel. Later still, she was the moving figure in a series of landmark cases, designed to unlock America's suburbs, upon which this account centers, an inspiration, even for calloused souls, and an unassuming hero for our time.

Contents

Acknowledgments

In the five years since this project first began to take shape, it has depended greatly on the kindnesses of both strangers *and* friends. Without financial support at critical moments from the Faculty Research Program and the Real Estate Center at the University of California, Rutgers University Press, and the Gerbode Foundation, the venture would never have gotten off the ground.

In New Jersey, dozens of people spent countless hours educating us on the folkways and law-ways of that singular state. Our special thanks to John Payne and Martha Lamar, who provided insight into, and lots of primary materials concerning, statewide efforts to promote affordable housing; Kevin Riordan, who offered wise counsel and an invaluable primer on Camden; Angelo Errichetti, who re-created Camden's tempestuous politics; Michael Doyle, who in word and deed represents clarity and justice in a derelict city; Carl Bisgaier, who walked us through the quarter-century history of the *Mount Laurel* case; Dan O'Connor, who tracked down crucial and elusive bits of data; Randy Primus, who offered both a Camden and statewide perspective on policy and politics; Ara Hovnanian and Richard Goodwin, who contributed the wise pragmatism of developers; Eugene Serpentelli, who provided a rich portrait of the exclusionary-zoning litigation over which he presided; and Thomas Kean, Cary Edwards, and John Lynch, who took us behind the scenes of the campaign for the Fair Housing Act.

Two people deserve special mention. Peter O'Connor, the lawyer and nonprofit developer whose efforts are central to the story, gave us invaluable introductions to key players and places, a committed advocate's sense of what was going on, and reams of source material. Without the inspiration of Ethel Lawrence—her tireless work over decades and her patience with those of us who came late to the telling—this book would have been simply an account of how policy gets made, not a textured human drama as well, which is why it is dedicated to her memory.

Colleagues at Berkeley and elsewhere patiently read drafts of the manuscript, offering interpretive insights, thoughts about structure, and corrections of potentially embarrassing factual errors. David Beers made essential suggestions about the structure of the book, reminding us that everything doesn't have to come first. Our thanks to Kristin Luker, John Quigley, Peter Jaret, Amitai Etzioni, Reid Cushman, Robert Kagan, Jennifer Hochschild, David Cohen, Katherine Newman, Lex Kelso, and Eugene Smolensky.

Our agent, Elizabeth Grossman, cares a great deal about writers and writing, a trait less common in the book business than one might assume; she offered smart advice and an occasional shoulder. At Rutgers University Press, copy editor Bobbe Needham tightened the prose; Karen Reeds, Kenneth Arnold, and Steven Maikowski, while never losing their enthusiasm, patiently shepherded a book that took longer in the doing and grew more intricate in the telling than anyone anticipated; once again, they have made publication as pleasurable an enterprise as possible. It is a special pleasure that the cover was designed by Adrian Card, friend and artistic fellow traveler.

OUR TOWN

Shades of Fear—
Mount Laurel and Beyond

Beat! Beat! drums!—Blow, bugles blow!
Thro' the windows—thro' the doors—burst like a ruthless force,
Into the solemn church, and scatter the congregation.

Walt Whitman, "Memories of Lincoln"

The day was unseasonably warm for an autumn Sunday in southern New Jersey. Inside Jacob's Chapel in the town of Mount Laurel, some twenty miles east of Philadelphia, the recently restored stained-glass windows were opened wide to catch the breeze. For the sixty members of the all-black African Methodist Episcopalian congregation who were present, this October 1970 Sunday was a special day. The congregation had invited a committeeman to announce the town's response to a plan to rezone thirty-two acres of land so that thirty-six garden apartments could be built for poor, mostly local, and mostly black families.

The pews were old and worn, salvaged from another church and sawn down to fit the small room, but the parishioners sat alert to what the committeeman would say. Prominent among them were Mary Robinson, one of the elders in the congregation, and her daughter, Ethel Lawrence, forty-two years old, who earlier that morning had played the piano, as she always did for Sunday services. Both mother and daughter were members of a community group that had written the housing proposal, then secured the funds needed to take an option on those thirty-two acres, and so what the committeeman had to say mattered especially to them. All around them, new housing developments, with their sprawling ranches and ersatz Taras, were transforming Mount Laurel from a small rural community to a booming suburb and pricing local residents out of their hometown. The new homes were vital if the next generation—Ethel's *children's* generation—were to remain in Mount Laurel.

The mood in Jacob's Chapel was guardedly optimistic. Despite some preliminary setbacks at earlier township council meetings, demands to redraw plans and then redraw them again, the parishioners believed things could be worked out; after all, blacks and whites in Mount Laurel were hardly strangers to one another. Black families had lived in the township since late in the seventeenth century, first as slaves and later as tenant farmers. To the most venerable of the black families, the Gaineses and the Stills, their manumission papers, which dated from the American Revolution, were their most prized possessions.

A third of a millennium is a very long time. The Quaker families, whose ancestry dated back an equally long time, knew the black community very well. Generation upon generation, blacks and whites had grown up together and worked the white families' farms together; in hard times they had helped each other out with food and firewood. There had been little overt opposition when, soon after World War II, blacks sought an end to racially separate public schools. Blacks and whites regarded one another as friends—though friends who knew, and kept to, their respective places—and surely friends didn't turn one another away.

But if the committeeman had this history on his mind, he didn't let on. Nostalgia was irrelevant to, even inconsistent with, suburbanization. As someone who was committed to the kind of growth that spelled prosperity— "good ratables," as New Jersey politicians said, meaning development that generates lots of tax dollars and requires few public outlays—he was unsympathetic to low-income housing. Such housing meant poor people, who carried with them the taint of urban miseries, who would harm the town's image and scare away the new money. In particular it meant poor *black* people, refugees from the upheavals in the derelict city of Camden, fifteen miles to the east, and that signaled trouble. Poor people, even those whose families had lived there for many generations, didn't fit into this pretty picture. The town's zoning ordinance didn't allow garden apartments or any other multifamily housing anywhere in Mount Laurel, and that, said the committeeman, was exactly how things were going to stay: the township council would never approve the community group's request.

Ethel Lawrence and the others in Jacob's Chapel recall what was said as if the words were a brand that sears the skin. After talking about all the changes that were fast coming to Mount Laurel, the new prosperity that this once sleepy farm town was enjoying, he came to the punch line. *"If you people"—you poor and black people, that is—"can't afford to live in our town, then you'll just have to leave."*

You people: The committeeman had transformed neighbors and helpmates into insiders and outsiders, those who belonged to "our town" and those who didn't. The bonds of neighborliness and friendship, the pull and tug of history—these went unmentioned, for they had all become irrelevant in a world where money was the single measure of status and belonging. In that world, the power of law would be used not to promote the idea of community but instead to enshrine exclusivity by walling out the poor.

An angry murmur arose among the congregation as the committee-man spoke. No one confronted him, because that wasn't how things were done, but his message outraged Mary Robinson and Ethel Lawrence. Later, when the news reached Reverend Stuart Wood, he was just as furious. Wood was a white Presbyterian minister who had come to this fast-growing town with the task of carving out a mission from the suburban wilderness. He had spent months drafting the housing proposal with the local community group, some of whose members lived in falling-down converted chicken coops, where the drinking water was polluted by human waste—tarpaper houses that could burn to the ground, with deadly consequences, in an instant. To reject the idea of housing the poor on grounds of simple economics seemed to the minister an unchristian act of selfishness.

The minister didn't hesitate to speak his mind—not only to his indifferent suburban neighbors but also in poverty-plagued Camden, where liberation-minded ministers and radical Legal Services lawyers were using demonstrations and lawsuits to promote a social agenda based on equity. The lawyers heard the Mount Laurel story and decided it was time to bring their equalitarian agenda to the suburbs.

"I thought they'd say, 'This is much too big!' " Reverend Wood recalls, thinking back to the first time he met with the attorneys in Ethel Lawrence's home. "Instead they said, 'When can we get going?' "

That fateful moment in Jacob's Chapel—the Sunday when it was decreed, on behalf of those who ran things, that "if you people can't afford to live in our town, then you'll just have to leave"—marked the beginning of fifteen years of path-breaking litigation. The *Mount Laurel* cases, as they came to be known, affected not just this one township. Those rulings put the concept of "fair share" on the public agenda and forced a wholesale revision of zoning across the state. Their impact reached far beyond New Jersey, affecting policies from Massachusetts to California, as *Mount Laurel* became the *Roe v. Wade* of fair housing, the *Brown v. Board of Education* of exclusionary zoning.

Ethel Lawrence was personally transformed in the process—from being a devoted mother and good neighbor who had lived her life in a little-known town, she became as well the symbol of a cause. She put aside the fretfulness of her family and the hostility of onetime friends, refused to be intimidated by threats of violence, and stayed committed to what she believed in perfect faith was the right thing to do. What Ethel Lawrence accomplished is as memorable and brave as, if less well-known than, Rosa Parks's refusal to move to the back of the bus for a white man in Montgomery, Alabama. A boulevard in Detroit, where Rosa Parks has lived for years, commemorates her courage and the civil-rights movement whose beginning is associated with her principled act of disobedience. If all goes well, Ethel Lawrence will soon have her own fitting memorial: 140 homes in Mount Laurel, set aside for poor families. Those homes will stand as a small but important rebuttal to what has seemed unstoppable: the secession of America's suburbs into racially segregated enclaves, a social development pernicious enough to warrant the name of apartheid—apartheid American style.

Fear and Loathing in Suburbia

Variations on what happened in Mount Laurel during the past quarter century occurred in and around New York City and Chicago, Detroit and Los Angeles—indeed, in almost every community in the country where poor and minority families have sought to find shelter. The story provides a lens through which to glimpse how the broader social contract has been rewritten—a lens through which to examine the demise of the historically urban impulse to boost the chances of the poor and of racial minorities, and the rise of a suburban majority, at once powerful and insecure, determined on separation and self-preservation.

For an instant in the nation's history, the period between the inauguration of John Kennedy in 1961 and the Vietnam-induced decimation of Lyndon Johnson's presidency barely seven years later, the passions of people like Rosa Parks and Ethel Lawrence became pivotal concerns for the republic at large, as Kennedy's New Frontier and Johnson's Great Society enlarged the national creed to include the poor and black. "What's good for General Motors is good for the nation," Charles Wilson famously said during his 1953 confirmation hearings as secretary of defense in Dwight Eisenhower's cabinet, but during the 1960s this view of government changed. While the fate of industry still mattered, what was good for the hollows and the ghettos—expanded opportunities for the poor and minorities—was *also* good for the nation. Out of this moment came federal initiatives like the Community Action Program, which reached into Mount Laurel to nurture Ethel Lawrence's Springville Action Council, and the Legal Services Program, which paid the salaries of the attorneys who challenged Mount Laurel's zoning rules in court.

Providing housing that poor families can afford and setting aside a fair share of suburbia for the impoverished: those items are now nowhere to be found on the national agenda. The language of equality is gone, replaced in policy-speak by buzzwords like *competitiveness* and *excellence*. Even modest attempts by Washington to provide something of value to inner-city teens, such as midnight basketball, are mocked as a waste of public dollars. The Republicans' "Contract with America," the dogma on which the party swept to power in Washington in 1994, is so unashamedly hostile to the claims of the have-lesses that it amounts to a declaration of class warfare.

That election confirmed the triumph of suburbia in American politics, a process that began at least as far back as Richard Nixon's "southern strategy" a generation earlier; and this triumph has been accompanied by deep antagonism toward the nation's poor and minority citizenry. In the 1992 presidential election, suburbanites cast the majority of votes for the first time in the nation's history. They rejected a lackluster Republican incumbent in favor of a challenger who campaigned as a new Democrat (as distinguished from a New Frontier–Great Society, tax-and-spend Democrat), a politician committed not to the ethic of redistribution but rather to the interests of a middle class that saw itself as under siege. One year later, Republican Christine Todd Whitman, a political neophyte, became New Jersey's governor on a platform that paid no attention to the impoverished cities of the Garden State, the most famous but hardly the only suburbanite GOP triumph that year; and in Michigan, a Republican governor made himself wildly popular by cutting off all welfare payments to adults without children.

Long-term New York governor Mario Cuomo's urbanness contributed to his defeat in 1994 by a little-known Republican from upstate named George Pataki, whose open hostility to New York City prompted that city's Republican mayor to cross party lines and endorse Cuomo. All across the country in the 1994 elections, Bill Clinton was repudiated by the voters, who for the first time in forty years gave the GOP a majority in both the Senate and the House of Representatives. So tainted was Clintonism that not a single Democratic nonincumbent was elected to a state or federal office. It was the president's "old Democrat" ways, the pundits said—his failure to "end welfare as we know it," as promised; his concern for gays in the military, not the middle class—that did him in.

The story of Mount Laurel—the township, the landmark case, the national symbol—implicates race as well as class. If the poor fare badly in this country, the *black* poor do much worse. Their realistic options for decent housing outside the ghetto, as well as for decent schools and jobs, are fewer, and the barriers to success are higher.

"We are rapidly becoming two societies, one black and the other white, separate and unequal": so the Kerner Commission, appointed by Lyndon Johnson to analyze the state of U.S. race relations, concluded in 1968, and that report commanded sufficient attention for a mass-market publisher to rush the report into print. In the twilight of Johnson's presidency, civil rights became a reality—blacks could vote and Jim Crow segregation was fast disappearing—but the economic condition of black America had not changed much. The gap between the black poor and the rest of the nation was apparently widening. The ghetto is a "prison," said the Reverend Martin Luther King Jr. in *Where Do We Go from Here*, his last book, which he wrote after the failure of his campaign to bring about integration in Chicago. The book's subtitle bluntly posed the choice: *Chaos or Community?* Then, the belief was widespread that if something wasn't done to better the lives of the poor, especially the black poor, the race riots of the sixties would be the prelude to an American doomsday.

This is the historical moment when the Mount Laurel story begins to unfold, with an appeal for social justice on behalf of blacks and the poor initially voiced in the political chambers of the town and the state, then in the courts. That moral claim was particularly strong in Mount Laurel Township, where a black community that had been in place for centuries was effectively being driven out of its own town, but the broader contention was that blacks everywhere deserved a fair share of the benefits of suburban life.

Today the view that racial justice requires intervention by government is anathema to the white middle class. While African Americans perceive little progress in race relations in the last twenty years, whites are inclined to the belief that racial discrimination is a bad memory. By now blacks have gotten their due, whites believe—more than their due, come to that. Middle America, which deeply distrusts the capacity of government, politicians and judges alike, to do good, places its faith mainly in the power of unregulated economic growth to solve our country's problems. Since the 1980s, writes Gary Orfield, a leading student of U.S. race relations, "the root assumption of educational and social policy [has been] that government [could] do little to produce social progress and that liberal reforms"—welfare and food stamps and subsidized housing—"had unanticipated consequences that made things worse. . . . The hope for a solution [has been] transferred to the market. If the economy could expand sufficiently . . . the savings would . . . produce an economic boom that would put low-income minority people to work."

Those who have moved to suburbs like Mount Laurel—who have sunk their life savings into their homes and mortgaged their futures as well—are motivated by a desire for a better life, not just a greener and more leafy place but one that is also more secure. Pointedly, they have left the city as blacks have been moving in, or else they have moved away from the innermost ring of suburbs, which in recent years has witnessed an influx of blacks. The very last thing they want to do is to assume responsibility for those whom they deliberately left behind.

The suburbanites' view, consistently expressed to pollsters and at the ballot box, is that their tax dollars should be returned to their own communities, not distributed in the fashion of a Lady Bountiful to the needy elsewhere. Suburban residents have been very ready to do whatever has seemed necessary, including spending large sums of their own money, to keep the disadvantaged at bay, to make them forbidden neighbors. In this, as in so much else, Mount Laurel was typical: when the *Mount Laurel* fight was being waged in the courts, the town reduced its usual array of public services in order to spend well over a million dollars on the cause; other communities, drawn into the fray, collected war chests of as much as two thousand dollars for every resident, a tidy sum indeed, to underwrite the legal campaign against housing the poor in their backyards.

These citizens regard such matters not in terms of policy choices, rights, and rules, but very personally, as intimately bound up with their own life stories. As one Mount Laurel resident, voicing a suburban commonplace, said: "No way do I feel I should subsidize a fifty-thousand-dollar home for them. Nobody's doing it for me. . . . Nobody has a right to say anybody owes them anything." The temptation is almost irresistible to construct one's own history as a triumph of rugged individualism, but the Mount Laurel chronicles show that, in this and so many other ways, something more than the pioneering spirit was at work. In fact, the rules of government and a rigged private market have greatly eased the way for white and middle-class families while shutting the door on minorities.

Partly this is a matter of social class, partly a matter of race. In New Jersey as elsewhere, public housing for the poor was rarely erected in suburbia because those communities refused to allow it. Public housing in the cities wasn't built to fit in existing neighborhoods but instead was constructed in such gargantuan proportions as to amount to separate worlds, and that housing was usually segregated. Sometimes the segregation was official (as in St. Louis, where in 1955 the mammoth Pruitt Tower was built for whites, the equally monumental Igoe Tower for blacks), while elsewhere segregation was predictable from the sites that were chosen.

Publicly subsidized housing for the middle class—Federal Housing Administration mortgages by another, ruder name—was an even more powerful force for separation. Since the 1930s the FHA has insured mortgages for suburban homes, and these have been much easier for whites than blacks, even with comparable incomes, to secure. In the suburb-shaping years between 1930 and 1960, fewer than 1 percent of all mortgages in the nation were issued to African Americans. Banks have regularly refused to make loans in neighborhoods populated by minorities—in the case of a heavily minority community like Camden, this "redlining" encircled the entire city—and so have contributed to their economic demise. Black families consistently report a desire to live in racially integrated neighborhoods, but whites' preferences for segregation have prevailed. Real-estate brokers have done their part to maintain the color line by making it a standard practice to deny blacks access to "white" neighborhoods. Because of these cumulative acts of prejudice, black families spend more on housing while getting fewer choices and worse quality; middle-class blacks wind up with housing no better than what poor whites are able to obtain.

Zoning has been the chief instrument by which suburbs have held themselves apart from the poor, which is why the *Mount Laurel* cases focus on the power to zone. Once, overtly racial zoning was routine and certain neighborhoods were designated as "white." While that practice was outlawed by the U.S. Supreme Court many years ago, subtler forms of discrimination, focused more on economics than on race, were substituted. Defenders of suburbia are fond of describing these rules—which, as in Mount Laurel Township, fixed a minimum house size and building-lot size and prohibited multifamily dwellings—as representing the will of the people. But since zoning decisions are made entirely by the town's present residents, they alone have the power to decide what is in everyone's best interest—to decide who gets to live in *our* town, now and into the future.

In many ways, blacks and the poor have been downed by law. Until the *Mount Laurel* case, judges in New Jersey and elsewhere had ruled that the "general welfare" meant whatever local residents said it did. Suburbanites in New Jersey and elsewhere also enjoyed the politicians' support. Despite repeated warnings from a succession of governors, Republican and Democratic alike, that fencing the poor into the dying cities meant eventual social calamity, legislators who represented the suburban interests succeeded in keeping things as they were; local authority—the authority to exclude—was the "Battle Hymn of the Republic" in state politics.

The separation of housing along racial lines, promoted through the rules of financing and zoning, shaped public-school enrollments as well. Although suburban politicians insist that it isn't local school boards but the housing market that causes segregated schools, this is sophistry. Towns typically draw their school attendance zones to coincide with segregated neighborhoods, and states routinely shape school-district boundaries to correspond with city limits. Decisions about who attends what school affect more than the racial mix; they also affect the quality of instruction. Since in many states public education is paid for mainly from local property taxes, schools with mostly white and middle-class students commonly have more to spend than schools where minority youngsters predominate. This pattern is vivid in New Jersey, where over the years wealthy suburban school districts have been able to spend two or three times more to educate each student than financially strapped cities like Camden.

The ramifications of segregated housing reach beyond educational opportunities to shape many other aspects of life, institutionalizing broader forms of segregation. Suburbs and the newer "edge cities" have, for instance, been able to attract business and industry that mean jobs by promising them relatively low tax rates. It is no coincidence that across the country there exists what social scientists describe as a "spatial mismatch," with blacks concentrated in the cities, far from the service-sector jobs in the suburbs, because "there are powerful relationships between residential segregation and the quality of education, the quality of housing, the availability of jobs, and income level." Meanwhile, as the suburbs prosper, all that remains for the Camdens of the republic are the burdens—the raw waste and, in the illusionless political calculus, the human debris as well.

Much of this is so familiar as to sound like a recital of the facts of life, but it doesn't describe the way things *had* to be. There is no necessary reason for school assignment to depend on residence, for example, nor is it axiomatic that cities must decay—elsewhere in the developed world, social patterns look entirely different. In these segregated U.S. communities, the cordoning off of whites from blacks, and the well off from the poor, has resulted neither from the wish of minorities to remain ghettoized nor from the invisible hand of a smoothly humming economy. Instead, that segregation has been the product of explicit policy choices. Division along the lines of race and social class, an American commonplace, has been deliberately brought about and maintained by rules of a game that operates as a subtle apartheid.

This is the story of Mount Laurel Township, which like so many other towns refused to allow even a handful of apartments for poor families to be built within its precincts. But while the drama of Mount Laurel is similar in so many ways to the suburban saga, the proverbial universe in a grain of sand, it is in the end a special and hopeful drama. Mount Laurel is the place where the commonplace has made history— where everything could conceivably change.

Going Home

Landmark cases and social movements as well have a way of beginning with small, seemingly insignificant events. The refusal of an all-white school board to replace a broken-down bus for the colored public school in Clarendon County, South Carolina, was the final indignity for African American parents in that rural community, who concluded that for their children's sake they had to go to court. They won their case and much more in 1954, when the U.S. Supreme Court in *Brown v. Board of Education* declared that government could not require blacks to attend separate schools.

So too in Mount Laurel, a minor incident in an out-of-the-way place reverberated—and reverberates still—across the nation's suburban landscape. What the New Jersey judges said in their *Mount Laurel* opinions about the obligation of suburbs to make it "realistically possible" for poor families to find homes there represents the most important zoning decision since the U.S. Supreme Court ruled, nearly three-quarters of a century earlier, that zoning itself was constitutional.

By moving aggressively to remake the suburbs, the New Jersey Supreme Court—like the U.S. Supreme Court in the segregation cases and in the school-prayer, criminal-rights, and abortion cases as well—opened a Pandora's box of questions about judicial activism and political authority. Of all these famously important and divisive cases, *Mount Laurel* strikes closest to *home,* literally and figuratively. It made America reconsider what it meant when it uttered that single, loaded word.

This tale of the making of that landmark decision, and all that has followed, is filled with the nuances of constitutional doctrine; accounts of the fleeting, fickle nature of prosperity; the impact of the next election on the actions of political leaders; the humdrum of bureaucratically managed policy. It also describes the thoughts and actions of the leading players in a long-running drama: a chief justice who ordered up a revolution, then backed away; a governor who denounced the court's decree as "communistic," then institutionalized key elements of that decree; a master builder who became the architect of the fair-housing bureaucracy; a single-minded law reformer committed to a socially integrated vision of America.

Perhaps the most important player of all is a woman abidingly concerned about her family's future in what, for generations, had been their hometown. Were it not for her persistence—the example she set for neighbors, lawyers, politicians, and judges—there might well be no *Mount Laurel* doctrine to dissect, no fair-share law to understand. While the story swings from township meeting to courtroom argument to legislative session, from Mount Laurel to Trenton, New Jersey's diminutive capital, then to Washington, D.C., and back again, it begins with the long series of events, in a city and one of its suburbs, that eventually led some unlikely guests to drink coffee and plot strategy in the cozy living room of Ethel Lawrence.

PART ONE
THE DEMISE OF A CITY, THE RISE OF A SUBURB

I guess we're all hunting like everybody else for a way the diligent and sensible can rise to the top and the lazy and quarrelsome can sink to the bottom. But it ain't easy to find. Meanwhile, we do all that we can to help those that can't help themselves and those that can we leave alone.

Thornton Wilder, *Our Town*

You could see a town lying ahead in its whole, as definitely formed as a plate on a table. And your road entered and ran straight through it, laid out for your passage through. Towns, like people, had clear identities and your imagination could go out to meet them.

Eudora Welty, *One Writer's Beginnings*

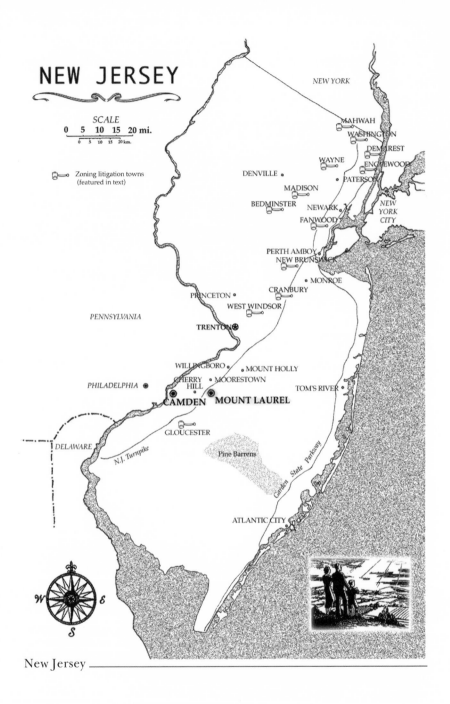

NEW JERSEY

SCALE

0   5   10   15   20 mi.

0   5   10   15   20 km.

Zoning litigation towns
(featured in text)

NEW YORK

MAHWAH
WASHINGTON
DEMAREST
WAYNE
ENGLEWOOD
DENVILLE
PATERSON
MADISON
BEDMINSTER
NEWARK
NEW
FANWOOD
YORK
CITY
PERTH AMBOY
NEW BRUNSWICK
MONROE
CRANBURY
PRINCETON
WEST WINDSOR

PENNSYLVANIA

TRENTON

WILLINGBORO   MOUNT HOLLY
CHERRY   MOORESTOWN
PHILADELPHIA   HILL
TOM'S RIVER
CAMDEN   **MOUNT LAUREL**
GLOUCESTER
DELAWARE
N.J. Turnpike
Pine Barrens
Camden State Parkway
ATLANTIC CITY

W   E

S

New Jersey

MOUNT LAUREL

1 JACOB'S CHAPEL
2 SPRINGVILLE
3 ETHEL LAWRENCE'S HOUSE
4 RUDDEROW FARM
5 LARCHMONT (HAINES FARM)
6 TRICIA MEADOWS
7 PROPOSED FAIR HOUSING SITE
   (IN MEMORY OF ETHEL LAWRENCE)
8 PROPOSED FAIR HOUSING SITE
   (IN MEMORY OF MARY ROBINSON)
9 RANCOCAS WOODS
10 RAMBLEWOOD
11 BIRCHFIELD
12 BETSY RANSOME'S NURSERY
13 MUNICIPAL BLDGS.
14 MOUNT LAUREL (164' elev.)
15 QUAKER MEETING HOUSE

    INDUSTRIAL/COMMERCIAL

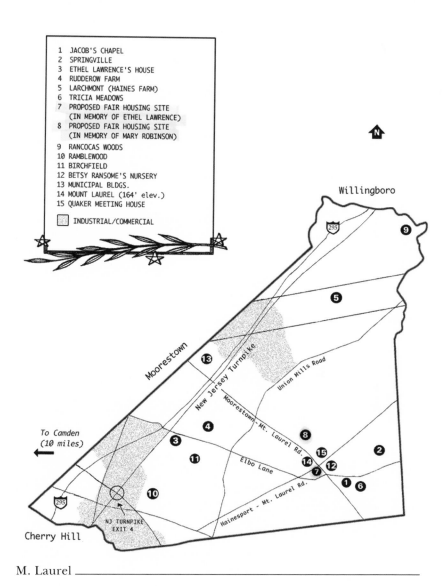

N

Willingboro

Moorestown

New Jersey Turnpike

Union Mills Road

Moorestown - Mt. Laurel Rd.

Elbo Lane

Hainesport - Mt. Laurel Rd.

To Camden
(10 miles)

295

NJ TURNPIKE
EXIT 4

Cherry Hill

M. Laurel

2

Camden: A City
Doomed by Design

Cities and suburbs in the United States are intertwined in a sometimes symbiotic, other times parasitic, relationship. Although they generally elect their own officials, set their own tax rates, and build their own public buildings, neither gets to shape its own future, for both are players in the larger drama of remapping the republic. In this ongoing theater, Mount Laurel and Camden serve as singular communities as well as stand-ins for many other locales. The swift and awful demise of all the Camdens in the nation has contributed greatly to the rise of all the Mount Laurels—and to the fierce suburbanite ambition to maintain a wall of separation between city and suburb.

It is the unhappy fate of some cities to grow up, largely unloved, in the shadow of greater cities. There is St. Paul, dwarfed by Minneapolis; Newark, overwhelmed by New York City; Tacoma, downwind from Seattle; and East St. Louis, the poor cousin of St. Louis across the Mississippi. Most famously there is Oakland, California, an ungainly span of steel and a cultural light-year away from San Francisco, forever cursed by Gertrude Stein's jibe that "there is no there there."

Camden, New Jersey, is such a place, unloved and mostly unlovely. Never mind the fact that, as the city's claque of boosters will point out, Walt Whitman spent the last two decades of his life there—that this poet who created chant-songs of America's great possibility used the money admirers gave him for a summer place to build himself a mausoleum in the local cemetery, that his odes to the strength of cities became memorialized in Camden granite. Never mind, either, those brave slogans in which from time to time Camden has cloaked itself—"the city of opportunity," "the city that makes everything from fountain pens to battleships," or, in a paean to its diminutiveness, "the biggest little city in the nation."

The very first sentence of Camden's official history, published in 1976, carries the defensive ring of a city perpetually victimized by its location directly across the Delaware River from Philadelphia: "For too long, the story of Camden has been obscured by that of Philadelphia." Fifty years earlier, W. C. Fields had made the same point more pungently. Camden, said the famously unkind comedian, "is the pimple on Philadelphia's ass."

For the better part of the present century, Camden has been trying to remake itself in the image of the new: first as the hub of industry and business; then as an urban enclave walled off from ghetto and suburb alike; nowadays as the latest exemplar of urban revivalism, the newest Baltimore, complete with its own aquarium. There have been moments when it appeared that Camden might find its niche—might become that "biggest little city" of its self-proclaimed fantasies—but these all faded. "Where there is no vision, the people perish": that biblical prophecy is chiseled into the eroding walls of city hall. In fact, Camden has mostly been a city of myopic and not visionary leaders, planners and politicians endlessly capable of self-delusion, promise makers with neither memory nor political sense.

To say it plainly, Camden, like many other cities, was doomed by design. For all the local missteps, its undoing has been mostly the work of outsiders—those who run things in the adjoining suburbs, in the state house at Trenton, and in the housing and highway bureaucracies of Washington. Initially they drew the boundaries that cordoned off Camden, hemming it in to less than nine square miles. Then the outsiders systematically proceeded to undermine, to loot, and finally to abandon it. In this, Camden differs from other municipalities only in the extent of the depredation it has suffered. "Our highly urbanized country has chosen"—*chosen*—"to have powerless cities," writes land-use scholar Gerald Frug, "and this choice has largely been made through legal doctrine that is neither a deduction from neutral principles nor a reflection of the development of modern society."

As Camden fell from grace, the surrounding suburbs were booming, first those in the inner ring and later towns like Mount Laurel a few miles farther away. This too has been by design. Just as bucolic Camden profited at the expense of plague-ridden Philadelphia in the eighteenth century, so too in the last half century the suburbs have prospered from the miseries of a metropolis that once entertained the fabulous notion of competing for trade not just with Philadelphia but with New York City itself.

At least since the 1920s, when the Ben Franklin Bridge linking Camden to Philadelphia was opened, in the process ruining a venerable residential neighborhood and allowing suburbanites to avoid Camden entirely on their way to Philadelphia, urban demise has been associated with suburban triumph. Then, when those suburbs refused to merge into a greater Camden, as was proposed a few years later, the city was effectively finished as a viable entity, a fact that became increasingly plain in succeeding decades. This is why, in order to understand the rise of suburbs like Mount Laurel, intent on keeping themselves apart from the nation's race and class woes, it is necessary first to appreciate how cities such as Camden were done in.

From Backwater to Boomtown

"Ye most invitingst place to settle by": that is how, more than three centuries ago, Quaker land-agent Robert Zane described the land around Camden. Of course there were *already* settlers, the Lenni Lenape Indians, who had been living on this land for more than a millennium when the Europeans, first the Dutch and Swedes, later the English, began to arrive. By 1677, though, the English had bought off the natives for a purchase price that encompassed all the temptations of modernity: blankets, kettles, needles, pipes, fishhooks, bells, combs, Jews' harps, brandy, and guns. Barely a half century later, the Lenni Lenape were mostly gone, decimated by smallpox and tuberculosis, and much of the land had been cleared for farming.

The attention of enterprising colonizers was fixed elsewhere, north to New York City or across the river in Philadelphia, while Camden was a backwater. The Duke of York had deeded all the lands between the Hudson and Delaware rivers, the territory that today roughly comprises New Jersey, to two courtiers who had given him sanctuary during the Cromwellian revolt against the monarchy. One of them, Lord Berkeley, soon became destitute, and in 1673 he sold his share to two Quakers, John Fenwick and Edward Byllynge. Although these early developers touted South Jersey as "the place / to add to beauty's brightest grace," the region that became known as Camden County played a more mundane role in colonial affairs. It was country cousin to Philadelphia, provisioning that bustling town with such staples as pinewood, melons, and pork sausage.

The network of turnpikes built shortly after the American Revolution, which directly connected the emerging cities of the Northeast, bypassed Camden, and so the city was consigned to continuing economic marginality. Only when Philadelphia was decimated by plague in 1793 did that city's residents come flocking in sizable numbers to South Jersey, urbanites fleeing "great Mortality and Sickness" for the healthier life of the country. Camden's first major developer, Philadelphia merchant Jacob Cooper, praised the site because it was near—but not too near—city life, the ideal setting for "gardening . . . the diversion of fishing and fowling . . . the pleasure of sailing on the water in summer." This new land of America, wrote Hector St. Jean Crevecoeur in *Letters from an American Farmer*, formed villages like Camden in a "pleasing uniformity of decent competence," its streets lined with plain-fronted, three-story brick houses. By the middle of the twentieth century, residents of Camden, which by then was a city in its own right, would resume this journey to the hinterlands, taking flight from perceived urban sicknesses of another kind.

In the aftermath of the Civil War, Camden enjoyed its first boom. Until then, the city's mayor candidly acknowledged, there had been few reasons "to dispose anyone to adopt this as a permanent place of residence" rather than a summer retreat, yet in just a few years a sewer system was installed, gaslights brightened the streets, and horse-drawn streetcars plied the avenues. There was already ferry service to Philadelphia, but new railroad lines greatly speeded and so expanded commerce. Factories began to open, among them the steel-pen company of Richard Esterbrook and the Camden Iron Works, as well as plants that produced lumber, woolen goods, carriages, and chemicals. Joseph Campbell started a modest canning plant in 1869, which eventually would expand into the soup business. On Cooper Street, named for the town's first developer, mansions were built for these merchants and industrialists, as well as for the doctors and lawyers who catered to them.

The city's centennial history, published in 1876, was largely devoted to celebrating this urban coming-of-age, and the 1880 census confirmed that Camden had made itself into the most important city in New Jersey. It was the forty-fourth-biggest city in the United States, with thirteen local schools and thirty-two churches. Its leaders hoped for much bigger things, predicting that within a decade Camden would challenge even New York City, with "water frontage . . . the equal of any harbor in the country." Companies that represented the newest technologies started moving to Camden. Victor Talking Machine Company, later renamed RCA Victor, built its first factory there in 1890; the New York Shipbuilding Company also broke ground that year, and a decade later, at the beginning of the new century, the firm launched its first ship. This was the city whose praises Walt Whitman had sung, and, when the poet died in 1892, in the city that local newspapers took to calling "America's Stratford," three thousand people filed past the casket of the man who had become the bard of democracy.

But economic transformation did not guarantee respect. Camden was "worse than Philadelphia" in its wickedness, the *Philadelphia Daily News* editorialized. There were frequent labor troubles, as newly organized unions—the Knights of Labor, later the American Federation of Labor—launched strikes to organize workers, and the unions encountered no little head-bashing resistance from the companies they struck.

Race relations in the city were strained and sometimes bloody. A century before the American Revolution, black families had lived in Camden as house and field slaves, and as late as 1820 there were still slaves on the local census rolls. Emancipated blacks were cordoned off into separate neighborhoods such as Kaignsville—a city map from the 1830s shows a garden there, set aside "for the people of color"—and in the years before the Civil War, the Underground Railroad ferried hundreds of escaped slaves through Camden, northward to New York and beyond. South Jersey had more than its share of pro-southern sentiment before the Civil War (the first Camden-to-Philadelphia ferry, launched in 1835, was named the *States Rights*), and few voters sided with candidates who favored abolition. During the Civil War, even as black Camdenites were putting their lives on the line, volunteering for the colored infantry brigades, a group of black men went to a South Camden bar and asked to be served. They were set upon and beaten by a mob of white patrons who pursued them to their homes. Some fought back, hurling stones and firing rifles from their rooftops; it took several days for city police and firefighters as well as the state militia to restore calm. Commenting on this episode, the *Camden Democrat* assailed the city's African Americans as "a brutal race," a racial libel that presumably reflected the predominant views of its readers.

South Jersey was part of a broad belt, from southern Illinois through Delaware, whose white citizens were hostile to civil rights for former slaves. New Jersey's blacks were finally granted the franchise in time for the 1870 election, but fights broke out at Camden polling places when whites tried to prevent blacks from registering. Well into the twentieth century, the regime of Jim Crow held sway. Blacks who wandered into "white" neighborhoods of Camden were driven off, and on several occasions lynch mobs were formed. "If I have any 'rights which a white man is bound to respect,' " a prominent black businessman named Dempsey Butler said despairingly, "I scarcely know what they are."

Corruption in Camden was entirely out of control, even by the freewheeling political standards of the era. "The worst of Public Robbers" is how the New Jersey state attorney, himself a Camden resident, characterized local officials. Philadelphia's *Daily News* looked across the river and held its nose. "Camden is a pest hole of political corruption. It is the sink into which all that is vile in politics flows. No hamlet, town or city in the whole union has such an infamous political history."

"Camden city government's attitude toward business is one of sincere, helpful cooperation at all times," became the political rallying cry, a homily that translated into favoring big businesses at the expense of the citizenry. In 1908, a street railway line was relocated for the convenience of the Pennsylvania Railroad Company, even though the change disrupted the settled patterns of a neighborhood. By no means would this be the last time the city's politicians gave the concerns of ordinary Camdenites short shrift.

"A Future So Great"

In Camden's long march toward recognition, Independence Day 1926 was widely seen as marking a decisive moment. On that warm and humid afternoon, the world's longest suspension bridge—the Benjamin Franklin

Bridge, almost two miles from end to end, 380 feet above the high-tide mark, built at the unheard-of cost of thirty-seven million dollars—was dedicated, linking Camden with Philadelphia. President Calvin Coolidge made an appearance at the festivities, and though it was a typically understated Coolidge performance, less than half an hour from arrival to departure and without an audible word, no one seemed to mind. As Philadelphians strolled across the span, many of them setting foot in Camden for the first time, a reporter jotted down a typical reaction. "It's just like Philadelphia, only it's cleaner." A jubilant spokesman for the Chamber of Commerce gushed that the Ben Franklin Bridge

> opened like a Sesame, the door of what almost overnight became a new commercial era to Camden and its surrounding suburbs. Commerce danced to the staccato of riveters' hammers on its sturdy steel frames, soon to prove as tuneful as a Pied Piper's pipes. Concrete and stone rose where shingles squatted. Country-rutted lanes sunk to oblivion beneath glistening coats of asphalt. . . . The country watched, waited, and prepared for the Bridge that in any accurate history must be recorded definitely as one of the most important events of the century, for whatever had been needed to awaken or revive the vitality of trade came with the completion of this venture into progress.

Philadelphia magazine waxed respectful, although reminding readers of Camden's decidedly mixed reputation. "No Camden joke on the vaudeville stage would be applauded if the audience knew Camden. Camden is serious business. It is a city of 105,000 busy people."

The opening of the bridge was the triumphal centerpiece of a campaign known as the Greater Camden Movement, which had been organized by a group of city business and government leaders. Two years earlier, at the dedication of the Walt Whitman Hotel—a million-dollar establishment described by the *West Jersey Press* as "a grand hotel, second to none in the state"—one local official delivered a purplish paean. "Today Camden stands upon the threshold of a future so great in its possibilities that no one will be so bold as to even attempt to outline the extent thereof nor the limit thereto." The new hotel was more than an urban wonderment; it also meant that world-class business had a hostelry in the city, and it sparked a downtown building boom. Horn and Hardart Automat opened a branch, and so did the Stanley Theatre, another million-dollar venture. Every major retail chain on the eastern seaboard had a store in Camden, and in the go-go years of the late 1920s, choice business properties were selling for several thousand dollars a square foot. The immodest intention of the Greater Camden Movement was to convert the city into a metropolitan center to rival Philadelphia. Already, ocean-going vessels were embarking for the Pacific coast from the city's expanded port; a new railroad terminal provided additional transportation tie-ins; and when an airport opened in Camden offering flights to Europe, Amelia Earhart and Charles Lindbergh flew in to deliver words of praise.

The Ben Franklin Bridge and the highway leading away from the bridge across New Jersey were intended mostly to benefit the suburbs just then coming into being—not villages like Mount Laurel, then regarded as too far away for commuting, but closer-in communities like Haddonfield and Delaware Township (later renamed Cherry Hill). The plan was to provide homes in these towns for some of the workers who would be needed by a city of "busy people." The leaders of the Greater Camden Movement hoped that eventually these suburbs would be annexed to Camden, making the linkage not only economic but political as well. The idea wasn't so farfetched. For one thing, Camden was wealthier than its neighbors, better able to afford the installation of public services, and so the match might well have been regarded as beneficial by both sides. For another thing, consolidation was logical. The city was tiny, not much bigger than a single neighborhood in Philadelphia, and to prosper it needed to expand. On a downtown office tower, the newest dream motto blinked in huge electric letters: "Greater Camden: The City of Opportunity."

Looking backward, though, the real impact of the Ben Franklin Bridge was perverse. Instead of launching Camden in the direction of prosperity, the spate of new construction marked the start of the city's downfall. The design for the on- and off-ramps to the bridge split Camden in half, and this dissection imperiled the city's identity. Building the Walt Whitman Hotel required tearing down a number of the lovely old mansions on Cooper Street; constructing ramps while following the cheapest route meant widening the same street. All these changes increased traffic, encouraged more tall buildings, and in a few years' time decimated the city's version of Society Hill. Seemingly overnight, recalls Edna Haycock, the septuagenarian historian at the Haddonfield Historical Society, "the aristocracy of Camden moved to Haddonfield."

While the bridge was supposed to bolster Camden's economy by tying city and suburb closer together, in fact it diminished suburbanites' dependence on the city. Now the only stop on the road to Philadelphia was to pay the twenty-five-cent bridge toll, and for the most part, the rapidly growing number of suburbanites preferred things that way. By the opening of the Ben Franklin Bridge, Camden had become a fine place to visit for a day of shopping or a night on the town. Besides the thirteen theaters in the city's Broadway district, which together seated twenty thousand patrons, the city offered an opera company and the nation's first drive-in movie. The sidewalks were so jammed on Saturday nights that people had to walk in the streets. But the smog, the polluted Delaware River, and the increasing crime—all the detritus of urban life—made Camden seem a less-than-ideal place to live.

A riot a few years earlier, in 1919 at the height of the post–World War I Red Scare, embedded this antiurban sensibility in the suburban mind. The clash, which began with a protest over a hike in trolley fares, was quickly attributed to "Bolshevists," and that raised the political ante. "Camden County has always been free from mob violence," intoned the local prosecutor, forgetting the white-on-black violence during the post–Civil War years, "and in the present emergency it will not be tolerated." Twenty-six Russian-born shipyard workers were rounded up by the police, prompting the city solicitor to opine that he "would have them shot first and send them out of the country as corpses." Meanwhile, the Ku Klux Klan made its presence felt, burning crosses to terrify black families and rout them from their homes, as advertising on buses proclaimed: "Every Loyal American Knows What KKK Stands For!" The advent of Prohibition bred violence as well as prosperity, turning the city into a haven for bootleggers, and this too was unsettling to those who numbered themselves among the decent citizenry. Philadelphia's public safety director issued a warning to criminals—"Let them go to Camden!"—and the insult seemed to stick.

Suburban communities were booming, with sixty thousand newcomers during the 1920s, even as the city's population grew by only two thousand. For the first time, more than half the county's population lived outside city limits. Increasingly, the split between city and suburb followed ethnic and racial lines—60 percent of the foreign born and 70 percent of the blacks in Camden County were living in the city—and that fact also made merger less attractive to the suburbanites.

Elsewhere in the country, cities were expanding apace, sometimes against the wishes of those who were annexed. Philadelphia swallowed up its surrounding communities in the nineteenth century; New York City took in Brooklyn and Staten Island. In 1917, suburbanites dissented when Baltimore wanted to expand, but a Maryland state court dismissed their complaints. "No principle of right or justice or fairness places in [suburbanites'] hands the power to stop the progress and development of the city, especially in view of the fact that the large majority of them have located near the city for the purpose of transacting business or securing employment or following their profession in the city."

In New Jersey, unlike most states, urban-suburban consolidation was legally difficult. But deconsolidation, splitting off, was easily accomplished by little groups of the like minded. Although the state's constitution requires towns to serve the "general welfare," that provision has seldom been given real meaning. Instead, towns have been encouraged to serve the narrow interests of their residents, ignoring and even victimizing outsiders, in the name of community sovereignty. Camden County alone has forty separate municipalities—including, remarkably enough, two towns almost entirely given over to golf courses, each created to thwart the blue laws that prevented Sunday golfing. Such fissioning is not atypical in a state where the biggest city, Newark, occupies only twenty-four square miles, where an industrial park and a race course have each become incorporated as separate towns. New Jersey is described as the most suburbanized state in the nation. That is another way of saying that it is the most municipally fragmented state in the nation.

When the idea of merging with Camden was presented to the nearby suburbs, they all demurred. Although the proposal was made in the midst of the Depression, when these towns faced hard times, local officials believed that even municipal bankruptcy was better than consolidation, so dubious had the city's reputation become. Many suburbanites had moved away from Camden to pursue a different kind of life, and they had no interest in being drawn back into the city's problems. As an editorial in the *Community News*, a suburban paper, pointed out: "Mighty few of us who live in the suburbs are inclined to favor 'moving into Camden,' no matter how it might figure out as an economy." A 1940 article in the *National Municipal Review* describing Newark's plight fit Camden's circumstances equally well. "A local patriotism, particularly in some of the wealthier and 'exclusive' communities, is of such intensity that many would justify the individual existence of these communities for the prestige of their name alone. Closely allied with these sentiments is the fear of joining with [the city] and its large foreign-born and Negro population."

These developments can be traced back to that fine and fateful Fourth of July in 1926, when the Ben Franklin Bridge was opened. "Everyone thought it was a commonsense thing to do, to build the bridge," says historian Edna Haycock, who remembers the event from her childhood, and perhaps it was the inevitable thing to do. "But they realized after the bridge was finished that it was just going to finish Camden." Nor was the demise of Camden unique to this one city. It was part of a new American dream, the suburbanized nation. "The ultimate solution," declared Henry Ford, whose automobiles helped make this migration possible, from cities everywhere, "will be the abandonment of the city, its abandonment as a blunder."

Stampede to the Suburbs

World War II seemed to offer Camden yet another chance at the gold ring of urban prosperity. While the pace of suburbanization had slowed because of the Depression and the imposition of gas rationing, the city's industry picked up as the shipyards and the Victor Talking Machine Company, now called RCA Victor, were kept busy in the war effort. Among the many locals who came to try their hand at city life was Ethel Lawrence, then a teenager just out of school in Mount Laurel, who took a factory job. At the dedication of the remodeled Plaza Hotel in downtown

Camden two years after the war had ended, the hotel's owner pronounced himself "justified in my belief that Camden will continue to be one of the leading industrial cities in the country"; the opening of a downtown campus of Rutgers University in 1950 indicated that the city might become a cultural and educational center as well.

But these episodes of good feeling proved to be not the harbingers of a bright future, just exceptions that predicted nothing. The modest wartime boom, Camden's last flash of glory, began to fade soon after the war ended; trouble quickly piled on trouble; a decade later, Camden was well on its way to becoming one of the country's first urban casualties. Almost every problem that an American city would confront surfaced early in Camden.

The suburbs started to grow again right after the war, and again migration fanned steadily outwards from Camden. Major new highways, first the New Jersey Turnpike and later a second parallel highway, turned what had been farm country into acreage ripe for development. As geographer Peter Muller writes: "High speed expressways ultimately expanded the all but frictionless urban region into the outermost suburbs. . . . The nation's pent-up housing demands, stifled by more than a decade of economic depression and war, were unleashed with a vengeance outside the city after 1945." William Levitt, whose first Levittown on Long Island became synonymous with suburbia, built another Levittown in South Jersey on a site twenty miles northeast of Camden, an unheard-of commuting distance at that time.

There have been tranquil enclaves outside congested cities for almost as long as there have been cities. "Our property seems to me the most beautiful in the world. It is so close to the city that we enjoy all its advantages, and yet when we come home we are away from all the noise and dust," a Persian nobleman declared to the king of Persia in a letter carved out of clay and written six centuries before the Christian era. In the eighteenth century, Camden itself had been such a place—"ye most invitingst place to settle by," as the developers of that day boasted—but after World War II, suburbanization in the United States accelerated to the pace of a stampede. Across the country, tens of millions of families flocked to the new towns, sometimes spending days camped out, patiently waiting in line for a chance to buy their own three-bedroom fantasy house on their own fenced-in quarter acre. Just 114,000 homes were built nationwide in 1944; six years later, that number had multiplied nearly fifteenfold, to 1,692,000. For the sixteen million returning GIs, interest rates were so low and down-payment requirements so modest on federally subsidized mortgages that buying a home actually became cheaper than renting. Moreover, as houses appreciated in value, their owners became wealthier; by refinancing their houses, they could send their children to college or buy themselves a summer cottage. Suburban homes became the biggest investment of the middle class. "If you seek the monuments of the bourgeoisie," historian Robert Fishman maintains, "go to the suburbs and look around."

While the suburbanization of America was partly accomplished by the lure of dollars, financial incentives alone could not do the trick. The suburbs were "a cultural creation, a conscious choice based on the economic structure and cultural values" of the middle class. When these families left behind the cities, with their crime, decaying infrastructure, poor public schools, congestion, and pollution, they were voting with their feet, opting not only for a modern house with more space and amenities than they had ever known but also for an entirely new way of living. The new towns were a tangible representation of deep changes in attitudes about raising families, the relationship between work and leisure, the importance of like-mindedness among one's neighbors, and, indeed, the very idea of community. The suburban home gave its residents "a public symbol of achievement, 'something to show for all your years of living,' " wrote sociologist Herbert Gans, who lived in New Jersey's Levittown for several years and came away favorably impressed. As developer William Levitt declared in 1947: "No man who owns his own house and lot can be a Communist. He has too much to do." Suburbia became an ideological Rorschach blot: conservatives applauded this realization of capitalism's promise of diffused prosperity, while liberals flayed it as a nightmare of provincial conformism come to life. That great lover of cities, Lewis Mumford, grew bilious on the subject, deriding the suburb as a retreat from reality, "an asylum for the preservation of illusion. . . . Here domesticity could flourish, forgetful of the exploitation on which so much of it was based. Here individuality could flourish, oblivious of the pervasive regimentation beyond. This was not merely a child-centered environment; it was based on a childish view of the world, in which reality was sacrificed to the pleasure principle."

Whether praised or damned, suburbanization proved to be both a way to plan a community and a powerful mind-set. As historian Kenneth Jackson observes in his aptly titled *Crabgrass Frontier*, suburbia became "the quintessential physical achievement of the United States . . . perhaps more representative of its culture than big cars, tall buildings, or professional football." It stands for and exaggerates "such fundamental characteristics of American society as conspicuous consumption, a reliance on the private automobile, upward mobility, the separation of the family into nuclear units, the widening division between work and leisure, and"— critically for the destiny of all the Camdens—"a tendency toward racial and economic exclusiveness."

Families hoping to finance a home in the city of Camden in the postwar years had a harder time than aspiring suburbanites, because all the incentives were weighted against them. Although the federal government had constructed the country's first public housing for civilian war workers during World War I—among the sites was Yorkship Village in Camden—that effort ended with the 1918 Armistice. The only other housing policy then on the books called for improving slum conditions through health and safety codes.

With the New Deal, though, federal involvement in housing increased. Slum clearance in the cities became the policy watchword, as hundreds of square miles of urban land were turned into public-housing projects meant for the working—the respectable—poor. "Salvation by bricks," city planner Jane Jacobs derisively called the strategy, which would be embraced a generation later in Camden to the detriment of the poor. While public housing could also be built in the suburbs, municipalities first had to apply for federal funds, and very few suburbs were ready to sacrifice their exclusivity.

In the far bigger private-housing market, the federal government put its seal of approval on racial discrimination. The Federal Housing Administration billed itself as a "conservative business operation"; in practice, this meant the agency subsidized segregation. Its policies promoted the abandonment of large areas of older cities, and because the behavior of private investors mirrored what Washington was doing, the impact of the federal rules was multiplied. Even more important, the FHA, which underwrote tens of millions of mortgages, regarded places like Camden as unacceptably risky. In the agency's judgment, the socioeconomic and ethnic character of a neighborhood—any "infiltration of Jews," for instance—rather than its housing stock, determined property value. Property owners were urged to insert deed restrictions barring "the occupancy of properties except by the race for which they are intended." In a 1941 memorandum concerning St. Louis, the FHA proclaimed that "the rapidly rising Negro population" has produced a "problem in the maintenance of real estate values," and federal officials said much the same about Camden. Any city block on which even a single black family lived was for that reason ineligible for federal mortgage guarantees. In Detroit, only after a wall was built to separate black from white areas was the FHA willing to finance white-owned properties there. These were terrible and durable official practices—"racial policy that could well have been culled from the Nuremberg laws," as Charles Abrams concluded in his classic 1955 study, *Forbidden Neighbors*, and the "evil" the FHA had done was built to last. "Thousands of racially segregated neighborhoods were built, millions of people re-sorted on the basis of race, color, or class, the differences built in, in neighborhoods from coast to coast."

Industry had been Camden's mainspring for nearly a century, yet there were hints after World War II that industry too would wind down. A series of protracted strikes in the late 1940s prompted some companies to leave, while others, eager to expand in order to meet the pent-up demand for consumer goods, couldn't find sites within the crowded enclave and so looked elsewhere. Armstrong Cork left, as did the C. Howard Hunt Pen Company and Highland Woolen Mills. Still, the biggest companies, with their huge capital investments, remained and prospered. RCA had its first billion-dollar year in 1955, the year it introduced color television; Campbell Soup Company recorded record sales; the local shipbuilding business had never been better. New York Shipbuilding Company, the biggest outfit, employed seven thousand workers, and through the 1950s as many as thirty-five thousand people worked in the shipyards, sometimes building eight ships at once.

At the dedication of the Holly Department Store in 1947, the city's mayor called Camden "one of the great shopping centers in America," and some retailers were still opening branches there as late as the mid-1950s. By then, however, the departing firms far outnumbered the newcomers. Fire gutted the ferry terminal and the slips in 1952, and the ferry company, which could not compete with the Ben Franklin Bridge, closed down completely. Three years later, the daily paper, the *Courier-Post*, built its new plant in suburban Cherry Hill. The grand convention hall and a major church went up in flames. The Towers Theatre, Savar Theatre, and Stanley Theatre, relics of the 1920s that had attracted thousands of patrons during Broadway's heyday, were unceremoniously leveled for parking lots in the early 1960s, while the Walt Whitman Hotel, once the pride of all New Jersey, became a seedy dowager and eventually a flophouse.

These developments frightened Camden's merchants. "Our downtown business community is apprehensive and alarmed over developments," declared the vice president of the Greater Camden Merchants Association. A realtor gazing down Broadway predicted that "this will be a blighted area"; another added that "it won't be long before the street is in darkness." When a mammoth enclosed shopping mall opened in Cherry Hill in 1961, one of the first in the nation, downtown vacancy rates spiraled.

Some realtors were not merely observers of but also participants in Camden's collapse. Stirring up and then taking advantage of the racial panic, they bought out anxious whites and resold the homes to black families at sizable mark-ups. Blockbusting, this tactic is called, and it worked all too well. In 1959, an enterprising *Courier-Post* reporter counted 332 "For Sale" signs just in North Camden. That neighborhood had never come back after being hived off from the rest of the city a third of a century earlier, when the on- and off-ramps to the Ben Franklin Bridge were built with so little regard for their impact on the future. The FHA dealt the final blow to the city's chances. Barely a generation after World War II, the federal agency redlined all of Camden as unacceptably risky, and consequently mortgage money dried up almost completely.

"City within a City"

The election of John F. Kennedy as president in 1960 signaled a national politics that was new both in style and substance—a New Frontier, Kennedy called it—and the agenda included reviving down-at-the-heels cities like Camden. "I urge you to do everything within your ability to eliminate delay," Kennedy wrote to Mayor Alfred Pierce. "I promise you the full cooperation of the Federal Government to this end." Partly this invitation made good policy sense, partly it was smart politics, for Camden had voted overwhelmingly for Kennedy, and the new president was ready to reciprocate.

Full cooperation: after years of neglect from Washington, city leaders salivated at the prospect of infusions of funds. A committee of Camden's leading citizens, primarily representing the downtown interests and drawn together by Mayor Pierce, produced a blueprint to remake the city in a generation. Its emphasis was on tearing things down and starting over again. Two hundred eighty acres of waterfront land in North Camden would be leveled to provide space for a shopping center meant to rival the mall in suburban Cherry Hill, high-rise apartment complexes for the urbanites who would work in new office towers, an Olympic-sized swimming pool, a marina, and even a Playboy Club—all this comprising a "City within a City," linked to the suburbs by a new highway. Jerry Wolman, the owner of the pro-football Philadelphia Eagles and mastermind of this plan, was hailed as the architect of Camden's renaissance, the worthy successor to Jacob Cooper, who two centuries earlier had also come from Philadelphia to bring civilization to downtown Camden. "Camden's Rebirth Will Be Evidence for All," announced the *Courier-Post* in 1967, and a year later the paper declared that "Camden Is Moving, Planners Believe."

But the idea of a city within a city was deeply flawed. It presumed that anything a planner might draw up could be made to happen in real life. It treated Camden as if it were a new town like Reston, Virginia, or Columbia, Maryland, places just then coming into being, rather than a community with its own history. The city-within-a-city notion also assumed, against all common sense, that it was possible to cordon off a sizable part of a city and pretend it was immune from the blight that lapped at its borders—to treat it, as a local critic said, like "gold fillings in a mouthful of decay." The scheme took no account of Camden's sorry economic realities, no account either of who was living in the city and the political claims that they might press.

Across the country, fifty-one thousand more housing units were pulled down by urban-renewal projects than were built as public housing.

It was easy enough to destroy the old Camden, but the money needed to build the new city, to render the dream into steel and concrete, to fill it with businesses and residents, wasn't to be had. The neighborhood called Kaigns Point (a century and a half earlier, when it was known as Kaignsville, it had been one of the city's first black communities) was leveled to make way for an industrial park. Three hundred ninety families lost their homes, and fourteen businesses were razed; for several years, the land stood empty; then a factory was built, but no one came. It was a decade after the decimation of Kaigns Point that the first commercial occupant, a pickle-making concern, moved in, one of a succession of tenants in a failed commercial venture.

Nor is the Kaigns Point story so unusual in the annals of Camden. Some seventeen hundred families saw their houses destroyed during the 1960s, about one Camden family in fifteen. In a single year, 1967, more than a thousand families were displaced as ninety-nine acres were flattened, yet nothing was done on almost all this land besides paving it over for parking lots. Developer Jerry Wolman went bankrupt. Meanwhile, two mainstays of local industry, the Esterbrook Pen Company and the New York Shipbuilding Company, shut down, putting thousands out of work. In 1953, at New York Shipbuilding, Mamie Eisenhower had cracked a bottle of champagne across the bow of the *Nautilus*, launching the nation's first nuclear-powered submarine, yet, less than a decade later, disputes about shoddy workmanship cost the shipbuilder its reputation and the business it needed to survive.

Nonetheless, there was a seemingly endless supply of people with new visions for Camden to replace the failed visionaries. Boosters urged that Camden become the region's medical center, anchored by prestigious Cooper Hospital and a new Veterans Administration hospital. But the VA hospital never came to pass; and while Cooper Hospital did expand its facilities, this had little effect on the city's economy, since the revenues lost by taking this prime real estate off the tax rolls weren't made up by money flowing into local commerce. RCA remained in Camden, as did Campbell Soup, and these firms became the mainstays of a group calling itself the Camden Centre City Corporation, which put forward still another downtown-redevelopment scheme.

Behind the glossy brochures and glowing promises was terrible, if unpublicized, news. Between 1950 and 1970, Camden lost over half its manufacturing jobs, more than 22,000 in all—a devastating number for any city's economy—while manufacturing jobs in the region more than doubled, to 197,000, as many businesses moved from the city to its surrounding suburbs. Even the ever cheerful *Courier-Post* began to express doubts about the city's prospects: "Some Find Camden's Urban Renewal Dreams Are Only Nightmares."

The Fire This Time

By the late 1960s, the patience of the city's worst-off residents had been tested too often. The nonwhite population grew from 27 percent to 40 percent during the decade, and now there was no work for many of them. While there had historically been a black middle class in Camden, minorities never had much voice in how the city was governed. For more than a generation, from 1936 to 1958, one man served as Camden's mayor, and his successor stayed in office for a decade. City government was fueled by patronage, with the old-line families gaining the biggest benefits.

In the space of a decade, though, this quiescence was replaced by civic interest. Expressions of interest shaded into protest. Then the protest turned violent.

White ministers committed to an agenda of social justice, liberation theologians such as Donald Griesmann of the Camden Metropolitan Ministry, found their vocation as organizers in the poorest neighborhoods of the city. Reverend Stuart Wood, who had been assigned to the nearby suburb of Mount Laurel, tried and failed to interest his neighbors there in the cause of civil rights. Wood took flight from that community, which he found spiritually arid, and gravitated to Camden, where exciting things were happening. Later on, the young minister would bring together activists from the two communities, an introduction that eventually led to the *Mount Laurel* litigation.

The clerics joined forces with reform-minded attorneys, as well as with leaders of civil-rights groups, among them NAACP, CORE and a local group called the Black People's Unity Movement (BPUM). They organized petition drives, gathering hundreds of signatures, then launched rallies and marches to city hall to complain about conditions in the city. At one demonstration, two hundred school-age youngsters carried hand-lettered placards protesting slumlords who made their lives a misery and city officials who denied them public housing. When Mayor Pierce accused the organizers of "hiding behind the use of little children," Reverend Griesmann had a quick retort: "The children understand the problem, which is simple. The problem is segregated public housing and slum housing." Later, when asked to testify about conditions in Camden before a congressional committee, Griesmann's vivid account of what was wrong with Camden put the city on the federal policymakers' map. Angry members of the local housing authority threatened to sue him for defamation, but Griesmann's lawyer reminded these officials that, to any such charges, truth was a complete defense.

Across much of the republic, the hope of the era was racial peace, shaped by Martin Luther King Jr.'s prayerful dream of equality and its expression in the 1964 Civil Rights Act. The reality, though, was heightened expectations among blacks, then rage at promises unmet. Between 1964 and 1967, nearly fifty cities were split open by acts of racial rebellion. While a measure of calm prevailed in Camden until 1969, when the violence did come it was not surprising, since in all the ways that mattered, the city was indistinguishable from Harlem or Watts, Newark or Detroit. Racial incident piled on incident, like dry wood that required only a chance spark to set it off. There were black-against-white clashes at Camden High School during the spring of 1968, and by the following fall, almost all of the 320 white students who had been enrolled at the school had transferred. That same spring, a few days after Robert Kennedy's assassination, blacks bitter about alleged police mistreatment of members of BPUM by city police clashed with police officers on the steps of city hall.

Then, a hot summer later, with more allegations of police abuse, another clash began after a fiery speech by black-power advocate Rap Brown. The violence escalated quickly, and before peace could be restored two police officers had been killed, scores of blacks hurt, dozens of buildings vandalized and torched. Nor was this episode the end of things. Two years later, in August 1971, came the most violent confrontation in Camden's history. It started familiarly enough, with an incident involving the police. After several officers who had been charged with beating a Puerto Rican man were let off—unfairly, many people thought—for five days and nights the city turned into a war zone. Whole blocks were smashed and burned, a state of emergency was declared, and civil law was suspended. After the first night of violence, the *Courier-Post*'s lead story read like a news report from Saigon: "A pall of smoke and tear gas hung over a smoldering Camden today."

That event convinced many of the die-hard urban loyalists that the cause was lost, that it was time—well past time, really—to leave Camden behind, for there was nothing for them to salvage. A Puerto Rican grocer named Alfredo Alvarado, who had lived in the city for more than twenty years, watched as his neighbors packed up everything they owned and departed for new lives in the suburbs. "You should have seen the people flying out of here," he told a reporter. "It was like a fast-motion movie, they were so afraid and so scared."

Back to the Future

In the summer of 1970, the summer between the riots, a lawsuit was filed against the city of Camden with the audacious aim of stopping the city-directed destruction of poor people's neighborhoods—even if this meant halting all urban renewal. Among the plaintiffs were NAACP, CORE, and BPUM; Donald Griesmann's Camden Metropolitan Ministry; the Neighborhood Apostolate, a Catholic organization; and the Martin Luther King Jr. Christian Center. Two hundred nine families formed a group called

Save Our Homes, which was a party to the case, as was Poppy Sharp, one of BPUM's founders, who had organized community housing demonstrations in the 1960s. These plaintiffs were represented by a federally funded law firm, Camden Regional Legal Services.

The idea that the poor and people of color had unrealized rights, and that courts, which had been the instruments of enforcing the status quo, could be used to redistribute political and economic power, blossomed in the heady sixties. New legal theories concerning entitlements to education and welfare, jobs and housing, were being spun out by a generation of law professors weaned on *Brown v. Board of Education* for whom the welfare state was a matter of simple justice, as well as by attorneys working in federally subsidized programs like Camden's. Remarkably enough, these lawyers were paid by a federal program, Legal Services, to invent new and even insurrectionary uses of the law.

Camden Regional Legal Services was famous for its reformist zeal— or infamous, depending on one's perspective. The young attorneys who staffed its law-reform unit were led by Peter O'Connor, whose scant three years of legal practice made him a veteran activist in this new order. O'Connor had already won the first New Jersey judicial decision authorizing tenants to withhold rent from landlords who refused to repair derelict housing; in another case, he had successfully challenged South Jersey election practices as racially discriminatory. Together with Carl Bisgaier, a recent law school graduate, he brought a series of lawsuits in Camden that prodded miscreant landlords and lackadaisical city housing code enforcers into action.

The complaint in *Camden Coalition v. Nardi* detailed the many things that were legally offensive about Camden's urban-renewal plan. The city had effectively turned urban renewal into a strategy for eliminating housing for the poor; then it lied flat out about those activities when requesting funds from the federal Department of Housing and Urban Development and the state's Department of Community Affairs. Official records showed the city knew that, in gutting neighborhoods, it was putting poor families on the street, even when it claimed otherwise. Public-housing statistics proved that the city-run projects were totally segregated; a news story detailed how a black family's attempt to buy a home in a white area had led to a cross burning—all this in the teeth of the city's insistence that housing in Camden was open to all. The complaint further pointed out that Camden Centre City Corporation, the industry-dominated consortium, had pressed for what it called an "Industrial Waterfront Highway," a self-serving venture that would be a "death trap" for the adjoining black and Puerto Rican neighborhoods.

"If the intent of urban renewal is Negro *removal,*" the legal complaint in *Camden Coalition* acidly declared, "then Camden is accomplishing its goal." None of the coalition's many efforts before filing suit had persuaded the city to behave differently: not written complaints about falsified statistics, a forty-six-point proposal to the city council, a request to work with the urban-renewal planners (as HUD's own rules required), nonviolent street demonstrations to protest city-ordered relocations—not even the highly publicized installation of the fourteen-member Shields family, who had been made homeless by urban renewal, in the once splendid Walt Whitman Hotel. Hence the litigation.

The trial court froze the city's ambitious plans for rebuilding, which called for a new highway as well as offices, a hotel, and a high-rise apartment building for the well-to-do. The city had failed to find replacement housing for residents displaced by urban renewal, the court noted, even though federal law required that, before Camden could receive the federal funds on which these new projects depended, the state had to certify that there existed a genuine plan for relocation. City officials claimed that there was no shortage of housing for poor Camdenites, pointing disingenuously to ads for rental apartments in middle-class Cherry Hill, but state Department of Community Affairs officials rejected that argument. Just days before a crucial court hearing in the *Camden Coalition* case, Mayor Nardi was reminded that, by law, the city had to guarantee a unit of housing within Camden itself for each displaced family. The frustrated mayor then took out a yellow pad, scribbled "I will build one unit of housing for each unit displaced," and signed it. "That's my relocation plan!" the mayor declared, but then he crumpled the paper and threw it away when reminded that this document might actually be introduced as evidence in the legal proceedings.

Two years later, Mayor Nardi backed down. The Camden Coalition dropped its lawsuit, thus allowing building to proceed, and in exchange the city agreed to reserve several hundred units of new housing for the poor, including a twenty-three-story high-rise apartment building called Northgate, which had been planned for the anticipated white-collar influx. The local Building Trades Council, which also had been a party to the lawsuit, agreed to hire and train black and Puerto Rican workers from Camden, who hadn't been able to break into the unions.

There are civic leaders from that era of bad feelings who remain convinced that the downfall of Camden is the direct result of Peter O'Connor's efforts in the *Camden Coalition* case. The poverty lawyer was personally vilified by Camden's mainstream politicians, who didn't know how to deal with a man who looked like a flower child, with his painter's pants and ponytail, but who talked like a power broker, at one point threatening to turn the proposed new highway into a bike path if his clients didn't get their way. "He wanted veto power over elected officials," complains Mayor Joseph Nardi, and for a while he got it.

While the *Camden Coalition* lawsuit makes a convenient scapegoat for Camden's problems, and the sometimes intemperate Peter O'Connor offers an inviting target for demonization, the city's demise had been mapped out years, decades really, before the legal complaint was ever filed. But the litigation did have a marked impact on the city and its surrounding suburbs. It effectively rewrote the rules of Camden politics to assure that the have-nots would finally have their day in city hall. The stark limits of their victory also prompted the lawyers at Camden Regional Legal Services to look beyond the city limits, to seek out such places as Mount Laurel for answers to the problems of their clients— with extraordinary consequences, for the region and for land-use law everywhere.

Jacob's Chapel A.M.E.
Church, Mount Laurel,
New Jersey. Photo by
Larry Rosenthal

Ethel Lawrence as a
teenager in the early
1940s. Photo courtesy
of the family of Ethel
Lawrence

The 1787 manumission of Philip Still, resident of the Township of Evesham (later renamed Mount Laurel). Members of the Still family have lived in Mount Laurel for more than two centuries, alongside the descendants of other freed slaves.

Exhibits from the first trial in the Mount Laurel case, comparing housing in Springville and newer residential developments. Photos courtesy of Peter J. O'Connor

Dilapidated housing, Springville area, Mount Laurel, 1994. Photo by Larry Rosenthal

The Benjamin Franklin Bridge, viewed from North Camden; Philadelphia skyline in the background. Photo by Robert Homan

Police attempt to maintain order during the August 1971 riots in Camden. Photo courtesy of [Cherry Hill] *Courier-Post*

Blocks of burning apartments in Camden during the August 1971 riots. Photo courtesy of [Cherry Hill] *Courier-Post*

Burnt and abandoned houses in North Camden, May 1978. Photo courtesy of [Cherry Hill] *Courier-Post*

Collapsed housing in North Camden; Peter O'Connor's Northgate apartment complex in the background. Photo courtesy of [Cherry Hill] *Courier-Post*

Ruins of the Campbell Soup factory in Camden after its 1991 demolition.
Photo by Avi Steinhardt, courtesy of [Cherry Hill] *Courier-Post*

Peter O'Connor (second from left), Carl Bisgaier, and Ethel Lawrence accept 1977 commendation from the Southern Burlington County NAACP for their work in the *Mount Laurel I* case. Photo courtesy of the family of Ethel Lawrence.

(Top, left) Justice Frederick Hall, author of the *Mount Laurel I* opinion. Photo courtesy of [Cherry Hill] *Courier-Post*

(Top, right) Chief Justice Robert Wilentz, author of the *Mount Laurel II* opinion. Photo courtesy of [Cherry Hill] *Courier-Post*

Thomas H. Kean, two-term governor of New Jersey during the 1980s, who negotiated and signed the state's 1985 Fair Housing Act. Photo courtesy of Thomas Kean

(Top, left) State Senator John Lynch, former mayor of New Brunswick and key player in the adoption of New Jersey's 1985 Fair Housing Act. Photo by Sheldon Linz

(Top, right) Judge Eugene D. Serpentelli, member of the three-judge panel charged with implementing *Mount Laurel II*. Photo courtesy of Eugene Serpentelli

Governor Thomas Kean (left) with his counsel and attorney general W. Cary Edwards. Photo courtesy of W. Cary Edwards

Ara Hovnanian, housing developer and influential member of the Council on Affordable Housing. Photo courtesy of K. Hovnanian and Sons

Inclusionary development in Mahwah built by K. Hovnanian and Sons. Photo courtesy of K. Hovnanian and Sons

"Yep...I believe it might be contagious!"

Three editorial cartoons on this page and the following page about the Mount Laurel zoning dispute by Robert Beckett, a long-time Cherry Hill resident. The cartoons originally appeared in the *Burlington County Times* in the two years following the *Mount Laurel I* decision. Cartoons courtesy of Robert Beckett

A few of history's lengthiest battles

The Crusades
11th-13th centuries A.D.

Napoleonic Wars
1799-1815

American Revolution
1776-1783

Civil War   1861-1865

Vietnam
1955-1974

Mt. Laurel Zoning War
1972-19??

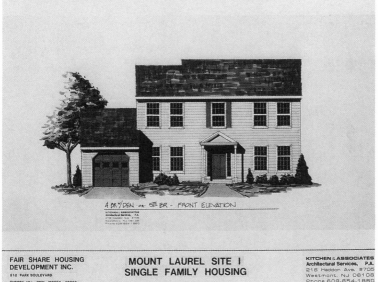

FAIR SHARE HOUSING
DEVELOPMENT INC.
610 PARK BOULEVARD
CHERRY HILL, NEW JERSEY 08002

MOUNT LAUREL SITE I
SINGLE FAMILY HOUSING

KITCHEN & ASSOCIATES
Architectural Services, P.A.
216 Haddon Ave. #705
Westmont, NJ 08108
Phone 609-854-1880

Aerial of parcel for Ethel Robinson Lawrence affordable housing project in Mount Laurel. Photo courtesy of Peter J. O'Connor

Architect's sketch for proposed house in Peter O'Connor's fair share development in Mount Laurel. Illustration by Kitchen and Associates Architectural Services, P.A., Westmont, N.J.

In 1995, Carl Bisgaier (left) and Peter O'Connor view the site of the future Ethel Robinson Lawrence housing project in Mount Laurel. Photo by Robert Homan

Ethel Lawrence in her home, 1991. Photo courtesy of the family of Ethel Lawrence

3

Mount Laurel:
A Suburb at Odds

Mount Laurel residents regularly tell a self-deprecating story about their town. Every time they plan a Fourth of July parade, they say, there's an argument: since there is neither a main street nor a town square, no one can agree on where the parade route should begin or end. This story carries the sting of a deeper truth, for in all respects, not just geographic, Mount Laurel has no center.

Only in the 1980s were township offices put up, hacked out of the surrounding woods, and these offices seem as disconnected as Brasilia from the ordinary life of the community. Despite the fact that the first white settlers came to Mount Laurel in 1688 and the township itself was incorporated over a century ago, this town of thirty-four thousand really isn't a town at all.

This identity confusion dates to the town's beginnings. The hill that gives Mount Laurel its name was originally called Mount Pray, in pious hope; then it became Mount Evans, after the first settlers, William and Elizabeth Evans, early believers in George Fox's new Quaker religion, who had spent the winter of 1683 huddled in a cave; later it was named Evesham Mount. In the late eighteenth century, local people started referring to it as Mount Laurel because of the laurel that grows wild on its slopes, and this was the name that stuck.

There is no coffee shop where the locals hang out, not even a real grocery store—for those things, you still have to drive to neighboring Moorestown. Mount Laurel used to be a chain of hamlets ringed by farms. In the nineteenth century there was an iron foundry and a schoolhouse in a crossroads known as Masonville; Centertown had the area's first small chemical plant and a lumber yard; in Hartford there was a telegraph office and another schoolhouse. But these hamlets are now just names on old maps.

Massive housing developments have doubled and redoubled the township's population over the past three decades. Office blocks and high-tech industrial complexes euphemistically described as parks occupy prime real estate near the major highways. Mount Laurel is neither a farming community nor a suburb that sends its breadwinners off to jobs in the nearby cities. It has become an amalgam of city and suburb—not quite so futurist as an "edge city" but rather the kind of place that urban planners, meaning no compliment, call a slurb.

Today this town has acquired an identity, though surely it is not the identity that the political managers of its future had in mind. Mount Laurel is known as the defendant in the zoning case that went on forever—the town where the dug-in resistance of well-off landowners and new homeowners to housing even a tiny number of poor families brought on a famous courtroom battle over the nation's suburban soul.

Fast Forward

Communities create their own myths, "an imparted sense of the story of themselves as characters in a drama." During the centennial celebrations in 1972, the citizens of Mount Laurel Township tried to recreate its past as a prosperous farm village whose pride was Rancocas Woods, which once attracted summer visitors with games of chance and open-air dancing. At the centennial there were four band concerts and a beard-growing contest, a turkey shoot and a kite-flying contest. But the pageant was as much a reflection of contemporary life as an exercise in nostalgia. Instead of the exhibition of prize farm animals traditional in rural communities, there was a pet show featuring well-coifed and mannerly dogs and cats. By 1972, there were almost no farm animals—almost no farms either—left in Mount Laurel.

For almost three centuries, from the founding of the community until the 1950s, change came exceedingly slowly—the radical transformation took place in the brief span of a single generation. During the American Revolution, the community had strategic importance because of its high ground. Its best-known citizen at the time was Nathan Haines, the "fighting Quaker" who broke with the pacifism of his faith to organize a militia unit. From Nathan Haines to William Haines Jr., eleven generations of Haineses lived in Mount Laurel; the Rudderows, another family that has had a powerful hand in the contemporary transformation of Mount Laurel, trace their ancestry back to Elizabeth Evans.

Beginning in the mid–nineteenth century, a stage coach stopped regularly on its way to Camden, and for years it was the one real tie between this up-with-the-sun farming community and the city. Decade upon decade, farmers planted corn, tomatoes, strawberries, pumpkins, and string beans and raised chickens, hogs, and dairy cows, hauling their produce to market by wagon and later by truck or selling it to Campbell's in Camden.

While Mount Laurel Township was formally created in 1872, there was seldom much official business to conduct, either for the council, which met once a month, or for the single police officer, whose responsibilities included herding cows across the road. The *real* town was Moorestown, envied and resented in equal measure for having a genuine main street and a more refined populace. Mount Laurel was the poor relation, and as late as 1950 its population stood at just two thousand eight hundred.

The changes marked since that date were so basic that it was as if someone had pressed the fast-forward button, and every trend, every aspect of the nation's coming of age that had bypassed the town, manifested itself in a single generation. Outside events partly shaped this transformation, because Mount Laurel was not isolated from the surrounding world. Major new highways, originally slated to slice through Moorestown, were shifted south to Mount Laurel when residents there complained: Exit 4 off the New Jersey Turnpike opened in 1952, and in the early 1970s came Interstate 295 barely a mile away. While the highways bisected the township, denying it the possibility of physical cohesion, they also gave Mount Laurel a direct link to the northeast corridor. RCA had already opened a major plant nearby, and the interchanges offered a logical site for the offices, the hygienic-looking manufacturing plants, and the hotel chains that were to come.

Meanwhile, a Levittown, that quintessential suburban venture of the postwar era, was built a few miles to the northeast, and in short order forty-five thousand people, many of them soldiers assigned to nearby Fort Dix and their young families, moved in. Developers who had earlier dismissed the region as too remote began to eye Mount Laurel as a giant in-fill, virgin land that was a manageable commute to Camden and Philadelphia. The near inevitability of suburban development is plain from aerial photographs taken in the early 1960s, which show suburbanization fanning out from Camden, then a gradual thinning to a swath of inviting greenery— the farms that still made up the township—then more suburbanization beyond, in Levittown (which by then had been renamed Willingboro).

But the way in which Mount Laurel was remade was no act of submission to the gods of development. The community willed the changes upon itself and made them happen. It got exactly what it wanted: tract housing, economic growth—and nothing for the poor.

As early as the mid-1950s, well before suburban development had reached the town, a Philadelphia developer took an option on two thousand acres of prime agricultural land. Although nothing came of that venture because the builder went broke, it shows that, from the first signs of development, practical-minded Mount Laurel farm owners would not let sentiment intrude on the new economics that made housing tracts a more valuable cash crop than tomatoes. Soon thereafter, Mount Laurel's first development opened on the easternmost fringe of the township in Rancocas Woods, which at one time had been the town's recreation spot. This was hardly another Levittown—most of the new homes were log cabins, and their owners were dubbed "woodies"—but it marked the beginning of an influx of newcomers.

Commercial development was also on the minds of local officials. At a township council meeting in 1963, the Republican mayor boasted of "several hot business prospects" that were considering building offices near Exit 4. Just a few years later, as housing projects much more ambitious than Rancocas Woods were being launched, the new mayor, Bill Haines—whose family's farm, consisting of several hundred acres, was soon sold for $1.88 million to the biggest of the new developers—began to promote a braver vision of Mount Laurel's future, one that combined residential and commercial growth. Haines was less interested in conventional suburban tracts than in something that was new then, even visionary, called planned unit developments (PUDs). Patterned after Reston, Virginia—more grandiosely, after Italian hill villages and New England towns—PUDs are large-scale, self-contained communities within a community. When Larchmont opened in Mount Laurel in 1970, it was only the second such complex in the state. Its advertising boasted that it was ideally placed between city and country, though by now *city* had taken on a new meaning—not Camden or Philadelphia, whose proximity was no longer so relevant to the calculus of the would-be resident, but instead the Cherry Hill Mall, among the first enclosed shopping malls in the country, located in a more built-up suburb.

This tendency to embrace the new, with all of its ambiguous blessings, already apparent at the time of the centennial celebration, has accelerated since. Mount Laurel's business directory boasts health spas, a tanning salon, and a bar where upscale corporate employees meet for "food, drink, and great times," all located near the turnpike exit. The township's population increased at a faster rate than that of any other community in this rapidly suburbanizing state. It nearly doubled between 1950 and 1960, to 5,249, then doubled again in the next decade. By 1980, the population had grown to more than 17,000, as nearly three thousand new housing units, many in the new planned unit development, were built; in the next decade the population doubled yet again, to 34,000.

The demand for public services similarly mushroomed. The township outgrew its two prewar schools—one became a senior center, the other an administration building—and built six elementary and middle schools. The continuing pursuit of what local politicians call "good ratables," properties that generate lots of taxes while not demanding costly public services, has provided a stream of tax revenues. In a single year, 1985, the assessed value of Mount Laurel's twenty-five square miles of real estate increased more than 12 percent, to more than half a billion dollars; and during the preceding decade, the value of taxable real estate in the township had shot up by 330 percent, a growth rate more than three times that of the rest of surrounding Burlington County.

Three industrial parks in Mount Laurel house twenty companies, including Honda, Bell Atlantic, and National Football League Films. A Holiday Inn, a Quality Court, an Executive Motor Lodge, and a Hilton were all operating in the mid-1980s, mostly to accommodate visiting corporate executives. All told, there were two million square feet of office and industrial space—and this was supposed to be just the beginning, for plans were announced in 1985 for eighteen million additional square feet. With nearly six thousand acres of developable land still available and prospects bright for continued growth (the coming recession was not even a blip on the economic forecasters' radar), Mount Laurel set up New Jersey's first Long Range Planning Commission to project development into the twenty-first century. While growth in Mount Laurel, as elsewhere, has slowed almost to a standstill in recent years, the township's current population is almost twice as big as neighboring Moorestown's, and it is richer in terms of property value per resident, a fact that gives satisfaction to old-timers who recall when they were treated as Moorestown's poor relations.

All the familiar problems of growth have accompanied this prosperity. Traffic jams, once unknown, are twice-daily occurrences, and the number of car accidents has climbed too, to more than a thousand in 1990, a 20 percent increase in just five years. Drugs, once thought to be a city vice, are used by teenagers who complain that they're living in Dullsville. Crime has increased as well, and the much-expanded police force in Mount Laurel now carries automatics rather than revolvers. In place of the farms there are only pastoral names like Apple Way, Quail Run, and Orchard Court that developers, hoping to evoke nostalgia, assign to their brand-new streets.

Mount Laurel's history bears some resemblance to the story of Grover's Corners, the mythical New Hampshire community close by the Massachusetts border, pop. 3,149, where Thornton Wilder set the American classic *Our Town.* Both were settled in the late 1600s, and at the beginning of the present century, both were sleepy villages, neither growing nor shrinking much in size, surrounded by farms, overwhelmingly Republican in their politics. All the change comes later, in our time—it's as if, instead of looking backwards, the all-knowing stage manager who narrates the play is gazing into the future, not at all sure that he likes what he sees.

Grover's Corners is by and large a really nice place, as the stage manager tells the audience. Dr. Gibbs makes house calls and bashful boys treat their high school sweethearts to strawberry sodas, everyone looks after the town drunk, for "he'd seen a peck of trouble," and almost none of the residents lock their doors at night (though even at the turn of the century this trusting practice is beginning to disappear as the town starts to "citify").

Yet one of the first things the stage manager says about Grover's

Corners is that there's a bad neighborhood "across the tracks . . . Polish Town's across the tracks, and some Canuck families," and these ethnic families are stand-ins for blacks on the bottom rung of the social status ladder. Grover's Corners is also a place where money talks, though in muted tones. As a child, Rebecca, whose life history is traced out in the play, is forever saving. When her mother tells her "it's a good thing to spend some every now and then," she answers, "Mama, do you know what I love most in the world—do you?—Money."

An actor planted in the audience pesters the town's newspaper editor, Mr. Webb, to address "social injustice and industrial inequality," and he responds in a jokey way. "Oh, yes, everybody is [aware]—somethin' terrible. Seems like they spend most of their time talking about who's rich and who's poor." But the heckler is in no mood to be fobbed off with jokes. "Then why don't they do something about it?" he persists.

"Well, I dunno," Mr. Webb answers, "I guess we're all hunting like everybody else for a way the diligent and sensible can rise to the top and the lazy and quarrelsome can sink to the bottom. But it ain't easy to find. Meanwhile, *we do all that we can to help those that can't help themselves and those that can we leave alone.*"

That answer—Thornton Wilder's answer—mixes an appreciation for the vicissitudes of life, which don't always reward the deserving, with a lively social conscience. Among the well-off families in Mount Laurel, however, no similar sense of social obligation is apparent. By the time the committeeman stands up to address the black congregation in Jacob's Chapel, money and exclusivity are all that matter. *"If you people can't afford to live in our town, then you'll just have to leave."*

Quakers and Blacks: Sometime Friends

From the outset, the Quaker settlers in the Mount Laurel region depended on the help of nonwhites, initially Native Americans and later blacks, for their survival. William and Elizabeth Evans would have died were it not for the Lenni Lenape Indians, who provided them with food, taught them how to survive in a cave, and helped them build their first cabin. A few years later, when William Evans bought a thousand acres of land, he paid not only the Englishman who held formal title but also the Lenni Lenape king, Himicon, whose claim Evans valued at five pounds sterling.

Quakers brought the first African Americans to Burlington County as slaves as early as 1664; a county court judgment in 1685 enforced a verbal contract in which two slaves were traded for "6500 good well-burnt bricks." Although the Quakers were morally opposed to slavery, their sense of economic necessity came first. While the slaves were emancipated a century or so later, after the American Revolutionary War, most stayed on as tenant farmers, re-creating their economic dependency in a relationship that lasted for well over a century. The freedmen and freedwomen formed their first congregation in 1811 and later named their African Methodist Episcopalian church Jacob's Chapel, after Quaker farmer Albert Jacobs, who paid three dollars for the land on which the church presently sits and then contributed the property to the congregation.

By the 1840s, Mount Laurel had become a haven for freed blacks, as each new settler was given a quarter of an acre by the Quakers. It was also a stopping point on the Underground Railroad, which ran from Delaware through Woodbury in Gloucester County, then on to Mount Laurel in Burlington County and north to Mercer County, ferrying slaves to freedom. Traces of that hiding place remain underneath the floorboards in the vestibule of Jacob's Chapel. In the graveyard alongside the church, a dozen tombstones are inscribed with testimonials to the men who fought during the Civil War in the Colored Infantry, and alongside each of these stones rests the star of the Grand Army of the Republic.

So many bodies have been buried in that graveyard that the precise location of all the grave sites is no longer known, and when a member of the congregation dies the grave digger has to tap out an unused plot. The church's written records are gone too, tossed out in a flurry of housecleaning awhile back, but Mount Laurel's black community keeps its memories alive in stories handed down from generation to generation.

Ethel Lawrence, who became the pivotal figure in the struggle for affordable housing in the town, traces her own roots in Mount Laurel back six generations, to a white Virginia woman who came in the 1850s on the Underground Railroad to have her half-black baby. Born in 1926, the second of Leslie and Mary Robinson's eight children, Ethel Lawrence remembers growing up in the 1930s, in a tenant house on Frank Watson's farm, mostly as an idyll. "We were poor but it didn't matter so much. There was always food on the table, vegetables and fruits we canned for the winter. We chopped down firewood to keep warm. We took the feed out of those old muslin bags and bleached them to make sheets and tablecloths. If there was a hog killing, three or four families would join in. Since black families like the innards . . . when [white] farmers killed pigs, they'd give them to you. Everyone knew everybody else and if you were in trouble, everybody helped. We got along beautifully."

The same kind of story is told by old-time Quakers like Buddy Rudderow, who remembers "rubbing shoulders with the black families of the community. . . . We all knew each other." Yet when Ethel Lawrence pauses to reflect on precisely how blacks and whites in Mount Laurel lived side by side, it is not as equals but rather as people who knew in their bones their assigned stations in life. "We got along together, just as long as

I remembered who I was and they remembered who they were—as long as I remembered to stay in my place and they remembered to stay in their place, then we got along fine."

The ownership of property was one thing that defined a person's status in the community: it was the white farmers who owned the land and the black farm workers who depended on the farmers' largesse for a place to live. Law and custom were place definers as well. Although New Jersey is conventionally considered a northern state, North Jersey, which clusters around New York City, is in this respect very different from South Jersey. In its geographic location, no farther north than Maryland, and in its social etiquette as well, South Jersey has not been much removed from Dixie. The Ku Klux Klan was active there in its several incarnations, and the identities of local Klansmen are known to the black families: during the 1980s, a high school classmate of Ethel Lawrence's youngest daughter, Renee, a girl whose father is an ex-Klansman, fled from an abusive home to live for two years with the Lawrences. While skinheads have supplanted the Klan among today's teenagers, they pose a similar menace, getting their kicks from beating up black and Jewish children and planting crosses on black families' lawns.

Until World War II, blacks were obliged to sit in the last rows of the Moorestown movie theater, and Riley's, the local drugstore, wouldn't let blacks sit at the soda fountain. Mount Laurel's schools were officially segregated, as a colored school and a white school operated until the late 1940s. This was what the blacks wanted, some whites claim, but that is wishful remembering. Quaker patriarch Buddy Rudderow recalls that one family sent its blond daughter to the white school, but when the teachers found out that one of her parents was black, the girl was forced to attend the colored school. South Jersey was nothing like South Carolina, however—it didn't take sit-ins or fire hoses to change some of the folkways in Mount Laurel. Well before the swellings of the civil-rights movement, the black community got the simple justice it asked for. The schools were integrated, Riley's opened its lunch counter, the movie theater let blacks sit where they wished, and all the while a semblance of civility was maintained.

Economics, not Jim Crow, took the hardest toll on the black families, whose lives began to unravel with the opening of the Mount Laurel exit off the New Jersey Turnpike in 1952. The state claimed some farmland to build the highway, and, while the surveyors were careful to protect the old farmhouses, some of the tenant houses were plowed under for the roadway. The white farmers didn't complain because they were compensated for their losses, but they began to let the tenant farmers go. When Interstate 295 was constructed a few years later, the state took more land and more tenant farmers were displaced. There was no place in the township for them to move—no place, that is, except a handful of shacks in a shabby neighborhood known as Springville. Eventually those shacks would become the springboard for the *Mount Laurel* lawsuit.

Ask old-time Mount Laurel residents where Springville is and you'll likely draw a blank stare, then a flash of recognition. "You mean Jewtown," they say, entirely unselfconsciously, providing yet another insight into the social consciousness of the community.

Springville was originally farmed by homesteaders, but they couldn't make a living because of the high water table on which these 422 acres mostly sit. In the first decade of the present century, most of them sold their land to Jewish families who had emigrated from Russia and were living in the slums of Philadelphia—hence "Jewtown." The Jews mostly kept to themselves. They formed an Orthodox congregation, Agudas Achim, and opened their own school, which their gentile neighbors called the "black-shutters school" as a way of remarking critically on how separate it was. A cottage sewing industry was started, with rows of sewing machines lining the main street. The corner store was owned by a Jewish family, as was the local bar, Martin's Tap Room, but most of the newcomers made their living raising chickens. Later, the year-round residents were joined by other Jewish families fleeing the heat of Philadelphia summers. They lived in modest cottages, hastily cobbled together and not suited for winter use.

Those were the halcyon days in Springville, but the neighborhood began to slip after the Second World War. The chicken business, always a small-scale operation, became unprofitable because of automation. The children and grandchildren of the families who used to spend their summers in Mount Laurel were now grown up with their own families, and they wanted someplace nicer. The synagogue shut its doors, and over time the building found new uses as a storehouse, a window shop, and a mosque. The end of the war also brought an influx of GIs to nearby Fort Dix, and, with housing in the area extremely tight, the abandoned chicken coops were converted into residences. These were tiny, just a couple of rooms that had rudimentary plumbing or no plumbing at all, a single door perilously close to the kerosene heater, but they were cheap and also filled a need. The GIs moved in, transients with no ties to the town. Poor families, white and black, mostly migrant workers, moved in as well. The taproom attracted a rowdy crowd. People in town started seeing Springville as a slum and an embarrassment. Although a single Jewish landlord and a few poor Jewish families stayed on, the era of "Jewtown" was fading. Locals began referring to Springville as "Tobacco Road."

Cleaning up Springville became, in the mid-1960s, a crusade for local health officials and politicians alike. It was a way to improve the town's image and in the process alter the character of its population. Much of the housing there was substandard: a survey showed that half of the eighty-eight homes were, by the state's building-code standards, either deteriorated or dilapidated. The wells used for drinking water were contaminated by human sewage. Several of the converted chicken coops had burned down, killing some of the people who lived in them. Town officials felt these places should not be rehabilitated. The only thing to do was to tear them down. *"A mission of mercy"* is how Joe Alvarez, who was then the town's zoning officer and later was elected to the township council, characterizes this campaign. But those whose lives were directly touched felt otherwise. According to state law, local officials had to ensure that the housing was made fit for people to live in or else make other arrangements for displaced residents. Because they were unwilling to do either, local officials usually waited until a family had moved out before conducting their inspection. Then, with no tenants whom they were legally obliged to relocate, they plastered the dwelling with yellow stickers that read "Unfit for Habitation" and razed the condemned homes.

"I know we had a very effective program," says Alvarez. "It may have resulted in eliminating a few homes, but then it was a good reflection on the town."

Colliding Dreams

Mary Robinson and her daughter Ethel Lawrence kept watch on these developments. Both mother and daughter had sought to secure their own futures against the changes taking place in Mount Laurel. Theirs was the credo of the blind man on the corner who sings in *Beale Street Blues*: "I'd rather be here than any place I know. It's going to take the sergeant for to make me go."

By the standards of Mount Laurel, Mary Robinson, then nearly sixty years old, a widow whose children were all grown, was an activist. Two decades earlier, she had spoken out against racial separation in the schools and the refusal of Riley's drugstore to serve blacks; she had sent her daughter, then just sixteen, to protest a movie house in Burlington that required blacks to sit in the very front rows. She owned her own home, which she and her late husband, Leslie, bought in 1935 for a thousand dollars.

In 1954, Ethel Lawrence and her husband, Thomas, a welder who worked for United States Pipe and Foundry Company, rented a bungalow on an acre of land on Elbo Lane, in a neighborhood known as Little Texas. They dressed up the outside of their home with flowers and shade trees, raised a few rabbits and some chickens, planted squash, collard greens, tomatoes, cabbage, string beans, and strawberries in the backyard. Within a few years they had saved up enough to make the down payment on the six-thousand-dollar purchase price.

With farms shrinking and Springville gradually being razed, though, it didn't take a seer to realize that none of these families, not even those whose ancestors are listed in the Jacob's Chapel Bible, would be able to remain there. Unless something was done to bend the economic forces that were turning farms into subdivisions for the rising middle class, there would be no home they could afford—no place in Mount Laurel for the next generation, the eight children Ethel and Thomas Lawrence were raising on Elbo Lane. It was the thought of what might happen to those children that stirred Ethel Lawrence to do something. The formation of the Springville Action Council—the federal community-action program come to Mount Laurel—gave her the chance.

Community action was a new concept in the mid-1960s. Lifted from inner-city projects that the Ford Foundation had financed a few years earlier, the idea had been and incorporated into Lyndon Johnson's vision of a Great Society. It was a particularly foreign-sounding idea in a town like Mount Laurel. On the map, Camden was just a few miles away, but the social distance between Mount Laurel's placid public life and the angry voices being raised in Camden could be measured in light-years.

Ethel Lawrence was a logical candidate to become involved with this new enterprise. She had been active in Jacob's Chapel since she was a girl, and she was the first black woman in the county to lead a Girl Scout troop. Behind the scenes, she and her mother had been Democratic Party stalwarts during the long years when Mount Laurel was a Republican monolith, and when the Democrats took over in 1958 she was able to get her out-of-work uncle a job driving the town's tractor and grader. That track record was enough for both mother and daughter to be tapped for the Springville Action Council. As she remembers those events: "Reverend Wood, a white man who was on the council's board, told me that 'all these do-gooders really mean well but they can't know what it means to be poor or to be black, because they have never been poor or black.' That reverend was exactly what you would think a Christian would be. He saw no color. He just saw human need."

Stuart Wood had been sent to Mount Laurel in 1966 with an unusual assignment, to create a ministry without a church. He rented a house in Ramblewood, the development that was filling up with young executives' families, and set about looking for a mission. The day he was taken through Springville, he knew he had found his calling.

"Right away I thought, 'Something needs to be done here,'" and during the coming months Stuart Wood knocked on every door in Springville. "Here were poor Jews, Cubans, poor whites, blacks. The chicken coops they lived in were like places where you cage an animal." Later he would tell reporters that Springville was "a festering cancer, worse than the worst slums in New York City," where living conditions "made me puke." The minister usually spent his days in Springville, or else with the liberal Quakers from Moorestown, or in seething Camden. At night he returned to Ramblewood, where the lawns were perfectly cropped, gin and tonic flowed at endless cocktail parties, and the talk was about steadily rising property values.

The first project of the Springville Action Council, which Wood helped to launch in 1967, was a Head Start program for children who, their teachers reported, were more sluggish and apathetic than youngsters from Camden who every day had to struggle for their lives. Ethel Lawrence decided she wanted to teach those youngsters; she commuted to Manhattan every day, months on end, to earn her teaching credential at the Banks Street College of Education.

The community group stayed financially afloat with barbecues and rummage sales. Its members knew that decent shelter for the town's poor families was a prime need; the critical question was how to make this happen. Town officials played along, believing that the group was harmless, until it received a six-thousand-dollar grant from the state's activist Department of Community Affairs for the state's first low-cost rural housing development. This was only seed money: the ultimate aim was to tap into federal subsidies for low-income rental housing to build two- and three-bedroom garden apartments. Planners volunteered their time to design the complex, and the state funds were used to take out an option on a thirty-two-acre parcel in Springville, then on the market at a thousand dollars an acre.

"The landowner told me I was next to God for wanting to help the people of Springville," Reverend Wood recalls. Yet before the apartments could be built, Mount Laurel would have to amend its master plan, because the zoning law on the books allowed for only single-family residences. Ethel Lawrence and Mary Robinson were sure that the township council would go along. After all, Mount Laurel was their town too and had been for generations. Surely the unarticulated sense of community revealed in the painless desegregation of the schools two decades earlier would bring Mount Laurel's officials to accede to the reasonable wishes of the town's black citizens. But this perception proved highly romanticized. It took no account of what Kenneth Lockridge describes as "the depths of the American experience . . . a craving for peace, unity and order within the confines of a simple society" and "a willingness to exclude whatever men and to ignore whatever events threaten the fulfillment of that hunger."

The first sign of trouble came when the Department of Community Affairs announced the seed-money grant. The press release got the facts all wrong: the projected Mount Laurel apartments would be rented for next to nothing, it said, and people on welfare would be recruited to live in them. Although this was untrue—the housing was actually intended for the working poor who were being pushed out of Mount Laurel—the story made page one in the local press.

The firestorm it ignited set the tone for all the controversies to come. From 1968, when the state grant was announced, until today, when middle-class residents in Mount Laurel hear "affordable housing," they don't think about Ethel Lawrence and her generations of ancestors from Mount Laurel. Most of the people who have moved into the new, middle-class developments have no sense that their adopted town has any history—they would be dumbfounded to learn that free black families were living in Mount Laurel before there was a United States of America. Nor do they have in mind people like Ethel Lawrence's oldest daughter, Thomasene, a medical assistant who during the late 1960s was struggling to raise her children in one of Springville's converted chicken coops.

What the suburbanites *do* think goes something like this. Very poor people are coming . . . very poor outsiders . . . very poor outsiders on welfare . . . *lots of very poor and black outsiders on welfare are coming to Mount Laurel from places like Camden, and they will bring violence and drugs, and they will wreck our schools. They will destroy our way of life.* This mixture of paranoia and urban reality explains why so many homeowners in Rancocas Woods and Ramblewood, the woodies and the strivers who were otherwise so different, were united on this one issue. Housing for the poor should not—at all costs *must* not—be built in Mount Laurel.

All Politics Is Local

The Springville Action Council was slated to make its case before the township council in November 1969. The bad news was that Richard Goodwin, the developer of Ramblewood and a powerful influence in local politics, was also on the docket. Goodwin was an ambitious man—"My mother didn't raise an empty chair," he boasts—who had gotten involved in the township election campaign that fall, hiring a public relations firm to promote the Republican cause. Less than twenty-four hours after the election, when with his help the GOP ousted the Democrats, he submitted his plan for a massive planned unit development. The night the Springville Action Council made its appeal, this proposal was the initial item on the agenda.

What Goodwin had in mind was a new town, which ultimately would become the ten-thousand-unit PUD called Larchmont. To these newly elected politicians, Republicans who had campaigned on a prodevelopment platform with his backing, the pitch was irresistible: the new residents will have money in their pockets, they'll give a boost to the economy. It was very hard to follow this performance with a plea for a change in the zoning rules—a modest change, as well, in the direction the town was heading—put forward mainly by liberal white ministers and black women with neither money nor the influence that money can buy. Their only argument, really, was that this was the right thing to do, and that was hardly enough to sway popular sentiment.

From the outset, zoning in Mount Laurel was a way to exclude people regarded by the residents as undesirable. Until 1952, a $2.50

permit was all that was legally required to build a house in Mount Laurel. There was no zoning ordinance on the books then, no planning of any kind, no building inspection carried out. The clerk who handled the building permits lived in a falling-down house that wouldn't have passed even the most cursory inspection. But this attitude shifted when townspeople got wind of a proposed labor camp for migrant workers. Overnight, the township drafted a zoning law—a crude text that ran only a couple of pages—meant less to guide the township's future than to keep out the migrant laborers. The Rancocas Woods development, built a few years later on the site of what had once been an amusement park, was a planner's nightmare. The developers did not install sewers, and, because there wasn't enough drainage, flooding followed every rainstorm. Water pressure from the fire hydrants was so pitifully weak that the volunteer fire department had to pump its water from Rancocas Creek. Not until the mid-1960s, after Ramblewood as well as Rancocas Woods had been approved and the shortcomings of a laissez-faire approach to planning were very apparent, did the town draft a real master plan.

The official who took major responsibility for shaping this plan, Democrat Frank Mull, knew firsthand what was wrong with Rancocas Woods because he lived there; his background in building and surveying gave him some expertise. Mull's intention was to get land-use policy out of the politicians' hands and turn it over to engineers and architects. "There wasn't a bit of prejudice in that plan," he recalls. "We simply decided this is a likely place for this, that's a likely place for that, and so on." But planning and politics cannot be so neatly separated. Sound principles of planning hardly compelled the conclusion that there was no "likely place" for apartment-style housing—no place at all, actually, in Mount Laurel's master plan. Town officials said frankly that they wanted Mount Laurel to be transformed into an "executive-type town," a place like Moorestown. Garden apartments for the working poor were as out of place in this vision as dandelions in the well-tended suburban garden.

While small-town politics is often a somnambulant affair, Mount Laurel has been notable for the partisan ferocity of its public life. Planning and zoning have figured centrally in this political warfare. Beginning in the late 1950s with the construction of new homes in Rancocas Woods and the first influx of newcomers, a community that had been solidly Republican for generations became the setting for bloody partisan battles. Democrats took control for the first time in 1958, Republicans regained power in 1966, there was a Democratic sweep in 1970, and five years later the GOP was again in command, as the political pendulum continued to swing. These party labels, although regularly used in Mount Laurel, are misleading. The contests in Mount Laurel were not reprises of the great national campaigns of the era—Kennedy versus Nixon or, later, Vietnam and Watergate played out in South Jersey. Mount Laurel's elections confirmed the adage that all politics is local, for the dominant questions, the preoccupying questions, concerned property values, tax rates and assessments, allegations of overdevelopment, claims that incumbents were in the developers' pockets. Behind these issues lay deeper questions of political identity—how can we control our destiny?

Both Democrats and Republicans cast themselves as progressives and their opponents as dinosaurs in matters of development. The Republicans, whose core strength came from the old landowners, described themselves as the promoters of intelligent growth who believed that the way to woo industry was straightforward. Their message was: "We need you and we won't give you flak."

It was the Democrats, mostly newcomers living in the new developments, who wanted to slow the pace of growth. They were concerned about what the proposed planned unit developments would bring—"wall-to-wall housing," as Joseph Massari, an angry voice before and during the *Mount Laurel* litigation, describes it. "I came to Mount Laurel in 1962 because it was rural and peaceful," says Massari. "I became active in the Ramblewood Civic Association because I feared the creek behind my home could be turned into a drainage ditch. This led me to be appointed to the township's Charter Study Council, which recommended a town-manager type of government, and in 1970 I ran on the new form of government." Massari's career in local politics exemplifies what Alexis de Tocqueville in *Democracy in America* describes as "self-interest rightly understood."

The Republicans dismissed the Democrats as arrivistes who had purchased their own small piece of the suburban dream and selfishly wanted to fence out everybody else. The Democrats countered that their opponents, who when in office approved almost every new housing and commercial complex that the builders proposed, were not selfless purveyors of progress, for their financial self-interest was closely tied to their vision of the public interest. A number of prominent Republicans, including council member Bill Haines, who proudly refers to himself as the father of PUDs, owned hundreds of acres of farmland that developers coveted. They stood to become millionaires if their vision was realized.

"Our town was on the edge of a major development explosion," Frank Mull recalls, "and it just didn't seem to me that the people who were potentially able to profit from that were the best people to have the role of decision makers." But the Democrats who personally placed great value on Mount Laurel's small town atmosphere, newcomers who were eager to lift the drawbridge the moment they arrived, faced a similar conflict when they opposed a new development. Each side was able to equate the public interest with personal interest.

All politics is local in another sense: it is a mutual back-scratching enterprise that thrives on contributions from citizens who expect to be rewarded in kind by those they help elect. Democrat Alvarez recalls getting fifteen dollars for his campaign from a man for whom he had found work as the town's truck driver; Republican Haines remembers that developers contributed the liquor to hold cocktail-party fund-raisers and "we'd get to keep the left over half bottles." Hurt feelings also carried political consequences. In 1970, Haines lost a bruising Republican primary campaign to Bill Shields. Disputes over planned unit developments and tax assessments were the publicly stated reasons for the internecine squabble, but according to Haines the real issues were much more personal. "The chair of the Republican county council wanted a job as the town-hall receptionist, but she couldn't type; another party leader wanted his brother-in-law hired as a policeman, but I was after a state-of-the-art police force. If I'd appointed those people, I would have been fine."

The influence of the leading developers on township politics was bluntly expressed. "We had a marketing study done as to which direction we should go from the center of Philadelphia," says Richard Goodwin, developer of Ramblewood and later of Larchmont, "and the line cut right through Mount Laurel. It wasn't too difficult to get permission from the town fathers in those days. The leadership was Quaker farmers. They knew in the back of their minds that when they sold their land their pot of gold had arrived—payback for the struggles the farmers had all their lives to scrape out a living." Other tangible rewards accompanied development. One member of the planning board made a tidy living by selling fences to Goodwin, and one of the council members drilled all of the developer's wells. Even as Bill Haines was negotiating to sell his own acreage to Goodwin for the new Larchmont PUD, he backed a sweetener for the developer: the recently formed Mount Laurel Municipal Utilities Commission would waive its water and sewage hookup charges for Larchmont. That arrangement, later challenged by the Democrats and overturned in court, would have saved Goodwin several million dollars.

Such partisan antagonisms did not translate into opposing positions on whether the township should change its zoning law to authorize new housing for the poor. Not once did a voice in the political mainstream ever have a kind word to say on that topic. In the late 1960s, the members of a Republican-dominated council turned down the Springville Action Council's plans, one after the other. The Democrats who succeeded them, and the Republicans who followed the Democrats, eventually spent more than a million dollars in lawyers' and experts' fees to fight the proposition, propounded in the *Mount Laurel* supreme court decisions, that the township had a legal duty to a "fair share" of the region's poor.

Politics and Race

The Mount Laurel politicians' words and acts carry the sharp scent of race prejudice. When council members talked about Camden, they were talking in a code everyone understood—the meaning was "black." When Bill Haines said that he didn't want "what happened in [neighboring] Willing-boro to happen here," that statement too could be taken as referring to race, although Haines later indicated he only had Willingboro's monoto-nous tract housing in mind.

What happened in Willingboro was this: a black soldier was denied housing in that Levittown because of the color of his skin. Developer Wil-liam Levitt was blunt: "We can solve a housing problem or we can try to solve a racial problem," Levitt believed, "but we cannot combine the two." Equally bluntly, the state Supreme Court sided with the soldier; other black families, anxious to move out of the dying cities and into a community that wouldn't abuse them, began to buy homes there. By the late 1960s, at a time when the Burlington County Human Rights Commission, concerned about possible violence, determined that it was prudent to inform the Mount Laurel police department that a single black family was moving into town, Willingboro had become more than one-third black. It didn't matter that Willingboro remained a verdant and tidy place—the prospect of a comparable influx of blacks into Mount Laurel was enough to terrify local politicians.

In the Springville neighborhood, discrimination based both on class and race was old news. The area badly needed sewers, streetlights, and roads. "When we asked for something, it might have been wells, it doesn't matter, it was always the same," recalls a longtime resident. "When the mayor found out we were from Springville we met a stone wall. . . . They couldn't wait to get rid of what was already there. Why should they want more?"

Still, Bill Haines believes that "we would have worked things out," referring to the proposed housing for Springville, "because we under-stood each other." Perhaps his claque, the Quaker farmers with deep roots in Mount Laurel, would eventually have struck a deal. Ethel Law-rence would like to believe that "the old farmers would have had enough foresight to spend money in building homes for these people than spend-ing the money to pay lawyers to keep them out." But the Quaker farmers were no longer in charge, the new suburbanites were running the town, and that altered the equation. "Things changed as the newcomers settled in the community. The old-timers turned against us. All our support died as the old-timers stayed in the background, for they did not want to risk losing the support of the newcomers."

The generation of GOP politicians who came of age in the 1960s wasn't much interested in negotiating. One Republican councilman who lived in Rancocas Woods talks about campaigning in Springville as if the experience had left the taste of ashes perpetually in his mouth. "The conditions there turned my stomach. I remember each time I shook some-one's hand and asked for his vote, he'd ask for some favor in return." Although this was par for the course in Mount Laurel politics, he drew back. "I thought it was awful. I told them they could keep their votes and walked out on them." Republican William Shields, a Ramblewood resident who became mayor of the town, speaks sarcastically about the Springville Action Council as people who expected "a million dollars and an El Dorado Cadillac" for the asking.

The Democrats on the council held similar views, even though they came differently to their positions. Councilman Frank Mull, putting on his planner's hat, believed that building subsidized housing meant "instant slums . . . those people knew damn well we weren't prejudiced." Joe Alvarez says: "I come from a culture of helping people. But the township didn't create the problem, and the township has no responsibility to alleviate the problem."

"I moved to Mount Laurel on November 27, 1954," recounts Alvarez, a native of Puerto Rico, and he savors the exact date. "It was because of fate," he adds, but the facts are somewhat more mundane. He was working for Philco-Ford at the time, living with his family in a rented house in Philadelphia, and he didn't have the cash to make a down payment on a home. An old-time Mount Laurel resident named Earl Bartling was willing to donate construction materials and give advice to this self-described pencil pusher; all Alvarez had to contribute was sweat equity and the $350 cost of a half-acre lot. Alvarez is not the only person who Bartling helped this way—at least ten houses were built in Mount Laurel because of his remarkable generosity—but Alvarez sees no connection between these private good deeds and any public responsibility. And although he has financed a condominium in Mount Laurel for his son, who otherwise couldn't have afforded to stay, he has no empathy for people like Ethel Lawrence's children who lack the family money to bankroll their own homes.

During the years he has lived in Mount Laurel, there have been occasional racist jibes about Joe Alvarez's ancestry, antagonists who asked him, "Why don't you go back to Puerto Rico?" Yet he regards himself as an American who made it, not as an outsider—in Mount Laurel he insists on being Joe, not José. For six months in 1964, the family moved to Puerto Rico, but they returned when they realized that the New Jersey suburb had become their real home. On the day of their return, says Alvarez, the Holiday Inn's billboard read: "Welcome Back, Joe and Anna."

Like other ethnic Americans, Alvarez assimilated in ways that the descendants of slaves, whatever their wishes, never have been able to. But none of this personal history surfaces when Alvarez talks about people who were seeking affordable housing, like Ethel Lawrence and Mary Robinson. He relies instead on the language of disease and disorder. "It's like grafting a good healthy skin so you can graft in cancer skin and blend it in. Here you have a healthy area. Bringing these people in here, you don't know who they are," he says, with all the ominous implications of the unknown.

Sometimes the politicians spoke, as Republican William Shields did, about the community's willingness to "take care of our own" but not "having to take care of the world." This is a morally plausible position, the philosophy attributed to the residents of *Our Town*, but the politicians' perpetual antagonism to housing the poor—*any* poor, local or otherwise— unmasks this commitment as a pietism. At one township-council meeting, Reverend Stuart Wood remembers, when Springville housing was on the table, "the local health officer poked me black and blue in the chest while pinning me to the wall. He screamed at me, 'Why don't you just sit tight like everyone else until I can condemn all those places and get the people there out?' " The only principles that drove the propertied classes, whom the politicians represented, were efficiency and security, a desire to "keep taxes down and to keep them out," part of their "relentless quest for material benefit along with the promise of freedom—that is, the lack of encumbrances—to improvise fresh identities."

The engineers and planners who worked for the planning board and the township council lodged one objection after another, twenty-two in all, to the proposed housing. The community-action group was only "marginally competent" to build on wetlands, complains the head of the planning board. "They were naive, flying blind. . . . They should have hired a good engineer," adds the township's engineer. Yet competency was never the real issue. The community group received sound advice from able professionals who contributed their time; four separate sets of plans were prepared, and each was rejected. "We were beaten by other professionals," says Stuart Wood, "planners, architects, and PR men selling the dream of a new suburban community of newly upwardly mobile people. They bought that dream—and in the process they killed ours." Politics hid behind the mask of expertise to exclude unwanted neighbors.

The biggest technical problem was how to deliver water and sewage treatment. Because of the high water table, the new project couldn't sustain its own systems. The obvious solution was to tie it into existing utilities located in Ramblewood, but, while this was technically feasible, it was a nonstarter politically. "There was no political base in Springville, no voters there. They were just poor, ignorant people," says Dick Goodwin, who had built Ramblewood's water and sewage systems. "The newcomers in Ramblewood didn't want poor people in Mount Laurel."

Meeting after meeting, the township council dominated by Ramblewood and Rancocas homeowners kept stonewalling the community contingent, hoping it would tire and go away. The people who showed up got "very personal—it was better than a TV soap opera," recalls Quaker matriarch Alice Rudderow, who in 1967 sold almost all of her family's 220-acre farm to developers. "Stuart Wood was like a small salmon swimming upstream," observes Goodwin. "He couldn't see that failure was the handwriting on the wall." When the option on the thirty-two acres in Springville ran out, no one picked it up, and it lapsed. The New Jersey Department of Community Affairs didn't lose interest; state officials offered to advance more money if that would get the project moving. Yet by the time that project was revived nearly five years later, after the state Supreme Court decided *Mount Laurel I*, the land had appreciated in value so much that it was financially out of the question to be "next to God."

Meanwhile, the housing controversy was moving into a new forum. No longer was this a matter for the citizens of Mount Laurel to settle entirely among themselves. The problem was about to be placed in the hands of the judges, who played by entirely different rules.

Way Stations to Litigation

Lawyers and nonlawyers inhabit different worlds. Attorneys think about a lawsuit as a way to get what their clients want while they flex their professional legal muscles; the more novel the legal claim the more muscle flexing, and hence, if they win, the more gratification. But to the laity, lawsuits are fearful and alien events, prolonged battles over arcane territory fought by proxies who, expressing themselves in the obscurantisms of legalese, pitch their pleadings and their pleas to stern, black-sheathed judges. Better to work things out, people generally believe, better not to raise the stakes by invoking the majesty of the law. So it was in Mount Laurel—before a case could be filed on behalf of those who were being driven out, the Legal Services lawyers first had to win the trust of their new clients. The go-between in that enterprise was Reverend Stuart Wood.

Mount Laurel's tactics frustrated the minister and made him question whether he was being of service to anyone. Town-council members regarded him as weird, a hippie child of the sixties living in a community that carried on as if Dwight Eisenhower were still in the White House. His outspokenness made him a pariah in the Ramblewood development where he lived, and, while that didn't bother him, it put a strain on his wife. At one cocktail party, Wood recalls, she had been talking intensely with a couple who had just moved in down the block, but the moment they realized that she was Reverend Wood's wife, *that man's* wife, they turned away.

Wood had raised unrealistic hopes within the black community, he thought guiltily. Strains were also surfacing within the Springville Action Council, as a successful black merchant disputed the tactics favored by the Jacob's Chapel contingent. The entrepreneur realized that he could earn a nice income by getting himself named a consultant on the federal grant that would underwrite the Springville project. "You're a fool," he told

Wood, who refused to go along, "we could make real money from this." Secretly, the business owner began trying to cut a deal with the Republican council members whom Wood and Ethel Lawrence saw as their enemies.

When Camden Regional Legal Services' enterprising young attorneys, who had read newspaper accounts of the community group's abortive attempt to get affordable housing, met with Wood, he was delighted to hand over responsibility for Springville's future. "I had nothing left," he recalls. "I couldn't work up any enthusiasm for the litigation because I was sure the local community leaders wouldn't let it happen. My role was to line up the plaintiffs for the case. That was the end of my involvement."

The lawyers came away impressed when they talked with a contingent from the Springville Action Council at Ethel Lawrence's home. Many suburbs had zoning ordinances that walled out poor outsiders, and ultimately the reformers hoped to end this practice. But here was a community that seemed bent on growing faster than anyplace else, while simultaneously ridding itself of the poor families who were already there. Because the town was forcing its own poor residents to move, the attorneys felt that their cause might arouse more sympathy than a lawsuit designed mainly to let in poor and black outsiders.

But the local black community held decidedly mixed views. The older generation of Mount Laurel's black residents, people like Hattie Britt, perhaps the most respected black figure in the town, didn't want to push matters too hard. By then well into her eighth decade of life, Britt had taught for years in the old colored school, then instructed white as well as black children when the schools were integrated; after she retired, one of the elementary schools was renamed the Hattie Britt School. She was disturbed by the radical ideas that the lawyers and the community-action group were kicking around. "The older people were satisfied with their life-style. It was the younger people who wanted a change. I know the civic leaders [like Mary Robinson and Ethel Lawrence] worked very hard to get housing for the poor in Springville and eventually to be integrated in the new developing areas. But one could not expect low-cost housing to be placed in the big-homes area.

"They wanted a decent place, a convenient place and a nice place to live. But if you don't have the money," she adds, sounding not so very different from politicians like Joe Alvarez, "one should expect to stay in one's own area."

Some members of the Jacob's Chapel congregation weren't eager to get involved either. The church had been split for generations along family lines. On one side were the Gaineses and Robinsons. On the other side was the Still family, which traced its ancestry back to James Still, the self-taught doctor of the South Jersey pinelands during the late nineteenth century and the most famous black man of his day. By tradition, the church sets aside one Sunday every year for each of these families, and relatives come from hundreds of miles away for the festivities. The pastor's salary and the heating bills used to be paid from the money raised on those family days. Even now, though the rivalries have faded, the families try to outdo one another in the lavishness of their spread and their generosity to the church; and so it mattered that the Springville Action Council was mostly a Robinson, not a Still, affair.

One Sunday, the minister at Jacob's Chapel delivered a sermon doubting the wisdom of congregation members' devoting so much time to the housing fight. Even members of Ethel Lawrence's own family grumbled at her involvement; but when her children complained that she was foolish to get involved, since she already had her own house, she replied that she was doing it for them, and that stopped the criticism. Ethel's husband, Thomas, chewed out the lawyers for what he regarded as their trouble making, yet he was proud of what his wife was doing. "While he never told me so to my face," she says, "Thomas would brag about me when he went to see his brothers."

Throughout the lengthy struggle, the handful of black professional families who had moved into Rancocas Woods and Ramblewood remained mute. "Secretly they support the cause of housing for the poor," says Ethel Lawrence, "but they were afraid of ruffling the feathers of their neighbors, afraid of risking their positions." Perhaps so, though it is also possible that these successful black families had no wish to invite the ghetto back into their lives and so were entirely comfortable with the strategy that town officials were pursuing.

Blacks who lived in the Springville chicken coops potentially had the most to gain from legal action, but they were scared that their landlords would evict them if they complained; and so they endured, in places like the shanty on which Ethel Lawrence's oldest daughter, Thomasene, spent eighty-eight dollars a month for rent. "Everything leaked," she says, "everything got mildewed, the shower was corroded. The open sewer ran right in back, polluting our drinking water. I was lucky because I had real wood floors and heat in the winter. Others had dirt floors and nearly froze."

These families needed housing, not lawsuits. Suing the township on their behalf meant breaking new legal ground, but not necessarily new ground for housing. A final court decision was probably years away. It would surely be better to win something tangible, Peter O'Connor thought, than to risk everything on the receptivity of New Jersey judges. He hoped he could strike a deal with developer Richard Goodwin to get the units built, and so make a lawsuit unnecessary. For his part, Goodwin had good reason to appreciate O'Connor's skills as an adversary. The developer had been in the midst of constructing an apartment complex in downtown Camden, part of the city's urban-renewal dream, when the lawsuit filed by Camden Regional Legal Services halted that venture. Although most of Goodwin's building had been done in the suburbs—

Ramblewood in the early 1960s, another development in nearby Cherry Hill a few years before—he had grown bored doing traditional subdivisions. He wanted Larchmont, his next Mount Laurel project, to be a planned unit development, a new concept that he had first learned about as a member of the national builders' council. As Goodwin envisioned Larchmont, its homes would be concentrated in clusters, leaving more open space than in conventional tracts (in his plan, "open space" meant a golf course). It would be a "life-cycle community" that housed all the generations—the newly married, families with school-age kids, the empty nesters—and that called for more of an economic mix than is typical in suburban tracts.

The Larchmont plan was venturesome in all these ways, and O'Connor tried persuading Goodwin to go one giant step further—to set aside some units for poor families, subsidizing those units with market-price housing. The sweetener the lawyer proposed was an increase in the density of building, with more units, and hence bigger profits, in the developed clusters. "You'll make your profit," O'Connor declared, "and Mount Laurel's social problems will be cured." Nearly fifteen years later, in *Mount Laurel II*, the New Jersey Supreme Court would mandate a similar approach for the entire state. But in 1969, the idea was unheard of. While Goodwin was intrigued, he ultimately rejected the plan as politically suicidal.

Over the next few months, Peter O'Connor and Carl Bisgaier came frequently to Mount Laurel. They walked around Springville and attended church services at Jacob's Chapel a Sunday or two. The lawyers were received politely but skeptically. What finally gave them credibility was a lawsuit they brought on behalf of Ethel Lawrence's aunt, Catherine Still. She had gotten weary of making do in a house with no toilet and no running water, and when her landlord refused to make improvements, she brought her grievance to Carl Bisgaier. The lawyer put her rent money in escrow, then took her case to court to test the state's new tenants' rights law. In 1971, Bisgaier won the case: the judge permitted Catherine Still to withhold her rent until the landlord brought her home up to code.

Word quickly went out in Springville that these attorneys weren't empty vests, that they could accomplish something with their legal arguments. Catherine Still's complaint was infinitely less ambitious than the township zoning challenge the lawyers were preparing. But for many years it was the only housing litigation that made any tangible impact on the town. The case known as *Southern Burlington County NAACP et al. v. Township of Mount Laurel,* filed in May 1971, would continue not just for a few years but seemingly forever. It became a Dickensian *Jarndyce v. Jarndyce* of land-use justice, a lawsuit that tested the mettle of the state courts—tested, as well, the character of those communities, black and white, well-off and poor, that together made up Mount Laurel.

PART TWO
RIGHTS, POLITICS, AND MARKETS

Courts do not build housing.

Southern Burlington County NAACP v. Township of
Mount Laurel (1975)

*We may not build houses, but we do enforce the Constitution. . . .
[I]f the poor remain locked into urban slums, it will not be because
we failed to enforce the Constitution.*

Southern Burlington County NAACP v. Township of
Mount Laurel (1983)

*We are under the Constitution, but the Constitution is what the
judges say it is.*

Charles Evans Hughes, *Addresses*

4

Simple Justice

In the annals of land use, the annals of poor people's justice too, the trilogy of *Mount Laurel* cases is renowned. Because these were state-court rulings, they never unleashed the national passions of cases like *Brown v. Board of Education*, which outlawed racial segregation, or *Roe v. Wade*, which made abortion a constitutional right. Yet these are the most critical judicial decisions on zoning in this country since the U.S. Supreme Court first announced, nearly three-quarters of a century ago, that municipalities could tell landowners how their land could, and could not, be used.

Like few other judicial decisions, *Mount Laurel* ignited powerful feelings. At church socials and backyard barbecues, at beach resorts and drinks at the nineteenth hole as well, even to say "Mount Laurel" was to start an argument. To some people it was shorthand for justice, while to others it stood for judicial busybodying that threatened a hard-earned way of life.

These disturbances in the field were felt most powerfully in New Jersey, since that is where the cases were decided. But what the state judges said about the legal requirement of making available a "fair share" of land for the poor, and about the moral obligation to do the right thing, also appeared on the front page of the *New York Times* and on the nightly television news shows. Lawyers and planners who worked on the case found themselves in demand in courtrooms elsewhere. Planning schools and law schools taught their students new ways to think about housing and the general welfare. Legislators from across the country borrowed the themes of *Mount Laurel* in rewriting their states' rules about land use. And phrases like "fiscal zoning"—less euphemistically, snob zoning—became policy commonplaces. Because of *Mount Laurel*, the relationship changed between cities and their suburbs.

Archaeologists in the Legal Trenches

None of these changes was remotely predictable to the lawyers from Camden Regional Legal Services who in 1970 were beavering away in the archives of Mount Laurel Township, pursuing what attorney Carl Bisgaier called an "archaeological dig." When they started out, these attorneys knew amazingly little about land-use law. "We didn't even know what zoning was," Bisgaier confesses—which was probably just as well, since it kept them from being discouraged by the utter lack of legal precedent for their arguments.

The press release accompanying the filing of their 1971 complaint called it "the first suit which asks a court to order a suburban community to develop an affirmative action plan for the construction of low and moderate income housing." That was a slight but pardonable exaggeration, for while similar cases were being brought elsewhere in New Jersey, the reform-minded attorneys did not discover one another until after they had filed the legal papers. These were truly legal innocents abroad in the land of reform. The task of researching the law was left to a Harvard law student named Ken Meiser, the house intellectual, who shuttled between Camden and Cambridge, and his inexperience showed. "It's all right here!" he exclaimed at one point, brandishing a New Jersey Supreme Court decision called *Vickers v. Gloucester Township.* Indeed, all the winning arguments *were* there, but in Meiser's excitement he failed to notice that he was reading not the majority opinion but the dissent.

While Meiser was guilty of wishful misreading, he was entirely right to focus on state, rather than federal, rulings. Because the issues in the Mount Laurel case potentially involved both federal and state constitutional law, the lawyers had to decide whether to take the dispute to a U.S. district court or to a New Jersey trial court. The former route was generally more familiar to reform-minded attorneys, and more glamorous too, since many attorneys think that federal court has more prestige and offers a more direct pathway to the U.S. Supreme Court. During the Warren Court era, federal judges had rewritten the law of equality, reconceiving the Constitution as an instrument to protect racial minorities and poor people against discrimination.

Yet even in its liberal heyday, the U.S. Supreme Court had been reluctant to say much about land use. Now, with Earl Warren replaced by conservative Warren Burger, there were unmistakable signs of retrenchment. In *James v. Valtierra,* decided in 1971, a closely divided Court upheld a California statute that required a public referendum before public housing could be built, rejecting the argument that this law effectively put a stop to such construction and so discriminated against the poor. That retreat in Washington, coupled with the emergence of newly energized state tribunals, meant that the advocates needed to change their tactics, to emphasize state rather than federal constitutional law. Justice William Brennan, who himself had served on the New Jersey Supreme Court in the 1950s, had the *Mount Laurel* case specifically in mind when he reminded lawyers that "state decisions [based on state law] not only cannot be overturned by, they indeed are not even reviewable by, the Supreme Court of the United States." In delivering this homily, Brennan was reminding reform-minded lawyers that the Warren Court was no more, and that they would do well to stay away from federal court.

For a generation, New Jersey's highest court had been as venture-some as any in the land. It was among the nation's most admired state tribunals, and judges in other states regularly followed its lead. While the court's opinions on land-use regulation had generally sided with the towns, recent dissents suggested that the New Jersey justices might be persuaded to change their minds. If that happened, there would be new law for the state and a model for the nation. That's why the activists began their legal campaign in the local trial court.

Jersey Justice

The New Jersey courts' fine reputation was of relatively recent vintage. In the 1940s, the august American Judicature Society pronounced those tribunals "the nation's worst." Then, the state's sixteen-member high court, known as the Court of Errors and Appeals and partly comprised of lay jurists—its membership changing from case to case as judges shuffled on and off the bench, its precedents almost unintelligible—was derided by the *New York Times* as "too large to be a court and too small to be a mob."

Below the high court in unwieldy hierarchy sat no fewer than seven-teen different kinds of specialized courts, law and equity tribunals rivaling one another, each court operating under its own distinct rules in a system as archaic as any that Dickens had described. As Denis Brogan, longtime British observer of American folkways, gleefully pointed out: "If you want to see the old common law in all its picturesque formality, with its fictions and fads, its delays and uncertainties, the place to look . . . is not London . . . but in New Jersey."

New Jersey politics was boss run then, and the state courts were a valuable tool for the bosses. Frank Hague, Jersey City's mayor and for years the most powerful man in the state, deployed the judges to control elections and then to block legislative investigations of the fixes. In 1938, the governor appointed Frank Hague Jr., then just twenty-eight years old and a five-time loser on the bar exam, to the state's highest court—in order to "please his daddy," the governor admitted.

It required immense effort, mainly on the part of a remarkable lawyer and politician named Arthur Vanderbilt, to rewrite the court rules. Beginning in 1930 with his election to the state bar association's Judicial Council, Vanderbilt, the founder of the state's Clean Government Move-ment who became president of the American Bar Association and dean of New York University Law School, issued reports lambasting the court system, proposing to bring it up to date through consolidation and central-ization. Boss Hague was, however, still running things from Jersey City—in a 1944 letter, Vanderbilt ruefully wrote that "the present chancellor [of the court of equity] has even outdone his predecessor in conforming to the readily ascertained wishes of the Hague machine"—and the politician kept the would-be reformer in check. In 1947, though, after several failed tries, a state constitutional convention finally pushed through Vanderbilt's proposals. The reformers showed that they had learned how to maneuver within smoke-filled rooms. To win Hague's acquiescence, they agreed to delete a measure authorizing the legislature to investigate local officials and to revise tax proposals that assured higher taxation of railroad-owned property in Jersey City.

Arthur Vanderbilt became the first chief justice of the made-over New Jersey Supreme Court, and he quickly moved to assert the court's independence. Even as, during the early days of the Republic, Chief Justice John Marshall of the U.S. Supreme Court had separated court from politics with a piece of legal legerdemain known as *Marbury v. Madison*, Vanderbilt insisted that the New Jersey legislature had no power to veto court-made rules governing procedure and practice, even though the state constitution suggested otherwise. More importantly, state politicians endorsed the ideal of judicial independence. In reaction to the political abuses of the Hague era, nonpartisanship became the norm for judicial appointments. Governors made it their practice to name an equal number of Republicans and Democrats to the bench; the senate confirmed those appointments and then, as the state constitution specified, routinely reconfirmed them for life terms seven years later, unless they had broken the rules of "good behavior."

This admonition to "good behavior" didn't mean a judge was expected to be Caspar Milquetoast—far from it. Policy-making was the proper business of the state's judges, Vanderbilt believed, because the law "derives its life and growth from judicial decisions which . . . abandon an old rule and substitute . . . a new one in order to meet new conditions." Each of his successors as chief justice has maintained an equally broad vision of what judging means. The Supreme Court has "creative responsibility for making law," insisted Joseph Weintraub, who was appointed to succeed William Brennan on the state bench in 1956, when Brennan was tapped for the U.S. Supreme Court, and named to head the court a year later when Vanderbilt died. As chief justice, Weintraub pushed the court to rewrite the law of torts to give consumers more rights against manufacturers, as well as to intervene in such sensitive policy areas as reapportionment and school finance. Richard Hughes, a former governor who succeeded Weintraub in 1974, carried the school-finance initiative forward; *Mount Laurel I* was also part of the Hughes court's judicial legacy.

"Judges have to mold the law into their concept of justice," one of Chief Justice Hughes's contemporaries on the bench told an interviewer. Another justice unselfconsciously marveled at how sensibly political the court could be—how "we can encourage the [state] legislature to pass laws or taxes without directing them to do that. This is the wonder of our system, and besides it works to accomplish our judicial objectives." While state judges, much more than federal judges, are expected to create public policy in their decisions, New Jersey's Supreme Court justices have been more openly political and politically strategic in their decrees than other states' judges.

By no means were this court's opinions uniformly liberal. "The Constitution is not at all offended when a guilty man stubs his toe," Chief Justice Weintraub wrote in an opinion narrowly defining the scope of legal protection accorded defendants by the *Miranda* warning. "On the contrary, it is decent to hope that he will." But the state's high court was best known for its rulings that made it easier for injury victims to sue government agencies, gave union organizers access to farm workers, and guaranteed the public greater access to the state's beaches. Judicial innovation was the byword in New Jersey.

All this was accomplished with little legislative direction or reaction. The great respect for the court and the politicians' desire to protect the judiciary's independence gave the justices maneuvering room. By the end of the 1960s, the New Jersey Supreme Court had grown accustomed to its role—not as the "least dangerous branch of government," as the U.S. Supreme Court had been characterized in the *Federalist Papers*, but as a policymaker acting in parallel with the governor and the legislature. Few indeed were the voices objecting that judicially led reform was antidemocratic.

"Suburban Blight" and the Court

The court's reformist bent did not, however, extend to zoning. On that subject, local autonomy became the dominant principle when, in its 1952 decision in *Lionshead Lake*, the state Supreme Court gave the suburbs carte blanche to write their own land-use rules.

The Township of Wayne was once a bucolic place, rhapsodized as "a wondrously beautiful valley" by the first English settler who laid eyes on it. But by the mid–twentieth century Wayne was beset by fear that it would be spoiled by development, and to prevent that from happening it adopted a zoning ordinance setting a minimum size for new homes. When a landowner who wanted to build modest summer cottages on his property tested the new rule, the court backed the township. Wayne officials' only legal obligation, the justices ruled, was to advance the "community as a social, economic and political unit." Across the nation, state courts cited *Lionshead Lake* when blessing zoning ordinances that required mini-mansions built on multiacre estates. A decade later, Gloucester, Camden's neighbor—"the first white settlement on the Delaware River," according to a local historical-society report from the era, and "still virile and forward-looking"—banned all trailer parks. In the *Vickers* case, the state Supreme Court upheld this ordinance, and that decision was also widely mimicked.

The New Jersey justices treated these disputes as pitting the rights of property owners to develop their land as they wished against the "general welfare" of the local community; and perceived that way, the correct result seemed obvious. A town should be able to "prevent suburban blight," said the court. There was reason to fear that, unless tough zoning measures were adopted, "the tide of suburban development" would "engulf the rustic character" of these bucolic places. Since zoning exists to create "community benefits," a town could exclude buildings—implicitly, people too—"repugnant to its planning scheme." But this formulation defines a "community" as consisting only of those already living there and financially able to stay put; anyone else is perceived as a stranger outside the gates. To those outsiders—to *"you people,"* as a Mount Laurel committeeman said to the congregation at Jacob's Chapel—the community had absolutely no legal responsibility. In this way, parochialism became enshrined in state constitutional law.

The state Supreme Court was not, of course, entirely to blame for New Jersey's famed localism. This fragmented state has relied heavily on local property taxes to pay for government services. With no significant source of state tax revenues until the mid-1960s, and then only a pittance of a sales tax, state government was kept small and ineffectual. Real politics mostly transpired in the state's 567 municipalities. The court did not create this system, but its zoning decrees of the 1950s and 1960s reinforced it.

For the young Camden Legal Services attorneys researching the court's discouraging zoning precedents in preparation for the coming Mount Laurel litigation, there were a few shards of hope amid the legal rubble. "If and when conditions change," the justices had declared in 1955, voicing Arthur Vanderbilt's activism, "alterations in zoning restrictions and pertinent legislative and judicial attitudes need not be long delayed." In the 1962 *Vickers* case, a strong dissent written by Justice Frederick Hall (who early in his career had worked in Vanderbilt's Newark law firm) attacked "community-wide economic segregation" and "unquestioning deference to the views of local officials."

Later rulings also contained language helpful for the Mount Laurel cause. "Regional needs" matter, said the justices in 1966, approving a variance to a zoning ordinance that allowed a mental hospital to be built. "General welfare . . . comprehends benefits not merely within municipal boundaries." A more critical ruling four years later involved the town of Englewood, which had donated ten acres of city-owned land to a nonprofit group. The intention was to build multifamily housing, mainly for black families displaced by slum-clearance projects, in a neighborhood that was then all white. Irate white property owners took the town to court, only to be smartly swatted down. This wasn't the Mount Laurel situation, to be sure—Englewood was supporting, not opposing, low-income housing in this dispute—but the Supreme Court spoke plainly about the need to build housing for minorities and the poor.

The dominant voice in this and later rulings was Frederick Hall's. Writing for a unanimous court, he pointed out that "the critical Englewood housing situation cries out for the active and continuous exercise of the highest responsible citizenship by all segments of the population and all governmental bodies." A denial of the zoning variance "could not well be sustained"—language that fairly invited *Mount Laurel*–type litigation. (The people in Englewood "were really protesting because they didn't want black families living outside [the ghetto]," Hall subsequently said.) Two years later, the justice went to work once again, this time condemning "fiscal zoning"—zoning designed to boost tax revenues and limit expenditures for local services—as a "legally dubious strategem." In fact, fiscal zoning was Mount Laurel Township's best and only justification for its zoning ordinance, its "strategem."

A bookshelf's worth of academic commentary on snob zoning sided with the *Mount Laurel* litigators. Charles Haar, writing in the *Harvard Law Review* in 1953, the year after *Lionshead Lake*, condemned judicial endorsement of "localism" and "economic segregation." Many suburbs would emulate Lionshead Lake, Haar warned, and turn to protectionism to "avoid excessive immigration." At about the same time, Norman Williams, a rising authority on housing law, argued presciently that "local and exclusionist purposes" were the forces driving suburban zoning. Poor families were being condemned to substandard housing while the costs of social services were being "increasingly foisted on financially overburdened cities." A decade later, as the racial and economic divisions between city and suburb became deeper and clearer, the critics took off the gloves. "The resident of suburbia is concerned not with *what* but with *whom*," Richard Babcock wrote in *The Zoning Game*. "When they protest that a change in dwelling type will cause a decline in the value of their property, their economic conclusion is based upon a social judgment." Norman Williams, by then a law professor at Rutgers and a good friend of Justice Hall's, was even more blunt: zoning "actually puts a premium on kicking the poor around." If state legislatures didn't limit local zoning authority, he wrote in 1969, the courts should declare exclusionary zoning unconstitutional.

When Ken Meiser, devising Mount Laurel legal strategy, came across this article, he and Carl Bisgaier made an appointment to meet with Williams at his Newark office. "We were in real deep water," Bisgaier acknowledges. "I was working with a kid who hadn't even finished law school." At the time, Williams was still writing his treatise on zoning, "and there were ten thousand note cards all over the place. He just brought us right in, said, 'How can I help you?' " Over the coming months, Williams gave the young lawyers a specialist's education. "He knew every land-use case written by every judge everywhere," said the awestruck advocate.

Activist lawyers and planners were already busily inventing litigation strategies to open up the suburbs. In the wake of Justice Hall's opinions and the spate of lawyerly critiques of localism, there followed what Norman Williams ruefully describes as the "great rush, in New Jersey and other states, to be the hero who slayed the dragon of exclusionary zoning, and all sorts of badly thought-out cases were brought by people necessarily in a hurry." The danger was that poorly designed cases would produce damaging precedents and so kill off the nascent reform movement.

Some of the first New Jersey lawsuits were brought by builders, prefiguring a later alliance between the developers and the dispossessed. After the population of suburban Madison Township leaped from seven thousand in 1950 to nearly fifty thousand in 1970, officials adopted a zoning ordinance meant to entice the kind of real estate—substantial homes, offices, and high-tech industries—that could be taxed to subsidize municipal services. The minimum lot size in some parts of town was two acres, and only a tiny amount of land was left for multiunit housing. Three-bedroom apartments were banned entirely, on the theory that this would keep out poor families with children, who would increase the financial strains on the public schools. Oakwood-at-Madison and the Beren Corporation, two builders whose developments had been blocked by the new ordinance, promptly sued the township. At the same time, in Bedminster Township, situated in rolling New Jersey countryside an hour's commute from Manhattan, Allan-Deane, a construction-industry subsidiary of Johns Manville, proposed to put up several hundred units of housing. The community drew together in outrage. This was a pastoral place where the population had grown by just 120 in more than a century, where the horses outnumbered the inhabitants and wealth was ubiquitous, if discreet; among the celebrities in hidden residence were Jacqueline Kennedy, Cyrus Vance, and Malcolm Forbes. Predictably, Bedminster said no, and in August 1971 Allan-Deane filed suit, claiming that the township's zoning ordinance was racially and economically discriminatory.

In Madison and Bedminster, the motivation for litigation was straightforward economics. Although poor people, would-be residents, were signed up as nominal plaintiffs, this was a merely tactical gesture. The developers' attorneys knew they had to demonstrate that their clients belonged in court—that, as lawyers say, they had standing to sue—and so they named people who could argue that, because of the zoning decision, they were denied a chance to live in the community. The real fight was between the developers and the old-guard townspeople.

In Mount Laurel, by contrast, the motivation for bringing the lawsuit was not to get rich but to do good, and the individual clients were entirely real. "Ethel Lawrence is a gentle and phenomenally wonderful person with integrity," Carl Bisgaier says of his client. "You could slice her up a hundred different ways, all you're going to find is integrity. She's a person of great personal strength, and the desire that things be right, and the willingness to take a stand. She did not fully comprehend what we [lawyers] were talking about, but she knew that this was wrong, what was happening to her people."

These three cases—concerning Madison, Bedminster, and Mount Laurel Townships—would simultaneously work their way up the judicial ladder. The Madison Township lawsuit was decided first at the trial-court level and at the time was the best known of the three; indeed, few of the legal high fliers could locate Mount Laurel on a map. But as things turned out, the events in Mount Laurel became the vehicle for ultimate judicial judgment.

"You Don't Have to Be a Weatherman"

With the community-action group's first attempts to build housing in Springville in the 1960s and all of the events that came afterwards, Ethel Lawrence found her true place in life. That observation does not detract from what she had already accomplished. As a teenager, she had gone with her mother to protest the practice of separating blacks and whites in a nearby movie theater. She had raised eight children and cared for her husband, Thomas, when illness made him quit work, and she would later spend many years nursing her ailing mother. She had been a Girl Scout troop leader, the first black troop leader in the region, had played the piano every Sunday at Jacob's Chapel, and had gotten out the vote for the local Democratic Party. When the Springville Action Council organized a preschool program, she earned the credential that she needed to teach there.

While those accomplishments would more than fill most people's biographies, Ethel Lawrence had not yet become a leader. When she was named to the community-action group, Reverend Stuart Wood remembers, she was quiet and deferential. The lawyers to whom Wood had introduced her, Peter O'Connor and Carl Bisgaier, were brash and smart, a couple of fast-talkers. She had never known anyone remotely like them. Because they respected her—not as the dutiful daughter, or the mother who baked the best rising bread around, or the wife who took good care of her husband, but as a wise woman who could describe the lives around her with richness and depth—they listened closely to what she had to say. And so she began speaking up, even as the attorneys started to construct a frame of legal rights around her story.

Plaintiffs in landmark cases are usually stand-ins, their identification a formality in what is really a dispute about principles, precedents, and policies. They are seldom fleshed-out human beings—a real black child barred from a segregated school, a real woman seeking an abortion—but instead someone named Brown or someone who gets assigned the fictitious name of Roe.

The Mount Laurel litigation wasn't like that at all. Ethel Lawrence was not a cutout on which the lawyers could paste their ideological agenda; she was a presence. Every single day that the case of *Southern Burlington County NAACP v. Township of Mount Laurel* was being argued in court—a matter of many months, stretched out over nearly a decade and a half—Ethel Lawrence and her mother, Mary Robinson, were there. Courtrooms were where she spent her vacations. While sometimes a handful of NAACP members were also present, mother and daughter were often the only spectators, sitting on hard wooden benches reminiscent of the pews in Jacob's Chapel. Whenever the judges looked up from the bench and saw these determined black women gazing back at them, it reminded them that lives as well as principles were at stake, that there were persons behind the tight-fitting masks of the law.

The Legal Services attorneys handling the litigation—Peter O'Connor, Carl Bisgaier, and Ken Meiser—represented a new generation of attorneys. They had gone to law school in the sixties, not with the intention of becoming partners in some stuffy Wall Street firm, but instead meaning to accomplish a quiet social revolution in the nation's courtrooms. These children of the Warren Court era regarded the law almost as a secular religion, and they had a faith in its power to undo injustice. The lawyers had already been successful in Camden, and more successes were to follow there, but now they were shooting higher. A triumph in Mount Laurel would be a frontal challenge to the ever widening divisions between blacks and whites, as well as between the poor and everyone else.

Peter O'Connor, who orchestrated the case and has made the cause of affordable housing central to his life ever since, excites the varied passions of others. "One of the most crazed and committed people to practice law," Bisgaier calls him admiringly, and his detractors say much the same thing, if with a less complimentary inflection. Characteristically, Ethel Lawrence, who has known him as well as anyone, describes a softer side. "If he had it within his power, there wouldn't be a hungry or a homeless person in the world."

As a boy growing up in suburban South Orange, though, there was little hint of a commitment to social justice. Throughout high school his passion was basketball, and he went to Holy Cross on an athletic scholarship. While he stood just six feet three inches, short by the standards of the game, he was a standout as guard, a natural leader who knew how to orchestrate his teammates on the floor, a player unafraid of elbowing his way past taller men when they tried to box him out of the flow of the game. Then and now, basketball has been a sport where black athletes excel, and for that reason many white players have found themselves enrolled in what amounts to Race Relations 101 on the court and in the locker room. "Basketball pricked my social conscience," O'Connor says, sounding like a better-known player from New Jersey named Bill Bradley. "Although things were fine among us as ballplayers, at the end of the game I went home to a very different place than the others did. Understanding just what that meant made the issues that the civil-rights movement was raising feel real to me, for the movement highlighted issues that I was living."

But civil rights was not yet his vocation. In the mid-1960s, during the time he was a student at Georgetown Law School, thousands of liberal northerners were putting their ordinary lives on hold, heading South to challenge Jim Crow laws by organizing voter-registration drives and freedom schools. Some, like Mickey Schwerner, James Cheney, and Andrew Goodman, murdered in Mississippi in the summer of 1964—Freedom Summer—became martyrs to the cause. Meanwhile, O'Connor took out every student loan there was, spent his days in class and his nights holding down three jobs, including a stint as a Capitol policeman, in order to make it through Georgetown. He was called up for the draft after graduation, but because of an old basketball injury the army turned him down. While he thought about joining VISTA or the Peace Corps, instead he wound up traveling in South America on a Rotary fellowship.

There were riots in the streets back home, and when the Latin Americans he met pressed him to explain why blacks were rioting, why there was so much poverty, he had no good answers for them, only new questions for himself. The racial conflagration that he witnessed firsthand in 1967 when he returned to Newark was the final push toward a lifelong commitment: he would be a lawyer who used his newly acquired tools to make things work better.

By the time he met Ethel Lawrence, O'Connor had packed a career's worth of legal hell-raising into a couple of years. As the senior attorney in Camden Regional Legal Services' law-reform unit, he had made so much noise that Vice President Spiro Agnew, on a fund-raising trip to nearby Cherry Hill, had lambasted Camden Regional Legal Services generally, and specifically the Camden urban-renewal litigation. That assault provoked a controversy in the chambers of the U.S. Senate, as Ted Kennedy criticized Agnew's heavy-handed attempt at intimidation. Back in Camden, the vice president's speech only boosted O'Connor's reputation.

Carl Bisgaier, who did much of the actual work on the Mount Laurel case, is a cooler customer. "I'm the cynic who was spurred on by Peter's perpetual enthusiasm," he says, and particularly at the outset of the case he was skeptical about the prospects for success. But Bisgaier too had what he calls his "personal epiphany," the moment when the rightness of what he was doing became transparently clear to him. During the fall of

1969, a year after beginning work with Camden Regional Legal Services, he took his family on a vacation to southern California. His experience in Camden had left him frustrated with cities, curious about the new towns that were then springing up in the West. But a visit to one of those invented places, Westlake Village, situated in the desert east of Los Angeles, "made me physically sick. 'My God,' I thought, 'there are no poor people here—the developers have created an environment that completely excludes the poor!' Then I realized that what this place had done overtly was why suburbs were what they were. It was all by design!" In the Mount Laurel case, Bisgaier would have his chance to expose that design.

The township's gentlemanly solicitor, Jack Gerry, defended Mount Laurel's zoning policies, not because he was personally committed to his client's cause, but because that was what he was hired to do—privately, he believed that the town *was* giving poor and black families the bums' rush. The local politicians would win their case, he anticipated, because the law was so heavily on their side, but that didn't make their conduct admirable.

The Legal Services attorneys charged that Mount Laurel's zoning ordinance unconstitutionally discriminated along race and class lines. But during the four-day trial in March 1972, town officials denied establishing "a pattern of economic and social segregation." The market, they insisted, had done that. They rejected the claim that the township had any "legal duty to house the poor." There was nothing "arbitrary and capricious" about what Mount Laurel had done, Jack Gerry argued, citing the standard and, until that time, the successful defense in land-use disputes. The township permitted building on smaller lots than did nearby communities and in this respect really deserved plaudits, but beyond that Mount Laurel was unwilling to go.

The township admitted every important fact in the plaintiffs' complaint—the sorry condition of the housing in Springville and the doubling in the number of Mount Laurel's housing units during the 1960s, with not a single dwelling built for poor families. In effect, the township asked: *so what?* "We didn't even have to present all our testimony," says Carl Bisgaier, "because the defense was willing to accept statements from witnesses instead of testimony. They didn't care. It would be like me telling you I was going to prove you were green and your saying, 'Go ahead, prove I'm green, I know what color I am. Go ahead, do what you want to do, I don't give a damn.' Their response amounted to a declaration that, legally, we were out of our minds."

Trial court judge Edward Martino had sat on the Burlington County bench for nearly three decades. A Camden native, he was the most powerful jurist in the district, responsible for assigning all the cases, and a man with a reputation for being a martinet. Because he knew the controversial Mount Laurel dispute would make his judicial colleagues queasy, he decided to hear it himself. Political pressure often sways trial court judges, but Martino was regarded as an exception. Though he was a Republican loyalist, on the bench he was neither particularly liberal nor especially conservative—just someone who let himself be guided by a sense of what seemed fair, within the boundaries of the law. Significantly, back in 1959, well before the heyday of activist judges in the field of civil rights, Martino found a Mount Holly restaurant guilty of race discrimination. In a statement that predates the national flap over racism in Denny's restaurants by more than thirty years, the judge declared, "Adequate service must be available to all citizens regardless of race, color, or creed, or national origin. The refusal of such equality of opportunity . . . is discrimination."

Martino had already been exposed to the Springville neighborhood's housing problems, since one of the plaintiffs in the lawsuit, Catherine Still, had earlier brought a case in his court that focused on conditions in the converted chicken coops. But the judge was nonetheless startled by the accounts of exploitation and ruined lives he heard during the Mount Laurel trial. "I took this never dreaming it was the type of case it turned out to be. I did not have any thought of taking care of the poor, but as I heard the testimony of the plaintiffs . . . and saw how the city fathers were treating a certain class of people, then I got a little agitated."

Judges are supposed to learn during cases, and profound judicial voyages of discovery do sometimes happen. At about the time Judge Martino was getting his lesson on misery in Mount Laurel, for instance, Stephen Roth, a federal trial court judge known to be unsympathetic to civil-rights claims, was learning to his amazement that the suburbs of Detroit practiced their own brand of apartheid—that they had contrived to keep black families out, forcing them to stay in the city, and so had helped to make the public schools racially isolated. That revelation prompted the Detroit judge to arrive at the novel legal conclusion that the entire metropolitan area, not just the city, which by then had few white residents, should take responsibility for desegregation (a decision later overturned by a bare majority of the Burger Court). In the Mount Laurel case, innovative legal arguments were less compelling to Judge Martino than the tangible plight of the people who came forward to tell their stories. "They were pushed around, and nobody came to their rescue. They were forced to leave their homes in a town where some of them had lived fifty years. Many of these people were born here, as were their parents and grandparents."

During his closing argument for the plaintiffs, Carl Bisgaier talked about how housing-design standards translated into tax dollars for the town's officials. "There was a money difference between a two-thousand-square-foot house and an eight-hundred-square-foot house, and that's the way they were thinking." He pointed to a map of the township that showed the approved planned unit developments. "It is just a matter of time before the whole town is closed off," he said, and then borrowed a refrain from the anthem of the day. "You don't have to be a weatherman to know which way the wind is blowing."

As the evidence piled up, abuse upon abuse, Judge Martino came to despise the politicians in Mount Laurel. "They were treating these people like cattle, even calling them scum of the earth and *telling them that if they can't afford to live in Mount Laurel they should leave*"—echoes of that fateful Sunday in Jacob's Chapel. The case, as the judge saw it, boiled down to this: "The defendants . . . wanted to uplift the municipality, and these people were not going to help them, and they wanted to get rid of them." The speeches they made at township meetings said as much. "They wished to approve only those development plans which were to provide direct and substantial benefits to their taxpayers. This angered me."

State trial judges mostly handle mundane matters on which the law is well settled. In this instance, though, Martino reached out to invent law. While he dismissed several developers as defendants, concluding that they had no legal duty to build housing for the poor, and also rejected the argument that the region, not just the township, had an obligation to plan for affordable housing, he pushed far beyond the limits of precedent when it came to Mount Laurel itself.

The judge saw the case not as a challenge to an isolated zoning matter but as a test of deliberate and deeply imbedded policy. "This was no zoning case, this was development of a whole municipality," Martino says. "They didn't dream that I would enter into the ultimate conclusion that discrimination has no place in America. . . . I had no hesitancy in determining that the attitude of the city fathers was contrary to the American way of life."

On May 1, 1972, six weeks after the trial and a year to the day after the lawsuit was filed, Judge Martino delivered his twenty-three-page opinion. It recites the damning facts lifted from the pages of the township council's minutes.

> Early in 1968 the mayor, when a discussion arose as to low income housing, stated it was the intention of the township council to take care of the people of Mount Laurel Township but not to make any areas of Mount Laurel a home for the county. At a later meeting of the township committee in 1969 a variance to permit multi-family dwelling units was rejected because the committee did not see the need for such construction. At a meeting in 1970 a committeeman, during a discussion of homes being rundown and worthless, indicated that the policy was to wait until homes become vacant before the township took action, "because if these people are put out on the street they do not have another place to go"

[and so, under the law, the township would have to take some responsibility for them]. At another meeting in September 1970 a township committeeman [said] . . . "We must be as selective as possible . . . we can approve only those development plans which will provide direct and substantial benefits to our taxpayers."

At that time, the judge points out, two-thirds of the township still consisted of vacant land, and nearly a thousand acres of empty land was zoned for houses.

In concluding that Mount Laurel's zoning ordinance was unconstitutional "economic discrimination," Martino had no New Jersey precedent to back him up. Instead the judge cobbled together an opinion that relied on dissents, decisions from other states, and law review commentary. Justice Oliphant's 1952 dissent in *Lionshead Lake* could have been addressed by name to Ethel Lawrence and her family. "Certain well-behaved families will be barred from these communities simply because the income of the family will not permit them to build a house [there]. They will be relegated to the large cities . . . even though it may be against what they consider the welfare of their immediate families." Justice Hall's dissent in the 1962 *Vickers* case (the opinion that Ken Meiser had once believed was a majority ruling), also quoted in Martino's opinion, was even more scathing. "[L]egitimate use of the zoning power by . . . municipalities does not encompass the right to erect barricades on their boundaries . . . where the real purpose is to prevent feared disruption with a so-called chosen way of life. Nor does it encompass provisions designed to let in as new residents only certain kinds of people . . . or keep down tax bills of present property owners. . . . [C]ourts must not be hesitant to strike down purely selfish and undemocratic actions. . . . 'The Constitution nullifies sophisticated as well as simple-minded modes of discrimination.' "

Through an abuse of the power to plan for land use, Mount Laurel had cordoned off poor blacks—assigned them to a zone of disregard—and this, Judge Martino ruled, had to change. Without specifically telling the township what it must do, the judge set a planning process in motion, ordering local officials to work with the plaintiffs in identifying housing needs and crafting an "affirmative program" to meet those needs.

Martino's decision completed the transformation of the issue from a dispute over a minor zoning amendment to an argument about the much larger municipal obligation to the town's poor. The long-term implications of that decision remained unclear—the state Supreme Court could still reject the reformers' agenda—but the matter was bound for the high court. Given that court's hints that fiscal zoning was unconstitutional, as well as the justices' inclination to wade into political thickets, Martino's ruling promised to be the opening salvo in a long war over local authority to fence out the poor.

"Not an Inch"

As Edward Martino closed the record, Mary Robinson, Ethel's mother, broke down in tears of relief. But the judge's order depended for its success on the cooperation of local officials, and that was not forthcoming. Between the filing of the lawsuit and the announcement of the decision one year later, the Republicans had been swept out of office and the Democrats were again running the show. While this changeover had a direct impact on the pace of development—the planned unit development ordinance was repealed, although an exception was made for already approved projects—on the issue of affordable housing, the new political cast meant only that public debates would be even nastier.

"There was much reactionary sentiment" after the Democrats took over, the town planner recalls, though in fact it wasn't the sentiment that was new, just the rawness with which it was expressed. "There were some very noisy, obnoxious rednecks showing up [at township meetings]. They had heavy accents, and they were saying that they did not want blacks in our community, and there was talk about not creating a new ghetto."

The Democrats saw their position not as insensitive or racist but as morally compelled, says John Trimble, who took over for Jack Gerry as Mount Laurel's lawyer after the trial. "They didn't think it was right to subsidize those who wanted something for nothing. They envisioned somebody getting a free house next to their own house for which they had worked and slaved, to get out to their paradise, which was a one-hundred-foot by one-hundred-foot lot in Mount Laurel." This sentiment may explain why, despite Judge Martino's order, there was no interest—none whatsoever—in negotiating with the plaintiffs. Soon after the judge ruled, Carl Bisgaier came to a township council meeting with a simple proposition: pass a Resolution of Need, the first required step in obtaining federal funds for affordable housing, and we'll drop the lawsuit.

"Bullshit!" responded the Democratic mayor, Joe Massari, who had run for office to stop just such housing. "We're not giving an inch on this thing. We are going to fight it all the way."

When news of that exchange filtered back to Judge Martino, he was livid. He summoned Trimble to his chambers, the attorney recalls, and "he told me he knew that the town officials were sitting on their hands, and that if I didn't get my clients to pass a new zoning ordinance I should resign as an officer of the court because they were not fulfilling their moral obligation. 'I am going to put them in jail,' he said. I told the council what the judge had said. They said I should tell him to go to hell."

Negotiating is how political business is usually done, of course; and negotiation holds pride of place in the politics of mutual advantage that typically operates in small communities like Mount Laurel, where everyone knows everybody else and today's adversaries are likely to be tomorrow's allies. But in this single instance, the town-council members regarded bargaining as compromising a moral position—as giving away housing to people who hadn't sweated blood for it and so didn't deserve it. They also saw negotiating as an invitation to political disaster, and at that they balked. In the battle of Mount Laurel, the trial court's judgment marked only the end of the beginning.

"Fair Share"

On issue after issue, from equal education to consumers' rights, the New Jersey Supreme Court has been a reformer among state tribunals. But even this activist court caused a sensation in March 1975—three years after the trial court's ruling; seven years after Mount Laurel Township first rejected the proposal to amend its zoning ordinance and permit thirty-six apartments to be built—when Justice Frederick Hall delivered the court's unanimous judgment in the *Mount Laurel* case. "I thought we had won the lottery," says plaintiffs' lawyer Carl Bisgaier.

The ruling was bolder in its rhetoric than the advocates ever hoped for. It demanded that developing towns across the state rewrite their zoning laws so that private developers, taking advantage of federal subsidies and market forces, could build homes for a "fair share" of the region's poor and moderate-income families. The decision drew national attention and quickly turned into a lightning rod; what *Brown v. Board of Education*, the school-desegregation case, had meant for southern whites, *Mount Laurel* became for suburbanites.

The case had been rushed to the state's highest court. When the township appealed Judge Martino's ruling, the Supreme Court, evidently eager to speak out on the issue, decided to hear the suit directly, skipping the intermediate appellate court. The justices had done the same thing in the *Madison* case, where the trial judge had sided with the developers and against the town, and both cases were scheduled to be heard by the high court, one after the other, on the same day in March 1973.

"Poor people simply can't afford to live in our township," Carl Bisgaier argued to the justices, speaking of Mount Laurel as "our town" as a way of emphasizing that his clients too had a stake in the community. "It's not because we've purposely kept them out, it's because the price of the land and the house is more than they can afford. . . . Mount Laurel is a typical town in New Jersey, and as long as the overriding factor [in the community's calculation] is the tax burden, the town has no obligation to provide for out-of-township residents. After all, we can't tax them."

Chief Justice Joseph Weintraub interrupted Bisgaier, to slice to the heart of the dispute. "What responsibilities does government have for low income housing," he asked, "and who has to pay for it?"

While still a law student at Cornell, Weintraub had acquired a reputation for precociousness when Supreme Court Justice Louis Brandeis wrote to praise a law review article he had written. A former law clerk of Justice Weintraub's, Eugene Serpentelli, who as a trial court judge would manage some of the toughest *Mount Laurel*–type cases a decade later, remembers that Weintraub "needed law clerks only to fill chairs, to sit at his feet as the master. And of course he also had the impatience of a brilliant person."

"Have you got a model opinion we can use as guidance?" Weintraub had brusquely demanded of an attorney who, in the companion case, was challenging Madison Township's ordinance. "If not, don't ask the court to do something you cannot do yourself. You should draft a model judgment explaining the fair share concept and send it to us." Now he was turning his fire on Carl Bisgaier.

Questions about duties and cost were the very issues Bisgaier dreaded, yet when he tried to wriggle around them, the justice bore in relentlessly. The advocate had no good answers; he fled from the courtroom, for a "lost weekend," the moment the session ended. A few weeks later, when tapes of the oral argument became available, Bisgaier and his colleague Ken Meiser spent a dispiriting afternoon reliving his humiliation in the same Trenton courtroom where the proceedings had been held. "It was," he says, "like hearing yourself going to the toilet over and over."

Bisgaier hoped for an opportunity to redeem himself, and while the law seldom gives such second chances, this time he got it, when the New Jersey Supreme Court ordered the lawyers to argue *Mount Laurel* and *Madison* again. Evidently, the justices had struggled unsuccessfully to reach a decision before the end of the term, when three of them reached mandatory retirement age. Hence the summons to reargument. "Cases of this magnitude should be decided by [judges] who have to live with the decisions," said Chief Justice Weintraub, who was one of those leaving the bench. More retirements followed in the coming months, and so, of the six justices who had served with Joseph Weintraub, only Frederick Hall, the leading land-use jurist, remained when the case was heard a second time, in January 1974.

Rutgers law professor Norman Williams, who was by this time a nationally known expert on land use, represented the plaintiffs in *Madison*. Williams was supposed to lead off the argument, tackling the hardest questions, while the *Mount Laurel* attorneys, as Carl Bisgaier put it, would be "second sisters." But moments before the oral argument was scheduled to begin, lawyers for Madison informed the justices that the township had recently amended its zoning ordinance in an ostensible attempt to comply with the trial court's ruling. The astonished judges took one look at the redrawn maps and sent the case back to be tried a second time in light of the rewritten ordinance.

Suddenly, the klieg lights shifted to the *Mount Laurel* case and its novice litigators. "Many of those in the courtroom . . . did not even know where Mount Laurel was," says Williams. He was standing outside the courtroom preparing to leave, when Carl Bisgaier rushed over and asked him to participate in his case. The justices quickly granted the motion. "Slam dunk that they would grant it," says Bisgaier, "they wanted to hear him." Then, however, the burden of argument fell upon the Legal Services lawyer.

With the catastrophe of his earlier performance before the high court still vivid in his mind, the young advocate struck boldly and directly. Government was institutionalizing poverty, he contended, zoning out poor people by design and so deliberately creating racial and economic segregation. Only if towns were legally obliged to act differently, required to reverse that pattern, was there any hope that things would change. The justices had few questions for Bisgaier, but they bore down hard on John Trimble, the township's attorney. Trimble stuck to the familiar text: the zoning laws represented sound fiscal and legal planning. While this was the line the court had taken in earlier cases, it was evident from the barrage of questions that the justices no longer believed fiscal responsibility was a good enough reason for zoning out the poor.

When lawyer Trimble contended that "the Supreme Court has neither the authority nor the means to review local zoning decisions," one judge retorted that "one thing we *could* tell you is you can't prohibit multi-family dwellings." Allowing such housing would be "political suicide" for suburban politicians, Trimble said in exasperation. Justice Morris Pashman, who in his short time on the court had already acquired a reputation for painting justice in its broadest strokes, responded: "I don't know why they think the court won't assist them in political suicide. . . . We may even take them screaming and kicking." That exchange encapsulated one of the most troubling and enduring issues in the case: the limits of judicial activism in defining and enforcing newly created social rights and obligations.

Justice Hall's opinion in the *Mount Laurel* case was his valedictory to the bench, and he used the occasion like a latter-day Sinclair Lewis, scolding the suburbs for their Babbitry. After reciting chapter and verse concerning Mount Laurel's callous treatment of its own poor families, Hall went on:

> Through its zoning ordinance, Mount Laurel has exhibited economic discrimination in that the poor have been deprived of adequate housing and the opportunity to secure the construction of subsidized housing, and has used Federal, State, county and local finances solely for the benefit of middle and upper-income persons. . . . There cannot be the slightest doubt that the reason for this course of conduct has been to keep down local taxes on property . . . and that the policy was carried out without regard for the non-fiscal considerations with respect to people.

Such behavior was not peculiar to Mount Laurel Township. "Almost every [municipality] acts solely in its own selfish and parochial interest and in effect builds a wall around itself to keep out those people or entities not adding favorably to the tax base."

A generation before, in the *Lionshead Lake* and *Vickers* decisions, the New Jersey judges had bowed to the wisdom of local governments, and courts elsewhere had followed their lead. But this was a tribunal that, since Arthur Vanderbilt's days, had made progressivism its credo. "Conditions have changed, and . . . judicial attitudes must be altered. . . . [T]he welfare of the state's citizens beyond the borders of the particular municipality . . . must be served." What the suburbs were doing, wrote Hall, was now legally unacceptable. It violated the command, inscribed in the state's zoning statute and implicit in its constitution as well, that government must serve "the *general* welfare," not just the interests of present residents or of the well off. The court's decision spoke to the ambitions of outsiders who wanted in—the general welfare, as Justice Hall constructed it, meant *regional* welfare.

The opinion was chock-full of the imperatives beloved by sermon writers and editorialists. "There cannot be the slightest doubt that shelter, along with food, are the most basic human needs"—but what about health, one might ask, or love, for that matter? "It is plain beyond dispute that proper provision for adequate housing of all categories of people is certainly an absolute essential in promotion of the general welfare required in all local land use regulation"—but if this were so plain, there would be no need for a *Mount Laurel* case.

Justice Hall did not even mention the *federal* constitutional rights of the poor, and there were good tactical reasons for this omission. The year before, in *Village of Belle Terre v. Boraas*, the U.S. Supreme Court had approved a zoning ordinance that permitted only families or unmarried couples, not groups, to reside in the community. The ordinance was needed, said William O. Douglas, the most liberal justice on the bench, to preserve "a quiet place where yards are wide, people few," where "family values"—family values!—"youth values, and the blessings of quiet seclusion and clean air make the area a sanctuary for people." The single-family home, Douglas opined, was a place of "blessings," a "sanctuary," language that "connotes the sacred." Zoning didn't affect any "fundamental rights" guaranteed by the U.S. Constitution, said the justices, and so, except where racial discrimination was deliberate, communities were left alone.

But the New Jersey constitution had sometimes been read as being "more demanding" than the federal Constitution, as Justice Hall pointed out, and he argued that it offered ample legal basis for striking down a local zoning law. Although there was no specific textual basis for the decision, just the capacious language of general welfare, the court established affirmative, constitutionally mandated municipal obligations. The state justices' strategy effectively insulated the *Mount Laurel* opinion from repeal by the legislators, who couldn't rewrite it by statute, as well as from review by the U.S. Supreme Court. This proved a prudent move when state politicians noisily if fecklessly complained; and just three months later the nation's high court held that neither poor city residents nor civil-rights-minded suburbanites could challenge a town's zoning ordinance.

In New Jersey, all the burgeoning suburbs, from the snootiest enclaves in Bedminster's fox-hunting country to executive-class wanna-be towns like Mount Laurel, were obliged to rewrite their zoning laws to assure that a "fair share" of the poor families in the region could live there. "Developing municipalit[ies]," Justice Hall concluded, "must make *realistically possible* the opportunity for an appropriate variety and choice of housing for all categories of people who may desire to live there."

Despite this boldness, there was much that the court chose *not* to specify. There wasn't a word written about racial discrimination, even though such claims were part of the plaintiffs' case—instead, the new judicial doctrine focused entirely on the legally more novel territory of economic discrimination. Critical technical details went undiscussed: how a "region" was to be defined, what "fair share" meant. Nor, most critically, did the court say how it might enforce the judgment.

Left mainly to their own devices, the opinion suggested, the suburbs could be counted on to accept their "moral obligation," to do what was right. The court's proper role was to do good by doing little: the justices struck down, as too judicially intrusive, that portion of Judge Martino's order that required Mount Laurel to develop a plan under judicial supervision. It was improper for a judge to get so deeply involved in land-use particulars, Justice Hall maintained, warning trial judges against brokering settlements. "There is no reason," Hall opined, "why developing communities . . . may not become and remain attractive, viable communities providing good living and adequate services for all their residents in the kind of atmosphere which a democracy and free institutions demand."

Given the prevailing politics of hostility, Hall's vision was as fantastic as believing that raptors would nibble gently from the hand of Saint Francis. Yet there were practical reasons for this go-slow approach. Despite their attempt to anchor the ruling in the past, the justices had to know that their new doctrine was a radical reversal of their own precedents. The decision subverted engrained habits of local control; and with such thin legal support, the court's bold move risked political trouble. Better to give townships the opportunity to comply voluntarily, the justices may have concluded—if the towns did nothing, there would then be better reasons for the court to do more.

In a concurring opinion, Morris Pashman urged the court to move even "farther and faster," to breathe "lifeblood" into "downright boring . . . culturally dead" suburbs. "Like animal species that over-specialize and breed out diversity and so perish in the course of evolution, communities, too, need racial, cultural, social and economic diversity to cope with our rapidly changing times." This Darwinesque passage was vintage Pashman. To his admirers, the justice's unabashed liberalism showed that he regarded "judicial activism" as something "not to be feared, but to be used to accomplish fairness," while to his critics, "[he did] not know what legislatures are for except to raise judicial salaries, and, since they do not do that fast enough, he would really like to take that function away from them too." His *Mount Laurel* concurrence gave ample ammunition to both camps. There is "an acute national housing shortage," the brunt of which is being borne by the poor, and "the growing movement of commerce and industry to the suburbs is imposing a heavy burden on employees who are unable to obtain housing in these suburban areas." That's why the court needed to "lay down broad guidelines for judicial review of municipal zoning decisions," including a declaration that, under certain circumstances, communities had "an affirmative duty to provide housing" for the poor.

In *Mount Laurel II*—eight years, several vacillating rulings, and much heartache later—the justices would embrace many of Pashman's ideas, setting up an elaborate structure of judicial management and laying out detailed rules to make the fair-share right a reality. Yet, as the judge reminded his brethren, "Even as we write [in 1975], development proceeds apace. . . . There is a hazard that prolonged judicial inaction" will permanently lock out the poor.

This was prophecy. While the justices zigged and zagged in the next batch of zoning cases, state politicians plotted to undermine them and federal financial support for subsidized housing dried up. At the same time, the building market, responsive to the rhythms of the economy, was going through its own cycles of boom and bust. Whatever the courts might say about rights, the economics of housing would largely determine whether new construction was feasible—for poor families or anyone else.

5

The Schoolmaster Court

In its 1975 *Mount Laurel* decision, the New Jersey Supreme Court spoke about the suburbs' moral obligation. Although *another* kind of moral obligation—a sense of duty to protect one's own family and home against threat—went wholly unmentioned, that concern profoundly shaped popular reaction to the ruling.

Home means so much more than four walls and a roof over one's head. It symbolizes a "haven in a heartless world"—the place where, as Robert Frost wrote, "when you have to go there, they have to take you in." Set aside all the terrible things that sometimes take place at hearthside, the rape of spouses and the brutalization of children: when linked to the home, these horrors seem perpetually to surprise. "He was such a good neighbor," it is invariably and wonderingly said as the drug kingpin or the kidnapper is led away in handcuffs, past the lawnmower and the minivan.

Viewed against the backdrop of less than entirely pleasing life histories, home becomes a token of one's status and success in the teeth of failure—of "dream [merged] with reality," as Charles Abrams wrote two generations ago in *Forbidden Neighbors*. "In its permanence the owner sees the stabilization of his own values; in the firmness of its foundation he follows his own roots into the community . . . in its ownership, he sees release from the fears and uncertainties of life." But home can represent risk as well as security, for "failure to pay a single [mortgage] installment may bring foreclosure, eviction, and despair." The arrival of unwelcome outsiders, people regarded as threatening the value of the homestead as an investment and a sanctuary, poses another kind of risk. Such fears, especially when heightened by propinquity and fanned by those who look to make political or economic capital from them, can evoke panic and worse.

The United States began as a nation with a "revolution in land" that paralleled the political revolution, whose "aim, not always fulfilled, was to put small holdings into the hands of the rank and file." Government would manage this distribution of land while otherwise staying clear. "The United States," said James Madison at the 1787 Constitutional Convention, "have a precious advantage . . . in the actual distribution of property . . . and in the universal hope of acquiring property," in a nation where the majority were "freeholders, or the heirs, or aspirants to Freeholds." Nearly 150 years later, at the President's Conference on Building and Home Ownership, Herbert Hoover echoed this theme, even going so far as to attribute it to the American "race": "That our people should live in their own homes is a sentiment deep in the heart of our race and of American life."

This passion for a home of one's own helped to power the exodus to suburbia after the Second World War. The new technology of tract housing, which cut construction costs, meant that ownership was within the reach of Everyperson, or almost Everyperson—two-thirds of all Americans, a proportion higher than any other nation's. But with the *Mount Laurel* ruling, it seemed as if government was rewriting this social compact. Now the court was telling people what they could, and could not, do with their land—telling them as well whom they had to accept as their neighbors.

To the law reformers and civil-rights advocates, this was a hallmark of social justice, the way out of the American dilemma. But to a great many others, this was dread socialism, a threat to their very identity.

One thing was certain: the transformation of "our town" as envisioned by *Mount Laurel* would not happen easily. "Courts do not build houses," Justice Frederick Hall wrote in the 1975 *Mount Laurel* opinion, and in the literal sense this is of course true. Courts can, however, influence the course and character of communities by fixing the outer bounds of the legally permissible; and they can alter the course of state politics, if sometimes in ways not easy to fathom.

In its 1975 decision, the state Supreme Court spoke of principles, of *what* should be done. *How* things should be done was a very different question, though—one that, as suburbanites and their lawyers soon realized, the justices had left unanswered. Evasions of the decree, both blunt and subtle, became the order of the day; and trial judges contributed to this hardening of suburban resistance. In Mount Laurel Township, the second trial over the town's exclusionary zoning practices was a potentially fatal setback for Ethel Lawrence and the others who hoped to be able to live there. Even the Supreme Court seemed to edge away from its *Mount Laurel* boldness, producing judgments that cut back the scope of its authority over zoning.

As the decade ended, the idea that suburbs would rezone their land to permit housing for people without much money seemed once again to lack plausibility. But in 1983 the Supreme Court crafted a decision that not only confirmed the principles of its 1975 ruling but also, more vitally, answered the question of *how?* in a way that at least temporarily routed the naysayers.

"We may not build houses," the justices declared, "but we do enforce the Constitution."

Landmark or Little Rock in New Jersey?

Justice Hall had only modest expectations for his handiwork. "It is a housing opinion, a rights opinion, put practically on a moral basis, but don't expect it to solve all problems. . . . It's just the beginning, as I look at it. It's a little bit like *Brown v. Board of Education* in the school desegregation field—a start to do something about the housing needs of the poor."

Many observers, both supporters and critics of Hall's opinion, were more skeptical yet. Zoning-law expert Norman Williams feared that, much as the governor of Arkansas defied a judge's school-desegregation order a generation earlier, some New Jersey town "will be a Little Rock and force a confrontation." For his part, George Sternlieb, an urban-policy scholar at Rutgers, anticipated that smart lawyers representing the suburbs would dream up endless strategies of avoidance, "like the dance of the seven veils. First they say it's a financial problem. Low and moderate-income housing can't be built. Then subsidized housing comes along and they say it's a zoning problem. Now that the zoning veil has been stripped away . . . a lot of towns are suddenly going to become environmentally conscious . . . [and] also make it difficult for developers by not providing the infrastructure." Rutgers planning professor Jerome Rose, a persistent critic of the judicial foray into zoning, believed that the justices were naive to assume that the suburban electorate, "many of whom . . . have fled from the perceived and real dangers of city living to find relative safety and comfort in their socially homogeneous communities, will respond to the judicial mandate with the question, 'What do we have to do to comply with the decision?' " The more likely question on the minds of suburbanites, he said, was "How do we postpone, avoid, or even defy this decision?"

In Mount Laurel Township itself, there was optimistic talk among those who had fought for affordable housing. Lawyer Carl Bisgaier predicted that the "landmark" decision would "finally open the suburbs to the poor." Catherine Still, whose ancestor had been the first black doctor in South Jersey and who had won her own dispute with a Mount Laurel landlord, had a more personal reaction. "My family has been in Mount Laurel for seven generations," she said. "I have eight children myself. When my children got ready to make a family of their own, there was no place in Mount Laurel where they could afford to live. . . . All seven generations are buried in the family churchyard. I want to be buried with them. This decision gives us hope."

Ethel Lawrence was more skeptical. When she traveled to Trenton, the justices in their black robes seemed to her as solemn and remote and powerful as priests, and the lawyers behaved as deferentially as acolytes. She was scared even to sneeze, barely able to take a full breath. Afterwards, she and her mother ran into three of the judges in the hallway outside the courtroom. "I was afraid to say something that might hurt my case, yet they were so very friendly. They gave us a book with a history of the court and they each signed it for us." The Supreme Court's favorable decision was not enough, she knew. Year by year, fewer poor families remained in Mount Laurel, just 80 families in 1975, as compared with 120 when the case was filed five years earlier. The town's approach to urban renewal, refusing permits to renovate and then condemning the deteriorated housing in Springville, was really "Negro removal"—and it was working. Town officials, she believed, "are going to delay as long as they can. Mount Laurel is not going to do us any favors."

No favors, indeed: whites in Mount Laurel read the ruling not as a final edict but as a declaration of war. "It's judicial dictatorship," fumed a Democratic council member, "a broadside attack against democracy. It's no accident that it started in New Jersey with a leftist judicial court with left-leaning legal beagles." Another council member added: "I don't think the real world was ever taken into consideration by the courts." This was the boilerplate among politicians who found it easier publicly to attack judges than poor black families.

Nor were the politicians the only ones riled up. The Ramblewood Civic Association, whose members had moved into their tract homes with the intention of leaving the poor and minorities far behind, vowed not to give in to the judges. One resident talked derisively to a reporter about "them." "No way do I feel I should subsidize a fifty thousand dollar home for them. Nobody's doing it for me. . . . Nobody has a right to say anybody owes them anything. They have the option of moving out of Mount Laurel if they don't like their housing here. Springville [the neighborhood where most of Mount Laurel's black families lived] is a pigsty, but they wouldn't live any differently if they moved to [upscale] Laurel Knoll. You are what you are."

At the end of 1975, seven months after the Supreme Court's decision, suburban mayors convened a statewide tribunal of war in Mount Laurel. Joe Alvarez, who a decade earlier had returned from Puerto Rico to his true home, who later had condemned every Springville chicken coop in sight, was now the mayor, and he chaired the session. (In subsequent litigation, Mount Laurel's lawyers would use Alvarez's Hispanic roots as evidence of the town's tolerance, but in fact the mayor's job rotates annually among council members.) From the suburbs of this most suburbanized state in the union, fifty mayors showed up. They issued a manifesto vowing to overturn the court's decree, even if that required amending the state constitution. The Supreme Court had inadvertently given an identity to a town almost no one had ever heard of. This is what could happen to any of us, these mayors said, these are the terrible things that runaway judges can do.

Mount Laurel Township appealed Justice Hall's ruling to the U.S. Supreme Court, but the justices demurred, since they had no federal grounds on which to hear the case. Embittered local officials complained that "the New Jersey Supreme Court did its very best to shaft us." Then the council asked Judge Edward Martino for more time—nine months more—to comply with the state Supreme Court's order to rewrite its zoning law.

"Ridiculous!" said the trial judge, who accused the politicians of "thumbing their noses" at the high court. "I'm fed up with it, and I'm not putting up with their snail's-pace attitude any longer," he told town solicitor John Trimble. "Everything indicates a deliberate stall. It's outrageous."

Ninety days was all that the judge would authorize for the zoning revision; and, showing his disdain, he demanded monthly progress reports. "You should give some thought to bringing contempt charges if the township misses its deadline," Martino told Carl Bisgaier, the plaintiffs' lead lawyer.

A town-council member fired back: "If the judge wants to become a legislator, let him come down here and get himself elected. We need a constitutional amendment to get them out of this zoning dictatorship."

Confronted with Judge Martino's determination to enforce the *Mount Laurel* decision vigorously, the town had to submit something by way of a revised zoning ordinance. What the Supreme Court demanded in its 1975 ruling was an ordinance that created a "realistic opportunity" for affordable housing. But what the township submitted was a farcical document, every bit as defiant of the judiciary as southern school districts' responses to desegregation decrees in the 1950s and 1960s.

The town rezoned three small parcels of land containing a total of twenty acres, a fraction of 1 percent of the township's acreage. While 103 low-income units could theoretically be constructed on this land (a number far below any plausible calculation of what was needed), in fact no units ever would—ever *could*—be built on these sites. One parcel, situated in wetlands behind an industrial park, was slated to be a stop on a proposed transit line; another was a successful nursery whose owner had no interest in selling to developers; and the third was part of the upmarket Larchmont planned unit development, which the developer had no intention of giving up. Even if a builder were idealistic enough, or else foolish enough, to take the zoning changes seriously, the town had inserted poison-pill provisions mandating detailed studies of the impact on traffic, the environment, and municipal services. These requirements, imposed nowhere else in town, would have sent the costs of development spiraling upward.

Mayor Alvarez acknowledges that the zoning changes were a sham. "We were going to do the absolute minimum we could get by with. Somebody would threaten to sue us. We'd say, 'Go ahead!' and so it went on and on." As if to stiffen the resolve of the council, the voters of Mount Laurel rejected even these trivial changes. By a vote of 4,420 to 885, a five-to-one margin, they declared that the correct response to the matter of affordable housing was to do nothing. Although this vote was only advisory, the local politicians read it as confirmation that court-ordered zoning was illegitimate. "Do nothing" turned into their marching song.

Back to court went the poverty lawyers with a new legal complaint. Their strategy, reminiscent of the tactic they used to great success in the 1970 Camden urban-renewal case, was to demand a total freeze on building—no more planned unit developments, no more Toyota offices or National Football League offices, no new sources of tax revenues—until Mount Laurel complied with the New Jersey Supreme Court's decision.

By then, the plaintiffs' attorneys had all left Camden Regional Legal Services. Peter O'Connor had opened a private law practice in neighboring Cherry Hill and was beginning to launch nonprofit housing projects on his own; someday soon, he hoped, he'd be building in Mount Laurel for the kith and kin of Ethel Lawrence. Carl Bisgaier and Ken Meiser both joined the state's Public Advocate Department, a new agency whose unique mission included bringing public-interest lawsuits, and they took the *Mount Laurel* case with them. Getting rid of exclusionary zoning and promoting the affordable-housing cause became a high priority for this fledgling agency. As Legal Services attorneys, Bisgaier and Meiser were obliged to pinch pennies, but now they had what seemed like "the deepest pockets in the world." In fact, because the suburbs fought back so hard, the housing advocates would need all the resources they could lay their hands on.

Justice Delayed—Again

If the Supreme Court's 1975 *Mount Laurel* decision was like winning the lottery, as Carl Bisgaier jubilantly declared, then the second trial, in the summer of 1977, was like discovering that the winning ticket was counterfeit. A new trial judge approved the town's sham zoning changes, and all the justices' fine words, all the expectation of a fair share for the poor, evaporated into the thinnest atmosphere.

The departure of trial judge Edward Martino was the first blow to the plaintiffs. This was the biggest case of his career, Martino knew, the one he'd be remembered for, but he had recently suffered a minor stroke and was feeling physically unprepared for the protracted litigation that town officials promised. Better to retire, he decided. The litigation was reassigned to Judge Alexander Wood III, a mild-mannered Quaker, himself nearing retirement age, and known for so disliking controversy that he had tried to get out of the assignment.

"He'll be horrible on zoning issues," Carl Bisgaier said of Judge Wood, while John Trimble, Mount Laurel's counsel, was chipper about his client's prospects. Both lawyers were right.

The second, seemingly more crushing, blow came from an unlikely source, the New Jersey Supreme Court itself. In three 1977 rulings, a badly split court fled from the boldness of *Mount Laurel*. It was as if the tribunal had had second thoughts, and its new decisions only encouraged the town's do-nothing stance.

The critical case was *Madison*, the same lawsuit that the justices had planned to hear, together with *Mount Laurel*, during the first round of arguments. At that time, town officials had amended their zoning ordinance and the Supreme Court had sent the case back for another trial to see whether the new ordinance was constitutional. Then, in his second ruling in that case, the trial judge rejected the new measure as inadequate. "The zoning objective [is still] . . . an elite community of high income families with few children. . . . The advances towards . . . low income housing opportunities [are] nil." That decision was now before the high court.

By a four-to-three vote, the justices undercut their own *Mount Laurel* doctrine. Concerning Madison Township itself, the trial court ruling was affirmed, but only on its narrow particulars. What mattered much more was the ruling that towns need not, and courts could not, quantify a town's "fair share" of poor families because that task was simply too hard. Experts' analyses vary so widely "as to preclude judicial dictation or acceptance of any one solution as authoritative," the majority insisted, while voicing skepticism about the capacity of trial judges to deal with "highly controversial economic, sociological, and policy questions of innate difficulty and complexity." The role of the trial court was only to consider whether a town had acted in "good faith," that ill-defined standard.

The point wasn't that trial judges aren't rocket scientists—or social scientists, for that matter—but that *Mount Laurel*–type questions are "highly controversial." This wasn't exactly news, and to harp on it indicated that the judges were growing skittish.

Two other zoning cases, decided a few weeks later, added to this sense of disorderly retreat. While the specific rulings had little practical consequence, the rhetoric was terrible from the housing advocates' point of view. The opinions emphasized that the suburbs truly know best—that it was reasonable to maintain the character of a community developed with "traditionally valued" single-family housing, rather than "deleterious" apartments—and stressed what courts could *not* do. "The judicial branch is not suited to the role of an *ad hoc* super zoning legislature." But as Morris Pashman, the most liberal member of the high court, insisted in an angry dissent, the justices were "strip[ping] the principles laid down in *Mount Laurel* of all practical effect." Sooner or later, he predicted, in towns where the zoning law was hostile to affordable housing, as it generally was, no one would even bother trying to challenge the law and build homes for the poor.

The Supreme Court in *Madison* also disowned the idea, advanced in *Mount Laurel*, that poor families were entitled to live in every developing community. It was enough to provide "least cost housing," the cheapest market-rate homes that could be built, rather than planning for housing that poor people could afford. By 1977, the justices had given up hope that developers would build for the poor. Federal funds to construct low-income housing were largely gone, and contractors weren't going to subsidize affordable housing from their own pockets. The lowered judicial expectation was that, if some new homes were built, eventually decent housing would "trickle down." This was the dampened expectation of the Public Advocate as well, which endorsed the least-cost housing idea as all that could realistically be done.

The only venturesome note was the decision to give the developer, Oakwood-at-Madison, what the court called a "builder's remedy": a developer who successfully challenged a local zoning ordinance—who "had borne the stress and expense of public interest litigation"—could be awarded not only a favorable court ruling but also, more concretely, the right to build the project, provided that 20 percent of the units were reserved for low- and moderate-income families. This guarantee offered a real incentive for developers, and, while the *Madison* justices envisioned the builder's remedy as "rare," just a few years later in *Mount Laurel II* the Supreme Court would make it the centerpiece of the relaunched judicial effort to open up the suburbs.

Despite this mostly bad news from Trenton, Carl Bisgaier and Ken Meiser at the Public Advocate went ahead with their plans to mount a new Mount Laurel trial. The original 1972 trial had been short, less than a week long, and nontechnical in character, as the testimony lingered on the sad stories of the dispossessed. This 1977 trial, by contrast, would consume more than a month of court time, including one day when the judge, himself a resident of genteel, neighboring Moorestown, toured Mount Laurel with the lawyers in tow.

The township had mounted only a perfunctory defense the first time around, but on this occasion it treated the lawsuit as if it were the Battle of Britain. John Trimble, the town's solicitor, was joined at the counsel table by John Patton, a high-priced attorney who had made a name for himself fighting *Mount Laurel*–type cases for North Jersey suburbs. Experts on the arcana of zoning and land use were summoned, setting up a duel with plaintiffs' experts. The trial transcript fills half a dozen thick volumes; several file cabinets are needed to contain all the exhibits. The $108,000 that Mount Laurel spent on its lawyers and witnesses forced the township to cut other items from its operating budget.

Bisgaier devoted several days to cross-examining the town's expert witness, demolishing Mount Laurel's contention that the three rezoned parcels could be used for affordable housing. Then, plaintiffs' witnesses turned up the rhetorical attack to full blast. University of Virginia law professor Yale Rabin decried Mount Laurel's "withholding of necessary facilities" such as fire protection as analogous to "a blockade in a war" and called its ordinance a "*negative* fair share plan." Planner Alan Mallach, who kept busy by working on similar cases across the state, recommended wholesale changes in the zoning laws, to allow nearly six thousand units of affordable housing—half of all housing that had been built in the town— by the year 2000.

There was high drama when Bisgaier saw his chance to play Perry Mason—to expose, beyond all deniability, the town's real intention to leave poor families out in the cold. The incident began when town attorney Jack Trimble casually mentioned to a lawyer named Frank Wisniewski that Mount Laurel had really selected its sites for affordable housing "to screw the plaintiffs." Bisgaier got wind of that exchange and subpoenaed Wisniewski, whose testimony was "a knockout."

"I ask him, 'Was a statement made to you regarding this case?' and he says, 'Yes.' I said, 'Was it made by a senior official of the township?' Again he says, 'Yes.' So I ask, 'What did he tell you?' *There's no objection!* And he says what Trimble told him about the township's plan to screw us. So I say, 'No further questions.' Then Trimble gets up and he's fuming. And he asks the witness, 'Who told you that?' Wisniewski says, 'It was you, Mr. Trimble.' I've never had an experience like this in a courtroom before or since."

But while Perry Mason regularly relied on such surprises to win his cases, Bisgaier got spanked by the court. Judge Wood, obviously ruffled, called a recess and summoned all the lawyers to his chambers.

"This is outrageous testimony," the judge said.

"I thought so too," Bisgaier replied, "that's why I called him as a witness."

"You don't understand," said Wood. "The witness is impugning the integrity of an attorney."

"But Wisniewski isn't saying *Jack* [Trimble] did anything," Bisgaier responded. "Jack just told him what his *client* was going to do."

The judge was implacable: unless Wisniewski's testimony was withdrawn, he would declare a mistrial. "You have to understand that I've already heard this testimony, but I can't have it stay on the record."

This threat of a mistrial, made after weeks in court, felt "like death" to Bisgaier. "What the hell was I going to do? I felt like I had no choice." Wood really would take the testimony into account, the advocate believed— surely that's what he meant when he said he had "already heard it"—and so he acceded to the judge's wishes, withdrawing the testimony, only to feel foolish when Judge Wood later ruled in favor of the town.

A year after the trial had wound down, in July 1978, Alexander Wood delivered his forty-three-page opinion. Relying heavily on *Madison Township* and the state Supreme Court's other 1977 land-use cases, the judge deferred to the town's own estimate of its housing needs. Since the rezoning was "bona fide legislative compliance . . . with the directives of the Supreme Court," the court's job was done. "The judicial branch is not suited to the role of an *ad hoc* zoning legislature," he wrote, quoting the high court's recent ruling. Although Wood rejected Bisgaier's arguments wholesale, he did grant some relief to a late intervenor. A contractor named Roger Davis had sought town approval to put up a development of 590 prefabricated homes, which he proposed to name Tricia Meadows, after his daughter. When the township council rejected the plan, Davis restyled his intentions, termed the mobile homes affordable housing, and joined the litigation. Ethel Lawrence's lawyers welcomed Davis's participation, because it showed there was a realistic alternative to "executive-style" houses in Mount Laurel. What they *didn't* anticipate was the court's decision, which favored Tricia Meadows while leaving the zoning plan otherwise undisturbed.

Even with the vague and somewhat confused state of the law, Judge Wood's opinion was indefensible. The township's rezoning was a sham, although the ruling pretended otherwise. Nor did the judge offer a scintilla of justification for granting Davis his rezoning—if the town had really complied with the Supreme Court's *Mount Laurel* edict, logically there was no basis to bestow anything on Davis.

The ruling made the lawyers miserable. When they drove to Ethel Lawrence's home to tell her the case had been lost, they were depressed, for they knew that they'd let her down. But she insisted that things would eventually work themselves out. "It's okay," she told them, "we're going to win."

"Ethel actually cheered *us* up," says Carl Bisgaier, shaking his head at the memory.

"I got a little stronger as I went along," says Ethel Lawrence matter-of-factly, and she remained uncomplaining through all the twists and turns of her case. "I am a great believer in prayer. I say, 'God, you know what I'm talking about, you know what we need,' and I leave the rest up to him."

Bisgaier was blown away by his client's strength, but for five long years he carried his disappointment like a sack of coal. He obsessed over what had happened, second-guessing himself for how he had "let this judge push me around"—particularly, how he had agreed to delete Frank Wisniewski's testimony from the record that the state Supreme Court would be reading.

"In the history of the *Mount Laurel* case," he says, "from first conception to today, it has not been that often that those supporting the concept have felt good about what was going on. We lost for the most part. It's a history of feeling like you had lost and were fighting an uphill battle—and then suddenly you'd win."

The Bumpy Road Back to the Supreme Court

The New Jersey Supreme Court was by no means finished refining the fair share doctrine. Chief Justice Richard Hughes had died, and in 1979 Robert Wilentz was named to replace him. Governor Brendan Byrne, a Democrat, didn't want a placeholder on the bench. "I'm looking for someone with the depth of a Weintraub, the authority of a Vanderbilt and the compassion of a Hughes," he said, pointing to the modern succession of chief justices on the New Jersey high court.

"The experience of the 1947 [judicial] reform is so strong, and its meaning so clear," Chief Justice Wilentz declared, "that it still moves us substantially in New Jersey." The meaning of this sea change in Jersey justice was also abidingly personal to Wilentz. His father, a state legislator and later attorney general during the Boss Hague years, was best known as the successful prosecutor of Bruno Hauptmann for the kidnapping and murder of the Lindbergh baby. In a less lofty moment, Wilentz *père* stymied a major legislative investigation of a rigged gubernatorial election when he ruled that the state police couldn't do the lawmakers' legwork unless Hague, who was accused of the rigging, personally gave his permission. During the 1960s, Wilentz *fils* followed his father to the state legislature and before his appointment as chief justice practiced law in the family firm.

Four years later, Wilentz would live up to Governor Byrne's high hopes, delivering an opinion on land-use justice known as *Mount Laurel II*. That decision gave developers, lawyers, and poor families eager to prise open the suburbs expansive declarations of rights, detailed remedies to make those rights real, and even the apparatus of a new mini-administrative system to enforce them. But as the justices were gearing up to rethink the question of land-use justice, the *Mount Laurel* case itself was nearly kept off the docket.

Under Wilentz's predecessor, ex-governor Richard Hughes, the state Supreme Court had become a politically embattled institution. Where once the court's activism had been a source of pride in New Jersey, more and more it was being criticized as antidemocratic. The court had begun to hand down an unbroken string of rulings, thirty-two in all, that reversed death-penalty verdicts, and this persistence was taken as strong evidence that the justices were out of touch and out of control.

Nor was capital punishment the Hughes court's only hot-button issue. For several years, the justices had been at odds with state legislators over how, constitutionally, to finance education. Like most other states, New Jersey relied heavily on local property taxes to pay for public schools, and consequently, even as the property-rich suburbs delivered a gold-plated education to their children, poor cities like Camden, with far fewer dollars, made do with underpaid teachers using outdated texts to teach overcrowded classes of students who started school academically behind their suburban peers, then dropped out or were pushed out in droves. In *Robinson v. Cahill*, the high court overturned that school-funding arrangement, determining that it was not the "thorough and efficient system of education" the state constitution required, but the legislature refused to revamp the school-finance law. The politicians' nose-thumbing inaction was followed by judicial deadlines, threats of contempt citations against the lawmakers, and judicially compelled tax hikes. No one had seen anything remotely like it in the state's history. While the legislature did make a last-minute gesture toward greater equity, the crusade left the judges weary, their reservoir of goodwill among lawmakers and the public practically empty.

When the first round of post–*Mount Laurel* affordable-housing cases reached the high court in 1977, the justices were in no mood for yet another politically bruising bout, which is one reason why, in *Madison Township* and the two related opinions handed down that term, the Supreme Court retreated from its *Mount Laurel* bravado. But the new chief justice hadn't been part of that donnybrook; and as one of his fellow judges says, "He pretty much runs the show." In the last days of 1979, less than a year after Wilentz's appointment and at his urging, the court decided to tackle exclusionary zoning once more.

Seemingly every unsettled issue presented by *Mount Laurel I* and its progeny was going to be heard, since Wilentz proposed to decide half a dozen cases simultaneously. At the Public Advocate, Carl Bisgaier and Ken Meiser were delighted. The office had invested heavily in *Mount Laurel*-type litigation. Right after the 1977 rulings, they sued all twenty-seven of the towns in Morris County, the very center of the ring of suburban development surrounding New York City. That legal complaint was intended to make a statement that reached beyond Morris County. If the *Mount Laurel* doctrine could be made to apply to the wealthiest and politically most influential communities in the state, then the judgment mattered— otherwise, it was useless law. That case was also teaching the Public Advocate a lesson in deep-pockets litigation. The townships hired social scientists to churn out documents contending that poor people were truly happier with their own kind; that living in the suburbs would be bad for them and, besides, would mean an end to the suburban way of life—a variant, for land use, of the infamous argument that blacks were inferior and so would be better off attending segregated schools. One defendant, the village of Harding, passed a $600,000 bond issue to fund its defense, thus raising the astonishing amount of more than $2,000 for every man, woman, and child.

Morris County was not one of the cases that the Supreme Court agreed to hear in late 1979, because the lawsuit hadn't progressed far enough. Inexplicably, neither had *Mount Laurel*; when the Public Advocate, bruised by Judge Wood's decision, petitioned for a hearing, the high court rejected the request. This was terrible news for the public-interest lawyers, the worst news yet in a case that already had eight years of history, much of it unhappy, behind it. A denial from the state's highest court is usually as final as the slow tolling of the bells at Jacob's Chapel on a funeral morning in Mount Laurel. Although a hearing before an intermediate appeals court with a subsequent appeal to the Supreme Court was still possible, prospects looked grim. In saying no, the Supreme Court seemed to be declaring that the trial court had read the legal tea leaves correctly—that Ethel Lawrence and the other plaintiffs would have to make do with twenty useless acres, that the Supreme Court's *Mount Laurel* doctrine had no practical meaning for the town itself.

Surely this was wrong, Carl Bisgaier believed, a fit of judicial absence of mind. Bisgaier had already had a second chance in this roller-coaster litigation, a second crack at making his argument in *Mount Laurel I*. Maybe he could wring out *another* second chance. "We did something brassy, which was to ask the justices to reconsider. In those papers, I basically said: 'How can you do this, put us on a slow boat to China, when you have the opportunity to hear *Mount Laurel* with all the other cases?' " The tactic worked as, without a word of explanation, the justices granted the petition.

"This was our final at bat," Ken Meiser says, a memory shared by planner Alan Mallach, who also takes his imagery from the world of baseball. "We were one strike away from going to a world where there never was a *Mount Laurel I*. This was our last crack at getting *Mount Laurel* back."

Arguing Mount Laurel II: *Fifty Parties, Thirty Lawyers, Twenty-four Written Questions*

When *Mount Laurel II* made its way to the Supreme Court, Chief Justice Wilentz took pains to remind the massed parties that the court was still a judicial tribunal, not a commission or a legislature. "We are not going to lose sight of the fact that ultimately" there are specific disputes to settle, the chief justice assured the anxious litigants. Confronted with the specter of more than fifty separate parties and friends of the court, represented by more than thirty lawyers in six cases, Wilentz departed from the normal appellate practice of lawyers arguing individually to judges, instead organizing something that resembled a seminar in planning or a legislative committee hearing. As the judges peppered the three-day proceedings with questions, the attorneys, rather like graduate students or expert witnesses, tried gamely to respond.

This format transformed six cases into tools for making policy, as the Supreme Court inverted Sergeant Joe Friday's admonition to read "everything *but* the facts." The role of the court had become, at least for this case, coterminous with the domain of government. The justices cared less about what had transpired in one or another verdant suburb than about the broad principles and rules for implementation they hoped would emerge from the cumbersome proceedings.

The initial hint that something special was afoot came in a document addressed to all the lawyers, which laid out twenty-four questions on which the justices were seeking enlightenment during three days reserved for argument. (By contrast, the U.S. Supreme Court typically allots just one hour for a case.) These questions ranged "from narrow to cosmic," writes Rutgers law professor John Payne, who later became counsel in one of the trials following *Mount Laurel II*. They were "an extraordinary compilation."

Queries about legal burdens of proof and who should be made a party to a case, the routine stuff of lawyering, were posed alongside unanswerable questions about the socioeconomic validity of the "trickle-down" theory of housing, which posits that as the well off move into new homes their former homes pass down the economic ladder, and the concept of "tipping," which holds that whites move out of a neighborhood when a certain percentage of blacks move in. "Is the underlying goal of *Mt. Laurel* economically feasible?" the court inquired. "Will attainment of the goal affect another important goal of this state—to rehabilitate housing?" During the first argument in *Brown v. Board of Education*, U.S. Supreme Court Justice Felix Frankfurter mused about how one might anticipate the "practical effect" of a decision on segregation; in *Mount Laurel II*, the justices asked for similar advice.

As a way of managing what could otherwise have been unworkable— imagine ten minutes apiece for each of thirty lawyers—the judicially posed written questions were useful. The attorneys were drawn away from the particulars of their client's case toward a broader mind-set aimed at solving big problems. In effect, they all were asked to be public interest attorneys. On both sides, responsibility for the judges' questions was divided up ("like a batting order," says baseball-minded public advocate Ken Meiser) and the resulting schedule, advocates assigned to speak on item III-E or item IV-A-2 for five or fifteen minutes apiece, read like a legislative committee's agenda prepared by an obsessive-compulsive.

The preparation for these hearings marked the first time that all the plaintiffs' lawyers—those representing developers, those arguing for poor families who had lost their homes, those representing civil-rights organizations like the Urban League—ever met. In the cramped Manhattan office of the Metropolitan Action Institute, a shoestring operation run by Paul Davidoff, a tireless advocate for low-income housing, they compared notes and hashed out strategy. The attorney representing the Urban League in one of the cases brought a national perspective to the table.

Stephen Eisdorfer, a former clerk to Justice Morris Pashman who had gone to work for the Public Advocate's office, had ideas about what the justices might really be looking for.

When there were disagreements in these strategy sessions—about how much housing should be guaranteed for the poor, for instance, and how much importance should attach to environmental concerns in a state with a substantial amount of ecologically fragile wetlands—Paul Davidoff refereed. "He was the Ralph Nader of the movement," Richard Bellman, one of the *Mount Laurel II* attorneys, says of the lawyer-planner. Davidoff had written the bible for the ethics-in-planning movement in the 1960s, an essay that argued that, when deciding how land should be used, the more voices that got heard, the wiser the result. He put those theories in practice, first in New York City, then throughout the New York metropolitan area, where he drove the suburban gentry to distraction with his grand and unrealized plans for democratic development—two thousand apartments in New Jersey, six thousand on Long Island, many of them intended for poor and moderate-income households. "There's that scene in *Monty Python and the Holy Grail*," says Carl Bisgaier, "where the king confronts this monstrous-looking knight in armor, and he cuts off one of his arms, then the other, and then he cuts off one leg, then the other, and the knight says to him, 'Don't come near me or I'll bite you.' That reminded me of Paul Davidoff. He may have just lost everything, but he's still enthusiastic, ready to go." Although Davidoff was besieged by organized suburbanites who demanded that the IRS eliminate his organization's nonprofit tax status and pressured foundations to cut off his funds, somehow he carried on. In his 1984 obituary, the *New York Times* called *Mount Laurel* his "most notable suit."

On the morning of October 20, 1980, as the argument in *Mount Laurel II* began, a weak light filtered through the grimy leaded windows of the grand old courtroom. The bookshelves in this dark-paneled chamber sagged under the weight of law volumes that dated to the state's earliest years, while on the walls hung portraits of justices past, their paint crackling, their carved and gilded frames peeling. As the seven justices peered out from behind the raised bench, with just a single clerk on hand to serve as a traffic cop for the proceedings, lawyers crowded around tables where usually just one or two attorneys would be seated. So many lawyers were on call that those not on the schedule of speakers occupied a roped-off area of the visitors' gallery. Among the handful of spectators was Ethel Lawrence, who had driven up that morning from Mount Laurel, so nervous that she was afraid to breathe too loudly.

Chief Justice Wilentz's first question to the attorneys was meant to confirm that the issue before the court wasn't whether "*Mount Laurel* [should] be overruled," but rather how to translate the *Mount Laurel* doctrine into a workable remedy. One by one, all the lawyers dutifully agreed with Wilentz's proposition—all of them, that is, except John Patton, representing Mount Laurel Township. His response suggested why, a decade after having been filed, this case remained mired in the courts.

"I simply don't think it's a function of the court to start . . . creating fair share numbers and creating regions," Patton maintained. "No, I don't think that's the proper judicial function."

"You don't think we should be in this in the first place, which gets to the question of the *Mount Laurel* doctrine itself?" Wilentz followed up.

Patton's reply was unequivocal: "That's right."

Several attorneys tried to allay the justices' apparent concern that a court-created right to housing was wild judicial overreaching. These cases are pretty conventional land-use disputes, one advocate said reassuringly. "We impose limitations . . . by the nature of zoning"—what the court was being asked to do now was no different. But Carl Bisgaier took another and braver tack. Maybe he remembered his first high court appearance, when his slip-sliding around the critical issue had gotten him nowhere. Or maybe he was thinking about his first encounter, long ago in Mount Laurel, with the person who remained his most steadfast client.

"In 1970, when I met with Ethel Lawrence . . . to discuss this problem she was having in Mount Laurel Township," Bisgaier began, "implicit— *explicit*—in everything that was being said was that government simply cannot sit back when it has the power to do it.

"To whom else should we look? To whom else are low and moderate income persons to look for the remedy to the conditions under which they are living today?"

Time and again during the lengthy hearings, while his cocounsel split doctrinal atoms, the lawyer from the Public Advocate concentrated on real-life stories. "It's not a question of *whether* people are going to live," he said, responding to a question about whether suburbanites would have to pay higher taxes if poor people moved in. "They're alive, and they're going to *be* living. The question is, whether they're going to be housed adequately." *Housed adequately:* those falling-down, fire-trap chicken coops in Springville leap to mind. When a justice asked Bisgaier whether he regarded affordable housing as a judicial or a legislative problem, he responded in a very unlawyerly—a very human—way. "The fundamental problem here is people. They're the ones we are collecting the taxes for."

The justices understood the connection between unbuilt houses and exclusionary zoning. "Do you think that experience now teaches us that . . . where you do not have an adequate number of low and moderate housing units in a particular municipality, one reason is almost certain to be the inadequacy of its zoning ordinance?" Public Advocate lawyer Ken Meiser was asked, a classic instance of leading the witness.

Much of the discussion focused on how to give legal bite to the court's ruling. Should there be "specialist" judges to hear *Mount Laurel*–type disputes, one justice asked, and how should fair-share standards be set for each town? As Charles Haar, revisiting the New Jersey scene four decades after his *Harvard Law Review* article condemning the exclusionary-zoning decision in *Lionshead Lake*, points out, "basic planning questions of defining the boundaries of a region, of predicting the future, of estimating the demographic prospects of a town, the quantum of housing need, the number of jobs, what was the likelihood of new people knocking at the doors and posing a regional need for shelter"—such "technical struggles were no longer confined within the covers of textbooks. Theoretical and conceptual issues that trouble professional planning experts . . . were suddenly thrust into the judicial arena—and not for philosophical discussion, but for decision."

The justices never said one word about politics, for that is almost never done in courtrooms, but the specter of politics lay behind the probing. These jurists knew they were venturing into turbulent territory—memories lingered of the suburbanites' outrage generated by the first *Mount Laurel* opinion. They were also keen to avoid a reprise of the school-finance wars with the legislature that had been sparked by *Robinson v. Cahill*, so they went searching for help from the other branches of government. Two studies prepared by the state's Department of Community Affairs in the late 1970s looked particularly useful. One, undertaken at the legislature's request, identified places where residential development should be encouraged and where builders should look elsewhere—this report would become the core of *Mount Laurel II*—while the other defined numerical housing goals, town by town.

Did these reports express "official" policy, the court wondered, and "how much actual public input was there?" The justices were really asking whether, by incorporating the findings of these reports in their decree, they would be gaining valuable political cover.

Cases are usually decided in the same term they are argued. But the 1980–1981 state Supreme Court term ended without a decision in *Mount Laurel*, and so did the next. Two years and a month passed without a ruling—"an extraordinary hiatus," court watcher John Payne wrote, "during which the court's ability to handle the remedial problem came increasingly into question."

Work simply halted on all the exclusionary-zoning cases in the lower courts, as trial judges awaited the high court ruling, but no judicial word came—not even a hint as to when word *might* come. When there are protracted delays, the most obvious explanation is that the court is having a hard time mustering a majority, but in this instance that seemed unlikely. During oral argument, the lawyers recalled, the justices had seemed to speak with a single voice. As Carl Bisgaier notes, they are "very expressive, not shy about dissension, but there was none of that."

Perhaps the judge assigned to write the opinion was suffering from writer's block, or perhaps it took longer than anticipated to sift through massive amounts of material. Guesses about who that dilatory author might be centered on the chief justice, who often assigned himself headline-making cases. Wilentz writes relatively few opinions, spending much of his time administering the state's judicial system, but the opinions he does write tend to be slow in coming and very long. All this was just guesswork, though, since no one outside the high court chambers really knew what was happening. Chief Justice Wilentz took, and continues to take, extraordinary measures—at one point asking now retired justices to keep their silence—to assure that, even today, New Jersey's Supreme Court remains as impregnable to public scrutiny as the Kremlin in its time of glory.

In Mount Laurel and in the other towns whose lawsuits had come before the high court, the plaintiffs' counsel had been on a high after the argument. "We were incredibly well prepared," Bisgaier remembers, "and we were just hitting home run after home run up there—so much different from my go-round with Justice Weintraub [in *Mount Laurel I*]." Besides, the court had thrown them lots of soft pitches. The lawyers convinced themselves that the justices would bury the 1977 decrees and reestablish *Mount Laurel I.* But as the time dragged on, they slid straight into fretful anxiety, then despair. Meanwhile, mortgage interest rates were also going down, after their stratospheric rise during the last year of the Carter administration, and lots of new housing developments were begun, none of which included housing for families of limited means.

"We were losing the land," Ken Meiser fretted, "and we couldn't do anything."

Finally, on January 20, 1983, the justices delivered their decree. The housing advocates believed it was worth the wait. "Let's put it this way," says Carl Bisgaier, "Wilentz is a lot smarter than I am. He'd decided we were right, and he did it his way. And it was better than I could have done it. So it was better than winning my case—we won his way."

"We Do Enforce the Constitution"

The New Jersey Supreme Court's judgment fills 120 pages of the official published reports, and it carries the whip and sting of the schoolmaster's birch. No other leading judicial opinion of modern times speaks so harshly and so personally about the public officials whose conduct the justices are reviewing. "The ordinance at its core is true to nothing but Mount Laurel's determination to exclude the poor," Chief Justice Wilentz wrote for a unanimous court, describing it as a document "papered over with studies, rationalized by hired experts."

Wilentz detailed the defects of one parcel that had ostensibly been made available for affordable housing when Mount Laurel amended its zoning ordinance and concluded that "[i]t would be hard to find . . . a less suitable parcel for lower income or indeed any kind of housing." Then he added the topping insult, that another of the proposed sites was worse! After scoffing at the tiny number of affordable-housing units the town nominally made possible through rezoning, Wilentz added that even this calculation was disingenuous, since not a single unit of affordable housing had been constructed or even proposed. "Mount Laurel's lower income housing effort has been either a total failure or a total success—depending on its intention."

What had transpired in Mount Laurel Township was not only mean-spirited, a cruel hoax on the poor; it also made the judges look feckless. "The [*Mount Laurel*] doctrine has become famous," the chief justice wrote; "the *Mount Laurel* case itself threatens to become infamous. . . . The obligation is to provide a realistic opportunity for housing, not litigation. . . . We may not build houses but we do enforce the Constitution."

The Supreme Court did much more than deliver a critique of one town's misbehavior. It also "put some steel" into its ruling by introducing a mechanism that used both marketplace and institutional incentives to make housing for the poor a reality statewide.

Most constitutional rights take the form of what philosopher Isaiah Berlin calls "negative liberty"—that is, they protect individuals *from* government. But *Mount Laurel II* called for "positive liberty," an affirmative requirement that every town take responsibility for its "fair share" of the state's poor. Gone was the wishy-washy language of *Madison*, which required only that towns engage in bona fide efforts to include the poor. "*Madison* has led to little but a sigh of relief from those who oppose *Mount Laurel*," the court confessed, thereby consigning that 1977 decision to the trash bin of abandoned opinions. A municipality must "*in fact* provide a realistic opportunity for the construction of its fair share of low and moderate income housing." Gone too was the "numberless approach" of *Madison*. "Figures speak," federal judge J. Skelly Wright declared in a famous civil-rights case, "and when they do, courts listen." So too here: the municipality has "the heavy burden of demonstrating . . . its satisfaction [of its fair-share obligation] and any justification of its failure."

Nor was the reach of *Mount Laurel* limited to "developing" towns, as the Supreme Court had earlier suggested. Instead, the justices seized and made their own the plan, prepared by the state's Department of Community Affairs, that specified where residential growth should be encouraged. The *Mount Laurel* obligation applied in all these "growth areas" and so would "depend on rational long-range land use planning . . . rather than upon sheer economic forces." It was not enough for communities to remove zoning barriers to affordable housing or to allow "least-cost" housing; they were also obliged to give builders incentives to build homes for the poor. Towns had to require that developers set aside one unit in five for low- and moderate-income families and had to allow for mobile-home parks as well. Towns were also instructed to award "density bonuses," boosting the number of housing units that may be built as a developer increases the amount of affordable housing in a development (shades of Peter O'Connor's proposal to developer Richard Goodwin before the *Mount Laurel* case was ever filed).

To some key questions—What is a region? What is a fair share?—the Supreme Court gave a structural answer, creating new specialist courts to decide these things. The justices divided New Jersey into three parts, and for each area authorized the chief justice to name a single judge, who would be responsible for determining everything from liability to remedy in a single proceeding. No longer would endless delays, appeal upon appeal, be permitted. Because their docket would mainly consist of affordable-housing cases, the Supreme Court reasoned, these "*Mount Laurel* judges" would develop the expertise needed to handle this complex litigation. In short order, it was anticipated, a consensus would emerge on the definition of a region and the method for calculating each community's obligation. There would be no more unsympathetic jurists obstructing progress toward affordable housing—no more fiascoes like Judge Alexander Wood's, in the 1977 *Mount Laurel* trial, when he threw up his hands in perplexity at the planners' testimony. Towns that were prepared to rewrite their zoning ordinances would get help from a court-appointed master and, more importantly, were promised six years of grace from any *Mount Laurel*–type litigation. But where local officials balked, the new *Mount Laurel* judges were assigned effective control over zoning and land use.

When Carl Bisgaier filed his pleadings in the original case in 1971, there existed decently funded federal and state programs that subsidized housing for the poor—that's how the original thirty-six-unit Springville project in Mount Laurel Township was to have been underwritten. The availability of federal subsidies would have generated affordable homes if towns had removed their zoning barriers. But these sources of funds began drying up during Richard Nixon's truncated second term in the White House. Having no authority to commandeer state funds, the court's only realistic option to pay for low-income housing was to harness the market itself.

Although developers had not built much affordable housing, except in publicly underwritten urban-renewal projects, the justices figured that builders would respond to the prospect of profit—that, if you offer opportunities to build, developers will come. The *Mount Laurel II* decision transformed the builder's remedy, first described in *Madison* as a rarity, into the principal technique for funding low-income housing. Developers who agreed to set aside 20 percent of their units for this purpose, fixing a price at below-market levels, were entitled to jump the queue for project approval. If they didn't get a quick okay from local planners, they could sue the township in a *Mount Laurel* trial court. Then, if they persuaded the judge that the town was violating the Supreme Court's fair-share housing rules, the trial court would set aside the local ordinance—and more. The builder won not only the legal case but, so much more importantly, the right to build.

If all went according to plan, there would be a suburban building boom in New Jersey, and poor families would emerge as winners.

Despite the barrage of legal arguments, the claim of Ethel Lawrence and the Southern Burlington County NAACP remained anchored in a moral imperative. "What [would] this state be like" if it rejected that claim? the opinion asks. There would be "poor people forever zoned out of substantial areas of the state . . . because they are not wanted; poor people forced to live in urban slums forever, not because . . . attractive locations could not accommodate them but simply because they are not wanted." As a matter of the simplest justice, that seemed wrong. Yet just as Felix Frankfurter, in the arguments over *Brown v. Board of Education,* was troubled by the possibility that the great principle of racial equality would be "evaded by tricks," housing advocates feared that *Mount Laurel II* might be undermined by the reality that, as Justice Frederick Hall conceded in the 1975 *Mount Laurel* opinion, "courts don't build houses."

Writing soon after *Mount Laurel II* was handed down, John Payne, the Rutgers law professor and affordable-housing advocate, sounded sanguine about the prospects for implementing the decree. This decision "suggests the end of the court's naive expectation that a political response will be volunteered and a determination to stimulate such response however possible," he wrote. "Legislative and political inaction has become much more costly to legislators and executives hostile to the *Mount Laurel* doctrine than before."

This was the hope. "If [the strategy] succeeds," Payne concluded, it "will chart the way for a new judicial role in stimulating legislative responses to a whole series of complex social problems that might otherwise go unresolved. . . . [T]his is a most pleasing possibility." The key word, of course, was *if.*

Killing Baby Seals

On the door of superior court judge Eugene Serpentelli's chambers, situated in peaceable Ocean County, there hangs a sign that reads: "Combat Zone: Enter At Your Own Risk." On no other occasion since Serpentelli's appointment to the bench in 1978 has warfare broken out with such frequency and such ferocity as in the affordable-housing cases that have come his way.

In *Mount Laurel II*, Chief Justice Robert Wilentz divided New Jersey, like Gaul, into three parts, and in the months following that decision he took great care in picking a trial judge for each region. Those personnel choices were critical because the new ruling was bold, and he did not want to see it nibbled away through timidity on the bench. The chief justice began his selection process with several dozen candidates, and the probing interviews he used to winnow this list sometimes lasted for hours. On three separate occasions, he summoned Serpentelli to answer questions. Wilentz wanted to know whether Serpentelli and the other candidates were good legal scholars and sensible courtroom managers. He wasn't looking for a crusader—during those interviews, he never asked about the plight of the poor or the need for affordable housing—but for someone strong enough to stand up against predictably fierce pressure from local politicians. "Do you have an automatic aversion to courts being involved in this sort of thing?" he inquired.

Like Steven Skillman and L. Anthony Gibson, the two other jurists chosen for the assignment, Serpentelli was relatively young. He had worked his way through college, then had gone to law school in 1959 on a college classmate's dare. There, he did well enough academically to clerk for Joseph Weintraub, New Jersey's chief justice and a fellow Cornell alumnus. Serpentelli had no history in politics; indeed, the fact that he was a member of neither party had posed something of a problem when he was initially nominated to the bench. His expertise was in municipal law, and he had been a partner in a four-man firm that mostly represented zoning and planning boards. When Wilentz offered him the opportunity to be a *Mount Laurel* judge, he took it, figuring it was like the zoning cases he'd handled as a lawyer. Quickly, he learned how wrong he was.

Into the three *Mount Laurel* trial courts came bushels' worth of lawsuits. Though the Supreme Court's ruling had been widely seen as a civil-rights suit, it was money, not principle, that talked the loudest. The builder's remedy that Chief Justice Wilentz had crafted, together with a vibrant housing economy, drove the litigation. A year after *Mount Laurel II*, 61 cases were pending: just 2 had been brought by civil-rights groups, both (including *Mount Laurel* itself) by the Public Advocate; developers brought all the rest. One year later, the number of lawsuits had more than doubled, to 125, nearly all of them brought by builders.

This flurry of developer-inspired legal activity showed that the exclusionary zoning laws, which had operated to prevent the construction of low-cost housing in the suburbs, were not a benchmark of the marketplace, as their defenders insisted; instead, they had been an impediment to the market. The new regime ushered in by *Mount Laurel II* was generating a miniboom in housing.

While some of the litigation, like the suit against Mount Laurel Township, had been around for a very long time, most of the lawsuits were new. Aggressive lawyers such as Henry Hill, who had been the developers' attorney in the *Bedminster* case early on, now turned *Mount Laurel*–type litigation into a mass-production operation. On one wall of his office, Hill hung a map of the state festooned with pins that represented his pending cases. His firm churned out what he called "strike letters," which threatened towns with litigation in just thirty days unless local zoning rules were changed to permit his clients to build. That demand went far beyond anything that the Supreme Court envisioned, but the possibility of costly, risky litigation made the towns listen. "It's not a threat," said Hill, talking about his infamous letters, "it's a promise." In a TV interview after filing one such lawsuit, Hill mocked the suburbs. "Nice, fat, profitable targets," he called them.

"They're like baby harp seals. They can slither and squeal, but no municipality seems to have won a *Mount Laurel II* lawsuit. The townships decide to give in fast because the killing is really much more merciful if it's quick. The municipality gets to choose where on the head they get hit."

Not every developer wanted such an aggressive advocate. Indeed, some of the most successful builders, such as Ara Hovnanian, who a few years later would serve on the state council created to promote affordable housing, persuaded local officials to let his firm build by coming across as more reasonable, in effect playing good cop to Henry Hill's bad cop. Yet whatever their preferred style, the developers took out their calculators and concluded that—even setting aside 20 percent of their units for low- and moderate-income families, as the Supreme Court's ruling required— there was good money to be made in the suburbs. Going to court, if they had to, really *was* as easy as, and surely much more palatable than, clubbing baby seals.

Many of these cases wound up in Judge Eugene Serpentelli's court in Toms River, the pleasant, out-of-the-way seat of Ocean County. The courthouse is a nineteenth-century period piece, with its high ceilings, fluted columns, and polished brass. But the region of New Jersey over which Serpentelli presided was far from quiescent, since it encompassed some of the state's most rapidly suburbanizing communities. Immediately, the judge was confronted with a pivotal issue that the state Supreme Court had pointedly ducked: How much did a particular suburb have to do by way of accommodating the poor in order to satisfy the command of *Mount Laurel II*?

America's most suburbanized state contains 567 municipalities. How should the fair share of affordable housing for each of them be calculated? Serpentelli's courtroom was being overrun with planners hired by each of the plaintiffs, prepared to press for more affordable housing, and planners retained by each municipality, equally ready to urge that fewer new homes be built. In a single lawsuit, the judge counted no fewer than twenty-one experts. But Serpentelli soon realized that a useful answer wouldn't emerge, case by case, in adversarial proceedings.

After all, what was fair for one town should have some relationship to what was fair for the other 566.

The technical difficulty of determining what "fair share" meant was imposing. Which census information provided the best indicator of housing need? Should the state's need be assessed overall or split up into regions? What about migration of low- and moderate-income households into and out of the state? Procedural business-as-usual would not yield answers to such questions, and so some alternative strategy was required. Rather than diving into these poorly charted analytic seas himself, Judge Serpentelli let the experts on both sides navigate collectively. By removing the lawyers—thus temporarily removing the adversarial character of the lawsuit itself—he permitted the planners to work as a team, pooling their knowledge and fusing different approaches to reach compromises on points of conflict. He anticipated that the process would produce not the "correct" answer but a consensus answer. That, the judge thought, was what fairness required.

The first lawsuit, brought by a developer against a single township, yielded only what Judge Serpentelli calls a "Model A plan," in acknowledgment of its primitiveness. It was substantially refined in the next case he heard, an ambitious complaint filed by the Urban League against all twenty of the townships in Middlesex County. This time two dozen planners, including experts not involved in the particular litigation who donated their time, met for days on end for a period of several months, as a planner hired by the judge coordinated the effort.

The planners felt like kids who had been left alone in their sandbox. Alan Mallach, a ubiquitous figure in the post–*Mount Laurel II* cases, recalls that "our first reaction was, 'Thank God the lawyers aren't here. Now we can talk about the real issues.' " Population projections and estimates of both present and prospective need were toted up; the state's development growth plan, which the state Supreme Court had referred to as a useful planning text, was dissected; units of substandard housing were counted; the "commutershed" around municipal centers was analyzed. "Almost everyone around that table focused on the methodological problems," Mallach says, "not on how the outcome would affect their particular client. The planners representing municipalities happened to be individuals of high levels of integrity or wanted to be seen by their peers as being such—so even those individuals inclined to be obstructionist felt, in that framework, that they had to act in a professional and collegial manner."

What emerged in July 1984 was a formula, incorporated by Judge Serpentelli in a 150-page decision that could be used not just in Middlesex County but across the entire state. In short order, and with modest variations, the two other *Mount Laurel* judges adopted what became known as the *Urban League* consensus methodology. "I was conscious throughout that there were no rules governing this new *Mount Laurel* litigation," says Serpentelli. "It really was an *Alice in Wonderland* type of thing. . . . We were making up the rules as we went along. Our authority was the inherent power of the court to shepherd any litigation before it in the interest of justice. I was also conscious that the methodology looked a lot like legislation, that whatever we did was likely to be picked up in any statute to come."

While the judge paid lip service to the procedural rights of the townships—even as, during the unorthodox *Mount Laurel II* Supreme Court hearings several years earlier, Chief Justice Wilentz had assured the parties that the court was still in the "cases and controversies" business—Serpentelli knew it would be almost impossible for any lawyer to overturn a methodology designed with such exquisite care by such a rainbow of experts. Many township officials despised the approach, which resulted in what they regarded as unrealistically big fair-share allocations. They complained that Serpentelli had abdicated to the planners—that he was just a rubber stamp, not a decider. "There were lawyers who questioned whether a court should do something like this," the judge acknowledges. "The planners were working in my courtroom, without any supervision from me." But Serpentelli is convinced that his unorthodox approach was really the only feasible one. "All the major players in *Mount Laurel* cases throughout the state were in that one room, and in future cases they'd be plaintiffs' experts or defendants' experts or court masters. I could never have gotten agreement on the methodology if I had relied on litigation alone. It would have taken me years to come up with something, and even then my own training was so inadequate in terms of what planners do, statistical analysis and all that stuff, that I might never have come up with anything useful. The expert help was critical. It's like needing to understand medical procedures in order to decide malpractice cases."

While Serpentelli relied heavily on the planners to develop a methodology of decision, he did not depend entirely on them for answers in particular cases. By habit he is the kind of professional who wants to get a feel of things for himself. In the 1960s, when he was practicing zoning law, he made it a weekly habit to take a drive with his wife to look at property that would be discussed at the next zoning appeals board hearing. Getting the lay of the land is a custom he has maintained on the bench: when called on to decide a much publicized and controversial case involving relocating radon-contaminated soil from one site to another, for instance, he visited the proposed locations. It was only natural that in *Mount Laurel*–type litigation Serpentelli's court would sometimes become a moveable feast.

Holding Court in a Mercury Marquis

Until the *Urban League* case was filed, the village of Cranbury, ten miles down a narrow, windy road from Princeton, prided itself on having changed little since the eighteenth century. Then, the Cranbury Inn was an overnight stagecoach stop on the journey from New York to Philadelphia. The inn is still a going concern, and up and down Main Street, past the old corner pharmacy and the public library, are mansions built in the same era. Partly because of the vigilance of the local historical society, mostly because of their owners' enthusiasm, the old homes are perfectly maintained. Good history has made for a good investment as well, and these days the homes on Main Street sell for half a million dollars. The state and federal governments have both certified the village as a landmark historical area worthy of preservation for later generations, and every year on Cranbury Day many of those homes are open for tourists to view.

Among the two thousand Cranbury residents, there was never much concern about crime. The first of the new generation of homes built outside the village during the 1960s posed no threat to the town's special character. Houses that borrowed their designs from the old colonials were erected on twenty-acre lots carved out of the farms and situated away from the village, sold to the kind of people who don't have to inquire too closely into the price of things.

But Cranbury is situated in Middlesex County; and so, when the Urban League filed its lawsuit, it was caught up in matters that townspeople hadn't paid much attention to. Less obviously, the lawsuit pointed out that issues of race and fairness weren't exactly unfamiliar. One of the plaintiffs was Guy Williams, who had worked at the Cranbury Inn since the days when, as he recalls, in order to achieve an "old-fashioned look" only black waiters and white waitresses were hired. Around the corner from the inn and next to the graveyard is the block-long stretch where Cranbury's black families, the Nixons and the Connovers, have been living in their wide-porch houses for generations, as long as Ethel Lawrence's family has been in Mount Laurel. Like Lawrence's kith and kin, the next generation of Nixons and Connovers can't afford to stay on in their old hometown.

Cranbury was prime territory for development, according to the "consensus methodology" developed in Judge Serpentelli's courtroom. More and more people were moving into the surrounding area, industry was also coming in, and there was substantial land on which housing could be built. The judge's planning expert concluded that the township's fair share amounted to 856 affordable units; and since, under the *Mount Laurel II* rule, developers got to build four market-price units for every low-income unit they put up, this meant a total of 4,280 new homes and apartments. In less than a decade, if the planner's recommendation became law, Cranbury's population would increase nearly sevenfold. With that news, the land rush was on. At a packed meeting in the normally staid village, when a Trenton realtor proposed developing eighteen hundred acres of farmland for new homes, he and a rival bidder started slugging one another.

By any calculation, 4,280 homes was an outsized number for Cranbury. As Judge Serpentelli knew, such a figure would "produce a great deal of resistance," especially in a town whose citizens were well versed in the public-relations game. Residents took to wearing "I Love Cranbury" buttons, and the charm of the village won it a sweet story in the *New York Times*, as the photographer climbed up a water tower to capture the Main Street panorama. When he was appointed a *Mount Laurel* judge, there had never been any talk of politics, Serpentelli recalls, and ever since, he and the chief justice had talked only about how to manage the cases. Sometimes, though, he wondered whether Wilentz meant him to factor politics into the legal equation.

Cranbury residents' insistence that "fair share" would mean historical sacrilege mattered more to the judge than the potential political fallout. Serpentelli is a history buff whose own home, he proudly says, is an authentic reproduction of a Williamsburg colonial. In another *Mount Laurel*–type lawsuit, the judge had visited the Revolutionary War battlefield at Princeton, to see for himself whether building affordable housing would be a blight on that piece of the past. (When he noticed that a development of high-priced homes had already been built equally close to the battlefield with no outcry, he became less sympathetic to the Princetonians' plea.)

In Cranbury, Judge Serpentelli decided once again to take a look. He arranged to be driven around the township, accompanied by his law clerk, his planner, the town's lawyer, and one of the developers' lawyers. The only car big enough to hold the entourage comfortably was a gray Mercury Grand Marquis that was owned by the wife of the town counsel. Reporters who covered the event rode in a trailing car. "I dictated my impressions as we moved along," Serpentelli recalls, and in the car court was in session, over the whir of the air conditioner. The lawyers became backseat advocates, speaking loudly so that their words could be picked up by the judge's tape recorder. The judge tried not to show his hand, although at one point, driving past a recently completed and conspicuously massive house that overlooked a wheat field, he turned to his clerk. "You can see why some people might be opposed to all this development."

"I was sure that I'd cut the [affordable housing] number in Cranbury," Judge Serpentelli remarked later, and his tentative ruling substantially reduced the town's obligation. But as events unfolded, he never had the chance to announce a final decision.

While the atmospherics of Cranbury are truly special, applying the "consensus methodology" to determine a town's fair share of affordable housing also meant marked change in other, less historically memorable, places. In Bedminster, situated in the state's horse-and-hounds country, a community whose zoning laws had been tested in the courts as often as Mount Laurel's, the planners' formula generated four thousand more houses and apartments for a township with fewer than a thousand residences and barely twenty five-hundred inhabitants. This expansion was too much, Judge Serpentelli concluded, because it "would bring about a radical transformation" of "a rural community which has not changed significantly for many years." Eventually, the township and the developers reached a settlement with which both sides were comfortable; the Public Advocate lent its support; and Serpentelli gave his approval.

But contention, not compromise, was the usual order of the day in Eugene Serpentelli's court. In the town of Monroe, also in Middlesex County, 774 new low- and moderate-income units, 3,870 new units in all, were required in the name of fair-share housing, and this meant a 50 percent increase in the town's housing stock. The town's mayor, Peter Garibaldi, urged the council to resist.

"I'll go to jail," Garibaldi pledged, if the judge held him or any other council members in contempt of court. The mayor of nearby Holmdel chimed in that he too would willingly go to jail "if I were faced with the same circumstances."

This demagoguery reminded East Brunswick's mayor of the vow that had been made by Alabama governor George Wallace a generation earlier, that he would "stand in the schoolhouse door" to prevent the public schools from being racially integrated. Yet Garibaldi was not only Monroe's mayor, he was also a state senator, for such dual office holding is permitted by New Jersey's constitution. And even though he didn't convince his fellow council members to take on Serpentelli—the council voted unanimously to comply with the judge's order while the mayor-senator was vacationing in Italy—conservative politicians across the state were starting to see things Peter Garibaldi's way.

Politics and Justice

In September 1984, shortly after Serpentelli had handed down his decision in the *Urban League* case, mayors from forty towns gathered with the extraordinary intention of bringing a lawsuit in federal court against the New Jersey Supreme Court itself. They contended that in *Mount Laurel II*, the justices had in effect become dictators and so had denied New Jersey citizens the "republican form of government" that the U.S. Constitution guarantees in all states. Constitutionally speaking, this argument was bizarre, for not in nearly a century and a half had the U.S. Supreme Court been asked to interpret this obscure provision, but that didn't appreciably slow the campaign. Twenty-two towns ponied up $250,000 to hire the New York City law firm of Mudge, Rose, Guthrie, Alexander, and Ferdon, Richard Nixon's old firm, and those attorneys commenced their legal researches.

The state Supreme Court justices appreciated from the outset that zoning questions were deeply political in character. That is why the court had been so careful to rest its rulings on state constitutional, not statutory, grounds—it would require a constitutional amendment to overturn the court's decrees. Yet in the wake of *Mount Laurel II,* such an amendment looked like a distinct possibility. Lots of legislators besides Peter Garibaldi were unhappy with the rulings that Serpentelli and the two other *Mount Laurel* judges were handing down. Assembly Republicans announced that they too would join the legal battle against the New Jersey Supreme Court, arguing that *Mount Laurel II* violated the doctrine of separation of powers.

Legally, those cases didn't stand a chance. But Republican governor Thomas Kean posed a more serious potential threat to the judiciary. Kean had won election in 1981 by the slimmest of margins, in part because of the popularity of his attacks on affordable housing in the suburbs. Then, two years later, came *Mount Laurel II.* The governor loathed that decision, even going so far as to describe it as "communistic." While Judge Serpentelli and his judicial colleagues were pondering the fate of towns like Cranbury, the critical and unanswered question was this: Would Governor Kean join with aggrieved legislators to do what had not been attempted since the days of Boss Hague—take steps to control the Supreme Court for its legal boldness?

6

The Politics of "No"

New Jersey's Republican governor looked at what was happening to his state—the dying cities, the blossoming suburbs to which cutting-edge industry and the middle class were flocking—and decided it was time to do something. Exclusionary zoning, snob zoning, was hurting not just the poor but working people as well, who couldn't find decent places for their families to live unless they submitted to endless commutes. For their part, the suburbanites were unsympathetic, since they believed that to build houses that these workers could afford would cause blue-collar disruptions in their lives. "There is lots of empty land and cheap housing further out," said the resident of a town that had recently attracted an IBM plant, "there's no reason why people should feel that they have to live here just because they work here." In his annual message to the legislature, the governor spoke about the need to develop affordable housing in suburbia. He warned that the state courts would "inevitably" step in if the politicians did not respond to the issue.

These events took place in 1970—thirteen years before the *Mount Laurel II* decree, some months, even, before Mount Laurel Township was sued in Burlington County court—and the Republican governor was William Cahill. The bill he drafted, which would have fixed a formula to apportion housing needs among the counties, never even made it out of its first legislative committee. For a decade and a half, this would be the pattern of New Jersey politics.

The civics texts assert that when it comes to complex issues like housing and land-use planning, legislatures are much better equipped to respond than courts. The theory says that because politicians, unlike judges, don't depend on particular cases, they can craft broader remedies. Those lawmakers can hold hearings to solicit views from all sides and can commission studies from experts to guide their decisions. Because they control the public budget, they can also put their dollars where their principles lie. While courts traffic in rights, which are often expressed in absolute terms, legislators are freer to compromise in the search for politically acceptable solutions; by the very nature of their calling, they must pay attention to the swirling political winds.

In New Jersey, though, the civics texts weren't entirely up-to-date. The New Jersey Supreme Court showed in *Mount Laurel II* that it was willing and able to craft broad remedies for systemic social problems and transcend the limitations of traditional litigation. It commandeered its own experts and forced the advocates to behave as policy mavens; it created a new institutional arrangement to implement its new zoning policy. The court's opinion reads much like a statute, and the judicially created builder's remedy was a plausible substitute for public dollars in changing the developers' incentives.

All the advantages a legislature theoretically enjoys don't mean much if the politicians are too weak, too paralyzed, or just unwilling to act—and, when it came to affordable housing in the Garden State, political paralysis set in. The legislature was unwilling to wrest control from the suburbs and establish a meaningful statewide rule that zoning must serve more than the needs of "our town"—that it promote the general welfare of New Jersey's citizens. As a result, the state's policy in this area amounted to no more than the sum of the exclusionary-zoning rules of its many municipalities.

New Jersey's legislature has a longstanding reputation for parochialism. With no statewide property tax or income tax, it generated little revenue until the mid-1960s, when it imposed a modest sales tax. "The Legislature is hardly equipped to compete with either of its sister branches in addressing itself to today's problems, much less those of tomorrow or the decades to come," a 1974 state bar association report concluded, while a majority of the assembly members sponsored a bill calling for a constitutional convention to strengthen that undangerous branch of government. A few years earlier, Robert Wilentz, who before becoming the state's chief justice served in the assembly, lamented those same infirmities. "When we want information, where do we go? To the executive. . . . Where do we often go for legislation? To the executive. Who explains bills before us, on both sides of the aisle? The executive."

Local wits are more scathing—because of the shenanigans that go on there, the Assembly is sometimes called the "zoo."

A number of legislators wear two political caps; they are both state and local officials, town council members and assembly members or senators. From the late 1960s on, these lawmakers were offered proposal after proposal by Republican and Democratic governors alike, but they did nothing. "Home rule"—local, not legislative, rule—was their prayer and their rallying cry.

It's easy enough to understand why. Supporters of affordable housing were mainly *potential* suburbanites, politically unorganized and without a bankroll, who had no say in selecting elected representatives from the existing suburbs. Their opponents were masters at making noise and getting out the vote. Backing affordable housing in the suburbs might be the right thing to do in some abstract philosophical sense, but politicians aren't thrilled by abstractions, particularly when embracing them means political catastrophe. Not until the 1983 ruling in *Mount Laurel II*, and the developers' gold rush that ensued in sleepy villages like Cranbury, did these lawmakers get involved.

The Governors Propose

Governor Cahill was not the first chief executive to urge that New Jersey's suburbs be opened up. The 1960s was one of those remarkable moments in time when poverty problems became not only discussible but politically fashionable. Solutions to those problems, wars on poverty, were everywhere in the air. From Washington, D.C., the Model Cities program poured dollars directly into poor neighborhoods, bypassing city halls, while the community-action campaign initiated by the Office of Economic Opportunity reached as far as the Springville Action Council in Mount Laurel. In New Jersey, Richard Hughes, Cahill's predecessor as governor and later the state's chief justice, launched a state-level OEO, the Department of Community Affairs (DCA). Its first chief was a planner named Paul Ylvisaker, whose brainchild, the Grey Areas program, which he developed for the Ford Foundation, later became the cornerstone for community action nationwide. Very much the urbanist, Ylvisaker believed it was "dangerous" to give zoning powers to suburbs. These communities will "have to rejoin the American union," he contended, if "we are going to keep a mobile society, if we are going to solve some of the problems of the central city."

From the DCA came legislation that, in its ambition to remake the state's housing map, foreshadowed *Mount Laurel II*. Exclusionary zoning was banned outright by this 1969 proposal, which obliged local ordinances to take into account "the need for various types of housing for all economic and social groups in the municipality, *and in the surrounding region*" (emphasis added). Would-be residents kept out by zoning requirements had the right to take their grievances to the state courts. Usually, plaintiffs must prove what they are alleging, but Ylvisaker's proposed legislation turned the tables, requiring suburbs to show their zoning laws didn't discriminate against the less than affluent.

The department's proposal was buried in the legislature, which then as now was dominated by suburban interests. Richard Hughes decided not to stand for reelection, and William Cahill, the GOP candidate, played on popular enthusiasm for local control to propel him into office. Ylvisaker was replaced at the DCA by an advocate of home rule.

Within a year, though, there was talk of a housing crisis in the state, as prices were rising quickly and first-time buyers were being frozen out of the market. At a 1970 press conference, the Republican governor sounded rather like his Democratic predecessor. "Zoning creates a real problem," Cahill acknowledged, "particularly in suburban areas where . . . sometimes two and three acres are required to erect a home, which prices the house beyond the pocketbook of the average man." Two years later, with the legislative elections safely out of the way and Republicans in control, came Cahill's housing initiatives.

Barely half of the hundred thousand units of affordable housing needed annually was being constructed, said the governor, referring not to public housing or even subsidized housing but to Levittown-type housing for the aspiring middle class. "No longer can municipalities afford the luxury of attracting business and industry and excluding housing. . . . You must provide housing." The governor called on the DCA to quantify regional housing needs. He also promoted a uniform statewide building code in place of local building codes that were sometimes being used to inflate the price of new houses under the guise of concern for health, safety, and aesthetics. The governor promised all things to all parties: his plan would relieve the housing crisis and help municipalities to end zoning abuses, while keeping control in local hands.

By this time, a trial judge had already thrown out the zoning law for Madison Township (the first *Mount Laurel* decision was still some months off), and the affordable housing advocates, Carl Bisgaier and Norman Williams among them, welcomed Cahill's gesture. Although the governor had proposed much less than they were asking for, the lawyers reasoned that state judges would be more influenced by Cahill's comments on the "housing crisis" than by the advocates' arguments and their experts' testimony.

From Governor Cahill's perspective, these pending lawsuits were another excellent reason for the legislature to do something. "The courts in this state, as in others, are striking at the heart of artificially conceived zoning and planning devices. . . . [T]he result of these judicial decisions can cause a zoning void and the ultimate destruction of local control." To keep this from happening—to preserve the legitimate core of local control—the towns had to "achieve a balance in housing: low, moderate, and expensive, single and multi-family." There was no reason why two-acre mini-estates couldn't coexist with apartments, if not on the same block then surely in the same municipality.

But suburbanites saw plenty of reasons to resist both the governor and the judges. United Citizens for Home Rule, a newly formed group, denounced the Cahill bill as "a power grab that ought to be resisted vigorously" and introduced a state constitutional amendment to guarantee that authority over zoning remain in local hands. Others began to raise environmental concerns.

There were indeed serious environmental problems to address: the New Jersey shore had been grossly overbuilt; toxic pollution from the refineries around Newark was a national joke; the state's fragile South Jersey Pinelands was threatened with development; and builders were coveting wetlands—like the property in the Springville neighborhood of Mount Laurel where Ethel Lawrence and the local community group had proposed building thirty-six apartments—even when construction was ecologically risky. During the 1970s and 1980s the state became a national leader in protecting the environment, as hundreds of thousands of acres of the Pinelands and wetlands were saved from development. But in the context of debates about affordable housing, environmentalism also was used as a strategic ploy. The green flag would be hoisted every time the issue was posed, often by advocates more interested in changing the subject than in promoting conservation.

Not only did the governor's proposal for statewide zoning authority fail; so did his political career. Cahill lost the 1973 Republican primary to a state assemblyman who made local control over zoning his hot-button issue. That fall, Brendan Byrne took back the state house for the Democrats, and Democrats regained control of the legislature. Yet in the New Jersey legislature, as in the township councils, party labels had little impact on the prevailing views about zoning: pro–home rule suburbanite Republicans typically were replaced by pro–home rule suburbanite Democrats. Governor Byrne would have no easier time than his predecessors in passing a measure that limited local zoning authority and imposed statewide housing requirements.

Besides, the legislators were preoccupied with school-finance reform, not zoning. In *Robinson v. Cahill,* decided in 1973, the justices declared that relying on local property taxes to fund public schools created unconstitutional inequalities between rich and poor towns. What followed was a three-year tug-of-war between the high court and the legislature, culminating with a judicial order that halted *all* spending on the public schools until the legislators funded a measure that moved toward equalizing school-district spending across the state. Extortion! cried the lawmakers, but in a special 1976 summer session they rushed through a personal income tax, the state's first, to pay the school bill.

Meanwhile, the *Mount Laurel* and *Oakwood-at-Madison* exclusionary-zoning cases had reached the New Jersey Supreme Court. Rumor had it that the justices would pursue a *Robinson*-style strategy and throw out the entire system of local zoning on the grounds of unequal treatment. Early in 1975, Senator Martin Greenberg, a Democrat and Governor Byrne's former law partner, introduced a bill giving the DCA the authority to determine statewide and regional affordable-housing needs, and then to set zoning requirements for each township, so that developers could build what was needed. The measure did not require towns to donate land or fund construction; they only had to remove the obstacles they had placed in the way of the housing market. All the familiar reasons for the politicians to act were recited. For one thing, Senator Greenberg said, change was needed: "Innumerable studies . . . amply attest to the unfortunate consequences of some of the existing uses of zoning powers in the state." Moreover, the courts were poised to do mischief unless they were headed off: "The state courts, rather than the state legislature, have recently become the principal public forum for deciding land use policies . . . a role which the courts, by their nature, are ill-equipped to perform."

Within a month, though, the Supreme Court decided *Mount Laurel I*, and the decision demanded far less than had been feared. Governor Byrne listened to well-orchestrated opposition to the justices' decision percolate upwards from the towns—listened, as well, to the absence of organized support—then proposed that suburbs be asked to take only small and voluntary steps toward meeting their fair-share obligation. To encourage such efforts, he offered a bill authorizing the DCA to conduct a survey that specified statewide housing needs. While the measure was toothless, since the townships could do as they pleased with the survey results, it too failed in the legislature. Suburban voters did not even want the facts made public, perhaps out of concern that, once the scope of the problem was clear, there would be pressure for a statewide answer.

The next year, Governor Byrne decided to make the cause of affordable housing his own. Instead of going to the legislature, the Bermuda Triangle of land-use reform, he drafted an executive order that tied the state's distribution of discretionary dollars to a community's voluntary compliance with *Mount Laurel I*. To pin down the meaning of compliance, he instructed the Department of Community Affairs to survey the state's housing needs and allocate fair-share obligations to each county; the counties, in turn, were expected to make similar allocations among the 567 municipalities.

The legislators were miffed at Byrne's maneuver. "This may be the bicentennial year, but that doesn't mean we have to bring back King George III," complained one senator, while another was less history minded. "It's another instance of kicking the middle class in the ass. The limousine liberals don't care, it doesn't affect them." Although the problem of exclusionary zoning and affordable housing affected not only the urban poor, the unhappy lawmakers saw it in terms of class and race. Seventeen GOP assembly members went to court challenging Governor Byrne's order, arguing that it was "blackmail" and insisting that zoning was really a legislative responsibility.

"If there is a problem," said Morris Township's assemblyman, John Dorsey, who would figure prominently in the bigger legislative battles following *Mount Laurel II*, "then the Governor's solution is far more radical than what we would propose." *If*: suburban lawmakers believed that the entire affordable-housing issue, like school-finance equalization, was being blown out of all proportion.

After a decade of doing nothing, there was hope in 1978 that the legislature might enact an affordable-housing bill. That term, the senate passed a measure, sponsored once again by Martin Greenberg, that would have the Department of Community Affairs set fair-share quotas for all municipalities. While the communities wouldn't have to pony up land or subsidies, the bill did authorize developers to secure court orders allowing them to build affordable housing.

The assembly—the zoo—was a different matter entirely. "Most towns are simply building new defenses," the head of the state's Builders Association observed. "They didn't want [zoning reform] to begin with, and they still don't want it." Through clever parliamentary maneuvering, Republican legislator Cary Edwards from suburban Bergen County killed Greenberg's bill. Edwards's strategy was consistent with his lucrative legal career, fighting *Mount Laurel* cases for exclusion-minded suburbs. Five years later, by then the counsel to Governor Thomas Kean, he would be the governor's man to see about housing and zoning.

Looking back at this political moment, Cary Edwards continues to believe that "Greenberg's bill was the wrong way to go. It didn't mean that *Mount Laurel,* or the fair-housing issue generally, would go away. [Chief Justice] Wilentz, in writing the [1983 *Mount Laurel II*] opinion, literally took Greenberg's bill and made that the public policy of the state. I believed that both the bill and the opinion were wrong—we were never going to resolve the issue of fair housing in New Jersey, where the dominant forces are suburban, without those forces actively participating in devising a solution. If the bill had passed, the human outcry in the municipalities would have been so aggressive that it would have self-destructed."

Perhaps so—or perhaps stronger leadership would eventually have carried the day—but the election of Republican Thomas Kean as governor in 1981 slammed shut the window of opportunity to boost affordable housing in the suburbs. In the universe of New Jersey politics, the Kean family is even more of a political dynasty than the Wilentzes. Kean's father was elected to Congress in 1938 and served for twenty years; his grandfather and great-uncle both served in the U.S. Senate; he's also descended from William Livingston, the first governor of the state. Thomas Kean had planned on a teaching career—he taught for a while at his old prep school, St. Marks, then started on a history Ph.D. at Columbia—but found the grind of a historian's life, all that rooting around in dank archives, too monastic for his tastes. Then came the assassination of John F. Kennedy.

"For the next two days I never left my apartment," he writes in his political autobiography, *The Politics of Inclusion.* "I watched television and did a lot of thinking. I didn't realize it at the time, but I suspect it was during those two days that I definitely lost whatever misgivings I still had about public service, and decided that if I ever got the chance, I would one day run for political office." Within a year, Kean was campaigning full-time for William Scranton, Pennsylvania's liberal governor, in his quixotic fight against Barry Goldwater for the Republican presidential nomination; and in 1967, Kean won a seat in the state assembly.

By 1970, the political wunderkind was picked as the assembly's majority leader, but he didn't have much use for the place. "The people's house," he called it, though his description sounds more like a monkey house on a bad day, "democratic government at its coarsest and most unrestrained, unruly, unkempt, and raucous." After four terms (and a seventy-vote loss in a House of Representatives race to Millicent Fenwick, immortalized in *Doonesbury* as Lacey Davenport), he quit politics for a while to deal in real estate. There followed an unsuccessful bid for the GOP gubernatorial nomination in 1977; four years later, he won the post.

Among New Jersey Republicans, Tom Kean has situated himself as a liberal, promoting education, environmentalism, and clean government. "I loved Ronald Reagan," he says, "but I hated his environmental politics." When he decided to make a second run for the governorship, consultants urged him to do something about his broad New England accent and to change the way he pronounced his last name (from "cane" to "keen"). The accent stayed, the consultants went. Sometimes Kean's liberal leanings have hurt him—his support for a controversial income tax to pay for public schools probably cost him the 1977 nomination—but, in a state where Democrats are in the majority, it has allowed him to play an artful middle game, the nonpartisan game.

On *Mount Laurel*-type issues, however, Kean was no liberal. Although he defeated his opponent, James Florio, by barely two thousand votes, he moved swiftly to rescind Governor Brendan Byrne's order that gave funding preferences to towns that voluntarily complied with *Mount Laurel*. He also dismantled the housing grants program in the Department of Community Affairs.

Those actions set the tone for the new administration on housing matters. Now the municipalities knew that the political branches of state government wouldn't interfere with local decisions regarding who was, and who was not, part of "our town." Perhaps this is what persuaded Justice Wilentz and his colleagues on the Supreme Court that, as the 1983 opinion puts it, "some steel" was needed to reinforce the *Mount Laurel* doctrine.

Fallout

In all the reaction to the New Jersey Supreme Court's second *Mount Laurel* decision, one key paragraph that appears early in that gargantuan opinion drew little attention. The court signaled that it didn't want to be a super–zoning board, that it hoped its ruling would prompt the state legislature to act in a way that might extract the judges from the fair-share enterprise. "Powerful reasons suggest, and we agree, that the matter is better left to the Legislature": so Chief Justice Wilentz wrote, and what came next suggested that these words weren't just boilerplate. "We recognize the social and economic controversy (*and its political consequences*) that has resulted in relatively little legislative action. . . . We understand the enormous difficulty of achieving a political consensus that might lead to significant legislation enforcing the constitutional mandate better than we can, legislation that might completely remove this Court from those controversies" (emphasis added).

This was an outcome devoutly to be wished, said Wilentz. "But enforcement of constitutional rights cannot await a supporting political consensus. So while we have always preferred legislative to judicial action in this field, we shall continue—*until the Legislature acts*—to do our best to uphold the constitutional obligation that underlies the *Mount Laurel* doctrine." To be sure, there remained critical questions of how much and what kind of legislative action would suffice. But the court did indicate that, at least when it came to zoning and housing, the justices were willing to share authority with, perhaps even cede it to, legislators to decide how to enact the broad principles of "fair share."

The justices had said much the same thing several years earlier about equal educational opportunity, and the Supreme Court did indeed accept, at least for a time, the state legislature's imperfect efforts to translate constitutional prescription into a new school-finance formula. Soon after *Mount Laurel II* was handed down, lawmakers on both sides of the aisle realized that, in housing as in financing the public schools, they needed to do something. The court's decision, with its potent builder's remedy and its regime of administrative enforcement, forced the legislature, which was caught between the justices' doctrines and constituents' demands, to try crafting a compromise.

Liberals hoped to preserve the central elements of the decision— the fair-share obligation, the builder's remedy—in legislation, and they also sought state money to build affordable housing. By contrast, conservative politicians were avid to gut the court's ruling, through a state constitutional amendment if necessary. What transpired, taking its final shape in the 1985 Fair Housing Act, was a classic political compromise between these two seemingly irreconcilable positions. The deal was brokered by a Democratic state senator, John Lynch, whose urban *and* suburban constituency pulled him both ways on the issue, and by a Republican governor, Thomas Kean, who relied on court-bashing rhetoric and the power of the veto to move in statesmanlike fashion toward modest increases in affordable housing.

"I don't believe that every municipality has got to be a carbon copy of another," Governor Kean told journalists after the 1983 Supreme Court decision was announced, "that's a socialistic country, a Communist country, a dictatorship." To a reporter from the *New York Times*, he delivered a punchier critique: *Mount Laurel II* was "communistic."

Liberal Democrat Gerald Stockman, the state senator who represented both the slums of Trenton and Princeton's ivied precincts, responded with language borrowed from the Kerner Commission's 1968 report on U.S. race relations. The governor was "under-recognizing the . . . two unequal societies in the state, urban and suburban." For Stockman, fair housing was really about race and poverty. But this was the 1980s, not the 1960s—even as Stockman's rhetoric, the marching song of the civil-rights movement, was being heard less and less, Ronald Reagan successfully revived the fearsome images of the cold war. From the vantage of the White House, the "evil empire" was headquartered in the Kremlin. To the occupant of New Jersey's state house, the state Supreme Court represented the heart of darkness; its *Mount Laurel II* opinion was an insult and a threat to domestic democracy. Kean won this war of words, because time and tides were powerfully on his side.

"This was safe political ground," says Cary Edwards, the governor's counsel and confidante, and his chief negotiator on housing matters. "The governor was really playing the court activism issue more than the *Mount Laurel* housing issue." In 1975, Kean recalls, when he was still an assemblyman, he had been "angry at the court" for its first *Mount Laurel* ruling. "The consensus in the corridors was that the court had overstepped its bounds." Now as governor he saw his chance to rein in the justices. "I had been in the legislature and already had reservations about what the court was trying to do. Though the hearts of the justices were in the right place, they couldn't achieve what they set out to do. . . . Coming into office, I knew we had to negotiate a legislative solution to the problem that was more workable."

Even before the *Mount Laurel II* ruling, Kean used his purse-string authority to limit the state's role in making housing policy. The Department of Community Affairs had operated in a political vacuum; when he became governor, Kean more than decimated it, cutting sixty planners from a staff of sixty-three. Planning, Kean believed, needed to take a "comprehensive, bottom-up approach," with state expertise regarded by local officials as useful, not threatening. "We needed state planning," says Cary Edwards, "but not the planning we had. So the best way to go was to eliminate it in its entirety, create a vacuum, and let people react."

Republican legislators pursued less nuanced approaches in the months following the court decision. Senator Thomas Gagliano, who was also the attorney representing his suburban township in its *Mount Laurel* litigation, proposed to ease the pain of the court's ruling by slowing the pace of implementation: just 10 percent of a town's affordable-housing obligation would have to be built within two years of a court order. The suburbs were enthusiastic, but critics pointed out the constitutional problems with such a radical attempt to change the terms of the court's judgment through legislation. The court might be prepared to compromise, they thought, but not to gut the basic constitutional obligation.

There was another, more frontal way to deal with the state constitution—change it. Senator John Dorsey, a veteran of the 1970s legislative wars over zoning, introduced a constitutional amendment to give municipalities complete zoning power; the courts, the legislature, and the governor would all be denied authority to intervene. Like the governor, Dorsey borrowed the verbiage of the cold war in making his case, equating *Mount Laurel II* with totalitarian communism. If the Supreme Court's judgment stood, "everything would be administered from the state level . . . like Russia."

In New Jersey, a proposed constitutional amendment passed by a majority of the senate and assembly in two consecutive years goes on the state ballot. Dorsey's strategy was to garner enough votes from Republicans and dissident Democrats to put the measure before the voters in 1984, when Republicans could be expected to turn out in large numbers to reelect Ronald Reagan. "If this issue would go on the ballot," said the senator, "the people would overwhelmingly approve it." Dorsey was plainly right—in 1985, in more than two hundred nonbinding local referenda, New Jersey voters favored limiting the court's role in zoning—but the Democrats controlled the senate, and some Democratic legislators, particularly those representing urban constituencies, were sympathetic to the courts' efforts to open up the suburbs. They kept Dorsey's constitutional measure bottled up in committee.

Yet stalling wouldn't work for long, the Democrats knew—there was just too much pressure on the lawmakers to act. "*Mount Laurel II* exploded in the state like a giant hand grenade," Thomas Kean wrote in his autobiography, *The Politics of Inclusion.* "Officials from every small town and suburb came to Trenton complaining that three judges were trying to make housing policy for every community in the state, and that generations of local planning were being overturned." Local politicians showed up at legislative hearings, busloads of their constituents in tow, to complain about the judges' mischief making. Officials from Cranbury detailed the imminent demise of their history-rich town at the hands of Judge Serpentelli. "I think it's a disgrace we're being forced to legislate the destruction of our town," said a council member from Mahwah, a suburb whose record of resisting affordable housing stretched all the way back to William Cahill's term as governor. "What is happening to us is un-American." The irony—that exclusion and segregation are un-American—was lost on the councilman.

With all this political pressure, with scores of builders filing suit throughout the state and the Mount Laurel judges coming up with huge fair-share numbers for suburbs, inaction was no longer an option in Trenton. Either the legislators would find a way to overturn the Supreme

Court's dictates or else they would have to establish some statewide planning capacity, create a mechanism to determine regional housing obligations, and confront the daunting fiscal problems of fair-share housing.

Enter Governor Kean.

The Courts Become the Problem

Using his 1984 state-of-the-state speech as his forum, Kean transformed the fair-share problem *Mount Laurel II* had addressed into another kind of problem—runaway judges. "I believe that the wholesale revision of local zoning ordinances by the judiciary is an undesirable intrusion on the home rule principle that has served our state well for many years."

This was a comfortable position for the governor to take, because opinion polls showed 70 percent of the voters on his side. Yet unlike Senator Dorsey, who preferred a constitutional amendment to remove the state from the housing business entirely, the governor was willing to talk about the state's responsibility for affordable housing. He proposed to create an agency whose only job would be statewide-growth planning. And to minimize the impact on suburbs that objected most strongly, Kean suggested allowing communities to buy their way out of their *Mount Laurel II* obligations by paying other municipalities, presumably cities like Camden, to take on the fair-share burden and build more housing for the poor. Such places were "best suited" for affordable housing. "What I'm trying to do is establish an incentive for planning," Kean explained after his address. "If there's no incentive for planning, this court decision eventually will end up as the antithesis of planning"—at least in towns that regarded affordable-housing obligations as a plague.

From a pure housing perspective, Kean's approach made considerable sense. It lightened the impact on the suburbs; it helped to defuse a constitutional confrontation between the Supreme Court and the legislature; and it provided money to rehabilitate urban housing without tapping directly into the state budget. What it *didn't* accomplish, however, was the social and economic integration of the suburbs. With the governor's intervention, the nascent tension surfaced between building subsidized housing, on the one hand, and opening up the suburbs to poor and minority families, on the other.

The Supreme Court had stressed economic integration—for that is what "fair share" implies—as the way to promote what the state's constitution refers to as the "general welfare." But this wasn't going to happen, said Rutgers planning professor Jerome Rose, a persistent and influential critic of the court. "The minority people whose interests the decision purports to serve" would, he predicted, be frozen out. For his part, Governor Kean was proposing to cement the divisions of class and race through the power of the dollar. "It is racist," said the assembly speaker, Democrat

Alan Karcher. Housing might be built, but a kind of apartheid would persist.

While the lawmakers tossed their rhetorical bombs, the number of affordable-housing cases steadily rose—sixty-one lawsuits filed within a year after the *Mount Laurel II* decision—and towns, behaving like the baby harp seals that builders' lawyer Henry Hill had mockingly called them, were easily clubbed into settlement, rather than submitting to whatever fate a judge might have in mind for them. In some instances, these communities agreed to accept developments that offered nothing to the poor but made the plaintiff-developers happy and kept the lawyers in fees; elsewhere, towns agreed to rezone and builders agreed to develop housing with a fifth of the new units reserved for families of moderate means. Almost no place did the needs of poor families get taken into account.

Politicians from both parties agreed that, at the least, a new statewide-growth plan was required to better manage the process. Senator Stockman, the Democratic lawmaker from Princeton, proposed a panel of experts to do that job. The governor signed on—the idea was consistent with his state-of-the-state proposals, and broad-based membership on the new panel would make planning "local"—and summoned Senators Stockman and Dorsey for a meeting. Dorsey, whose real agenda was an anti–*Mount Laurel II* constitutional amendment, had no objections to more planning—provided the *Mount Laurel* judges were put out of business until the new plan was approved. But on that point, Stockman could not give way, since a moratorium would stop whatever momentum the fair-share decisions had produced. A change in the state's constitution of the sort Dorsey was proposing would shut down the judicial enterprise for keeps and would create a troubling precedent for judicial independence. "You don't block housing for poor and moderate income people simply because it is upsetting to some people," Stockman said. "A moratorium on building for those who need it most would not make sense."

The talk in the governor's office turned harsh, voices rose, and eventually the Democrat from Princeton stormed out. The next day, Senator Stockman introduced his "long-range planning bill," which, as he explained to reporters, would "provide a necessary response to the *Mount Laurel* decision, one that will meet the needs of local officials who feel abandoned and naked before developers." Senator Dorsey and his colleagues offered a mirror-image measure, while adding a moratorium on judicial implementation of *Mount Laurel II.* They also used the occasion to spark reporters' interest in Dorsey's constitutional amendment. One of its sponsors was the senator who represented Mount Laurel Township; another was Peter Garibaldi, also the mayor of Monroe Township, who had become famous with his "I'll go to jail" speech in defiance of Judge Serpentelli. Now Garibaldi decried "builders waiting in the wings like vultures. . . . Forcing us to build affordable housing will create chaos, which we will never be able to dig ourselves out from under."

Much of this legislative speech making and the griping to reporters was really for show. Amid the bombast, many of the interested parties—among them planners and housing lawyers, representatives from the state's League of Municipalities, Democratic legislators, and staffers from the Kean administration—met privately in the spring and summer of 1984 to draft legislation covering many of the *Mount Laurel II* issues. The deluge of lawsuits had changed the atmosphere, the League of Municipalities lawyer said, and towns were now willing to talk seriously about affordable-housing quotas. Indeed, an ad hoc group of mayors had given its blessing to Stockman's statewide-planning bill, as a "necessary first step" to take planning out of the courts.

The participants in the backstage talks proposed a new fair-housing agency—the Council on Affordable Housing, or COAH, they called it—which would develop a statewide assessment of housing needs, then allocate those needs on a region-by-region basis. Municipalities would receive individual fair-share allotments and, in turn, would be asked to submit plans making affordable-housing construction possible. Towns whose plans were certified by COAH as fulfilling their fair-share obligations would be effectively immune from builders' lawsuits and would have six years to convert those paper plans into housing. A trust fund administered by COAH, underwritten by money from the state's real estate–transfer tax and supplemented with specially earmarked state aid, would make grants for affordable-housing projects.

In the legislature, both the *Mount Laurel II* moratorium bill and Senator Dorsey's constitutional amendment remained on the agenda. Concern persisted about how the threat of the builder's remedy was affecting the suburbs. "The builders' motivations in enforcing that remedy weren't exactly to plan the state in a way our grandchildren would appreciate," Governor Kean acidly commented. Conservative Republicans in the assembly announced that they were going to sue the state's high court in a federal tribunal, on the improbable ground that the justices had violated the separation-of-powers provision of the U.S. Constitution.

The proposed COAH legislation shifted the center of the debate away from critiquing the judges and back toward the substance of housing policy. The federal government had stopped underwriting housing for the poor, and so a pivotal question became, How much should the state spend? The measure's chief sponsors, Senator Stockman and Wynona Lipman from Newark, the only African American woman in the senate, appreciated that effective legislation required not only codification of *Mount Laurel II*'s fair-share principles but dollars as well. Around that fulcrum the divisions massed.

Deviltry in the Details

The progressive-minded bill carried by Senators Stockman and Lipman was known as the Fair Housing Act. It included money for affordable housing in suburbia and a state agency with the authority to make the fair-share hopes of the *Mount Laurel* cases a reality.

In less than a year, a bill bearing the same name and also creating an agency called the Council on Affordable Housing passed the legislature and was signed into law by Governor Kean. By then, however, the bill was really the governor's. It had been so transformed—so gutted, the two original sponsors believed—that, on principle, they cast their votes against it.

Committee by committee, chamber by chamber, the fair-housing measure made its way through the legislature. "This bill deals with *Mount Laurel II* by taking land use planning out of the hands of judges," Senator Lipman said, indulging in a mild bit of court bashing, "and it protects municipalities from the problems caused by too much housing growth too soon."

Along the way, the sponsors rewrote sections of the bill to pick up additional support. The composition of COAH's board was structured to include substantial local representation; the housing-subsidy program was pegged at a hundred million dollars, half of what the working group had suggested; the fair-share obligation on townships was lightened; most significantly, an extended phase-in period, up to twenty years in some cases, was written into the law over developers' objections that this would make it impossible to get financing.

At each step on the road to passage, the players had their eye on the governor's office. Kean was uneasy about directly subsidizing affordable housing in suburbia, preferring urban rehabilitation. The legislators pushing the COAH measure chose not to hear that message, hoping his position would prove flexible. But they failed to reckon with the political calendar, which put the fair-housing bill up for final decision during the governor's reelection campaign. Kean knew the calendar by heart, of course, and he also knew how to use it. Even as his counsel, Cary Edwards, was dealing privately with the Democratic legislators, the governor was playing to the crowds. In his January 1985 state-of-the-state speech, he thumped the *Mount Laurel II* decision once more for causing "judicial intrusion on an unprecedented scale." If the judges weren't checked, he warned, there would be "major damage to the environment"—an appeal to an interest group that hadn't previously been courted on this issue—as well as "sharp increases in local property taxes, a forced spreading of suburban sprawl, and a virtual abandonment of efforts to rehabilitate housing in our cities."

Developers came in for a gubernatorial hiding too. They had "run roughshod over the state's efforts to preserve open space, farmland and clean water"—more appeals to environmentalism. "One result of the 'builder's remedy' is a money-making windfall for a handful of private developers." Unless the builder's remedy was eliminated, the governor calculated, it would result in nearly a million units of housing being built in New Jersey in a six-year period, more than double the growth rate during the baby-boom years. Kean urged a moratorium on builder's-remedy lawsuits. Also, he suggested a constitutional amendment to keep the courts entirely out of zoning; that idea was borrowed from Senator Dorsey, but for a governor inclined to political balancing acts, it was more a feint toward the Right than a serious proposal.

All this left the affordable-housing advocates reeling. But Kean had a ready alternative to the constitutional-amendment route: permit the suburbs to "cooperate" with cities on rehabilitating urban housing as a way to satisfy their *Mount Laurel II* fair-housing obligation. The governor had broadly sketched out the idea of "regional contribution agreements," or RCAs, a year earlier in his state-of-the-state speech; this time he made the proposal specific. Such cooperation amounted to urban renewal by another name, with the important political advantage of never appearing as a line item on the state's budget. It "would give towns and counties an opportunity to reach agreements on what is really needed," he insisted, and would turn cities into "places to move into—and not out of." A representative of the League of Municipalities agreed with Kean, while tying his organization's support to adequate state funding. "If the Legislature funds this program as much as they are talking about, it should bring suburbs and urban groups together to build this housing where it is needed. If you build it out in the sticks . . . you are not going to get the people in the cities to move out to it. It is needed in the cities."

Others read the governor's proposal less benignly, as promoting do-nothingism through a moratorium and creating a market in gentrification. John Russo, the senate's Democratic majority leader, dismissed the speech as pure politics. "He doesn't want to say anything that people don't want to hear." The president of the state's Builders Association pointed out that, while "the builder's remedy is a club, a stick, a moratorium will only delay further the construction of affordable housing." Some legislators likened Kean's "cooperation" strategy to the discredited Civil War practice of allowing rich northerners to buy their way out of the draft. "All he wants to do," said one embittered Democratic assemblyman, "is keep black people from moving out of the cities."

Wynona Lipman, who had launched her successful bid for the state senate when the slow pace of the "old gentlemen" on the Essex County board got her down, was also unhappy. The implicit racial politics formed part of her unhappiness—back home, constituents in well-to-do precincts of her district were muttering about how *Mount Laurel* would bring blacks and crime to the suburbs—but only a part. Her fair-housing bill had already been amended to allow a municipality to transfer as much as a third of its fair-share obligation to another community in the same region. That made sense to Lipman as a way of sharing the burdens of growth, but the governor's alternative, which placed no limit on the amount of a locale's fair-share obligation that could be transferred or where it could be transferred to, "defeats the whole purpose of the *Mount Laurel II* decision."

This conflict between Lipman and Kean, which would continue until a version of the bill became law, encapsulated the big and unsettled underlying questions: Was the primary policy concern to provide affordable housing *someplace* in the state or to provide some affordable housing *almost everyplace?* Was the intention to help poor minority households or instead to give assistance to those a bit farther up the economic and social ladder? While integration and affordable housing were not incompatible aspirations, neither were they identical. When Governor Kean framed the issue, first in terms of out-of-control judges and later in terms of building housing, he effectively shifted the political debate away from the initial understanding of what mattered—away from the commitment of people like activist Ethel Lawrence and advocate Peter O'Connor to society's least privileged members.

After the 1985 state-of-the-state speech, negotiations between Cary Edwards, representing Governor Kean, and the legislators grew more intense. The New Jersey constitution gives the governor a powerful flexible veto, which Kean could use either to kill the measure outright or to veto it "conditionally"—that is, to say no unless the legislature amended particular provisions with which he was unhappy. This flexible veto was an impressive political tool, because it allowed the governor to endorse the principles of reform while putting the legislature in the unappealing position of spoiler. And so the horse trading resumed.

To Senator John Lynch, the governor's speech was excellent news. Lynch was bred to politics—his father had served in the state senate for twenty years—and the composition of his senate district situated him squarely in the middle of the fair-share debate. That district included the troubled city of New Brunswick, of which Lynch was also the mayor, partly a blue-collar ethnic town with a university campus and a growing minority population. Without outside funds, New Brunswick could never hope to build enough affordable housing to meet the need. Lynch had run for the senate because he believed that his city, like other cities in the state, was being shortchanged by Trenton. But his district also included the surrounding suburbs of Middlesex County, whose preferred future, a future without poor people, had been placed in jeopardy by Judge Serpentelli's post–*Mount Laurel II* rulings. Those towns had been victims of legal extortion, Lynch believed, pushed by the threats of developers' lawyers to permit housing they would not otherwise have allowed.

The senator was familiar with exclusionary-zoning issues from his days as a practicing lawyer in the early 1970s. Then, he had filed a lawsuit on behalf of a frustrated developer against the picturesque village of Cranbury, and his complaint cited Governor Cahill's early warnings about the "housing crisis" that the state legislature had ignored. Just weeks before Kean's 1985 state-of-the-state address, Lynch introduced his own housing measure, which was closer than Stockman's and Lipman's Fair Housing Act to the Governor's vision. Lynch favored the idea of city-suburb regional contribution agreements, not just because they would help suburbanites avoid something they regarded as bad, but also because they would help city politicians—including Mayor-Senator Lynch—build the kind of housing everyone considered a good thing.

Lynch was also driven by the calculus of state electoral politics. If the Democrats could keep control of the senate, then he was next in line to be named majority leader, but he feared that a backlash against *Mount Laurel* justice might unseat enough Democrats to give Republicans control. Easing the political pressure created by the fair-housing fight by defusing *Mount Laurel II* would be great for Democrats generally, great for John Lynch personally. He edged Stockman and Lipman aside to become the Democrats' chief deal maker on fair housing.

"Smoke-filled rooms follow Cary Edwards around," the saying in Trenton goes. When Lynch, equally renowned as a bargainer, entered into negotiations with Cary Edwards, the Governor's counsel, he favored a deal that neutralized the threat of more builder's-remedy litigation while getting a bigger state commitment to subsidized housing construction in the cities. "There is no question the court has attempted to depth-charge the Legislature into action," the senator remarked. "There are cases moving through the [judicial] system very rapidly and towns are getting hurt. . . . If you accept the fact that any attempt at a moratorium [which the governor had in fact urged] will not be accepted by the courts, then our number one consideration should be to provide a reasonable alternative to the builder's remedy."

The senator's strategy, rather like the governor's but pitched to different constituencies, was to divide and conquer politically by presenting each side with an intolerable alternative scenario. To Democrats who endorsed fair-share housing for the suburbs, Lynch played up the danger of a constitutional amendment, while to the Kean administration and Republican legislators, he decried zoning by litigation and extortion by developers. This required some delicate maneuvering. "We are walking a tightrope," said Senator Lipman, who watched her bill being rewritten; she suspected that the governor would never accept the critical component of a housing subsidy. For his part, Lynch meant to accomplish what no one else had been able to do—to steer a significant legislative package, one that was acceptable to the governor, through the assembly and senate.

The bill that took shape in the weeks following the governor's January 1985 speech appeared to satisfy all parties. It authorized regional contribution agreements, as the governor had proposed—but only within specified areas, not across the entire state, and for no more than a third of any town's fair-share burden. It also created a hundred-million-dollar Fair Housing Trust Fund. Cary Edwards sounded optimistic. "I have been on this issue for twelve years," he told reporters. "This is an issue that lends itself to political demagoguery and, consequently, there has been no action. . . . This is the first time I have seen such a consensus since I have been around. Now the Governor feels the consequences of the *Mount Laurel II* decision and the impact of the builder's remedy are such that the Legislature should act, not the courts."

Almost everyone was "prepared to deal," Edwards asserted, specifically citing suburbanites and conservatives. But this was wishful thinking, for right-wing Republicans were far from ready to buy into the compromise. John Lynch's bill was just another "punish the suburbs" measure, Senator Dorsey contended, and it was "socialist." That hoary criticism drew a horse laugh from assembly speaker Alan Karcher. "When zoning laws were introduced seventy or eighty years ago, the very people who now are attacking the *Mount Laurel II* decision were denouncing zoning as a communist plot. Now the most conservative legislators are saying they *want* government to interfere, to preserve zoning laws." Dorsey's allies argued, as well, that the proposed Council on Affordable Housing would cost the state "billions" in needless bureaucracy. Meanwhile, the conservative caucus in the legislature also tried to interest Governor Kean in backing a $20 million housing rehabilitation fund as a complete "alternative to court-imposed quotas."

John Dorsey and his colleagues lacked the votes to derail the Fair Housing Act, which was on its way to passage in the legislature with Governor Kean's backing. The governor had edged away from his embrace of a constitutional amendment—that, he said, should only be a "last resort" strategy—and a confident Senator Lynch dismissed Dorsey's proposal as something that "belongs in the comics section."

The housing subsidy remained a key sticking point. The bill approved by the senate authorized thirty-three million dollars for affordable-housing construction in the suburbs, a third of the amount specified in the initial legislation. The deciding vote was cast by a suburban Democrat who left his sickbed because he "wanted to do the right thing. I think the residents [of my district] know that we need housing that people can afford." This was one of the rare times during the legislative debate that anyone had thought to mention fairness.

Governor Kean was unmoved. He demanded that the state's housing funds be spent only to rehabilitate urban housing, as Senator Dorsey and his colleagues had proposed—anything more ambitious, like subsidizing affordable housing in the suburbs, invited a veto. The governor phrased his unhappiness in dollars-and-cents terms, while once again shifting the argument away from the activists' initial vision of social integration to one of refurbishing the housing stock. "The federal government couldn't afford to finance housing," he declared, a reference to near total cuts in federal construction subsidies, "and the state certainly cannot." To provide the quarter of a million units of affordable housing that *Mount Laurel II* contemplated would cost New Jersey $3.75 billion, he calculated, figuring on a state subsidy of fifteen thousand dollars for each unit, plus unknown billions of additional dollars for new roads, sewers, and other investments in the infrastructure. Far wiser, he believed, to spend the money on other services to help the poor than to dip a teacup into this sea of unmet need with a thirty-three-million-dollar appropriation, a fraction of a percent of what was needed.

"There is a lack of understanding of the court decision," Governor Kean said, referring to the senate measure. "It does not require the building of low- and moderate-income housing. It just says you can't zone them out." Although that observation ignored the unsubtle judicial strategy of builder's remedies, the Supreme Court's effort to assure that housing really got built, it contained a kernel of truth. If towns did in fact remove zoning barriers, *Mount Laurel II* did not force them to do much more—certainly not to build themselves—and this reality gave Kean's approach some chance of surviving its inevitable court test.

Assembly speaker Alan Karcher adopted an attitude of denial. "Unless the Governor tells me to the contrary that this is not what he wants, we are going to pass this program." Senator Gerald Stockman, one of the act's original sponsors, tried threats: "*Mount Laurel* will be an issue in the gubernatorial and legislative elections." This was undoubtedly true—but for Democrats, it represented more a danger than an opportunity. "It's real clear," as a Republican assemblymember pointed out, "that the Democrats don't want to roll the dice on this one."

Senator Lynch remained the indefatigable compromiser. While he recognized that Governor Kean could use his conditional veto to dictate the result he wanted, the issue wasn't necessarily a political lost cause for Democrats. "You can posture all day long about the Supreme Court, but you can't deal recklessly. Here's an alternative you can work with." Surely, from the suburbs' perspective, the bill that the Democrats had pushed through the senate was much better than the status quo. Maybe the voters would reward them for their good deed, Lynch thought, or at least not punish them for failing to act. "Instead of five thousand units, a municipality would be required to build a thousand, and they could be phased in over a significant period of time. . . . If we don't put in place a reasonable alternative, then the horse will be out of the barn. We should get away from the politics of zoning and think about municipalities under the gun."

Even as the governor and the Democrats were publicly lobbing grenades at one another, the backstage negotiations resumed. On neither side did the deal makers want a veto. Perhaps the legislature could swallow its concerns about invading the court's authority and accept a moratorium in builder's-remedy lawsuits, Democrats suggested, if Governor Kean would agree to a provision inviting quick judicial review of the constitutionality of that measure. Maybe the idea of a housing subsidy could be made palatable to the governor if the ceiling on regional contribution agreements—the proportion of a suburb's fair-share housing obligation that it could buy its way out of, by making a deal with a nearby city—was boosted from a third to a half.

The Republican leadership in the assembly also sounded a conciliatory (if elaborately metaphorical) note. "We are not only supporting the concept of taking down restrictive zoning barriers, we are supporting the concept of building low- and moderate-income housing," said minority leader Charles Hardwick. "That takes money. What Republicans are seeking to do is to make sure that the Legislature is not, in effect, throwing a defective life preserver to towns that are clutching for solutions while they are sinking under the Supreme Court's *Mount Laurel II* mandate."

The affordable-housing legislation was back on track, acknowledged Cary Edwards, speaking on behalf of the governor. "As soon as the Legislature is finished, it's my turn."

On March 7, 1985, the Fair Housing Act came up for a vote in the assembly. Everyone was feeling the pressure of the fall election campaign, and none of the vote counters knew whether the measure would pass. One of its backers, Wayne Bryant from Camden, reintroduced an old theme when he posed the issue in terms of social justice. "There were no poor folks who developed the Constitution," the African American legislator said, "there were rich white folks, your forefathers. It's time you stopped hiding under the Constitution . . . playing games with people who can't afford decent housing." When a Republican assemblyman demanded that the state impose a one-year residency requirement before a person could qualify for subsidized housing—"to prevent New Jersey from becoming one huge housing project"—a Democratic colleague took it as a personal insult. "I can tell you my grandfather was damn poor when he came to Ellis Island. . . . Bluebloods and polo ponies did not come with him."

Proponents needed forty-one votes for passage. They squeaked by with forty-two, all of them from Democrats, and only after promising two fence-sitting suburban lawmakers that Senator Dorsey's constitutional amendment to strip the court of power to review the constitutionality of zoning laws would be taken up at some future date. Down the hall to the senate went the measure. There, Senator Peter Garibaldi, the mayor of Monroe, once again delivered his standing-in-the-schoolhouse-door speech: "I would go to jail before I subject my town to the courts." But Garibaldi knew his diatribe was only for show. The senators, who had been in session awaiting the assembly vote, gave the bill quick approval.

"A big charade," assembly minority leader Charles Hardwick called the vote. "The Democrats know the Governor is going to veto the bill, and they are going to walk away from the problem knowing it has not been solved." John Lynch, ever the pragmatist, was more hopeful that Kean would sign what he called a "workable compromise," a way to avoid "the disastrous court-imposed builder's remedy that has led to so much over-development in the suburbs." Six weeks later, though, the governor sent the bill back, blue-penciled and with a conditional-veto message. He would sign the measure—but only if it was rewritten to his liking.

The biggest change Kean demanded was an increase in the portion of a town's fair-share obligation that could be transferred to another municipality. The bill sent to the governor's desk specified that one-third of the units would be the ceiling; the governor boosted that figure to one-half. Other items in the twenty-page message showed, however, that Governor Kean, like Senator Lynch, was willing to deal. He proposed to enlarge the size of the housing subsidy, drawing on funds from the real estate–transfer tax—as many as two thousand units of new affordable housing could be built each year, he predicted—while sticking with his pledge to make almost all of this money available to the cities, not the suburbs. He also dropped his demand for a moratorium on *Mount Laurel II* cases already in the courts, when his counsel, Cary Edwards (who after the 1985 election would be rewarded with an appointment as attorney general), convinced him that the justices would strike it down. Kean's changes gave COAH the power to set ceilings on how much housing a town could be asked to build, based on its present size. In his judgment, this was how to protect the bucolic Cranburys from being forced to double and redouble their size.

Reaction to Governor Kean's conditional-veto message was quick in coming. The state's Public Advocate had already resisted pressure from the governor's office and stayed involved in *Mount Laurel*–type lawsuits. Stephen Eisdorfer, a senior attorney with the Public Advocate, remembers Cary Edwards calling him in soon after Kean was elected, and browbeating him for bringing the countywide case in affluent Morris County. "Forget *Mount Laurel*," Edwards said, "that's no longer good law [after the 1977 *Oakwood-at-Madison* decision]." Now Eisdorfer publicly rebutted the governor's logic on the Fair Housing Act.

"The outcome is perverse," Eisdorfer said. "It puts arbitrary limits on how much housing can be required in any community. It tries to do exactly what the Supreme Court said couldn't be done. It rewards towns that have excluded low- and moderate-income housing in the past by saying they don't have to do it now. It says you can require new housing— after you consider open space, historic preservation, the environment, farmlands, recreation. The *last* thing anybody has to think about is low- and moderate-income housing."

John Lynch, the great negotiator, was more upbeat. "The bill is the only game in town," he said. Although in theory the legislature could still override the conditional veto, that wasn't going to happen. "The Governor made substantive and procedural changes, but the goal to create a reasoned atmosphere to remove the courts from basic housing decisions, to reassess the state's need for affordable housing and to provide a mechanism for funding remains intact." In effect, Lynch asserted, Governor Kean had signed on to the Fair Housing Act by issuing a conditional rather than an absolute veto, and this implied a "moral pledge" of state financial support for housing. Moreover, the version the governor rewrote had passed the legislature without a single Republican vote. Now the governor would have to rally GOP support for a measure that had in effect become his own bill.

In fact, all of Senator Lynch's various constituencies, both urban and suburban, benefited from Governor Kean's modifications to the Fair Housing Act. In the small and gossipy political world of Trenton, suspicions were voiced that the two politicians had engaged in what Republican assembly leader Hardwick called a "big charade." The rumor was that Lynch had maneuvered his bill through the legislature while knowing that it would be vetoed by the governor. Then, after the conditional veto, the senator could sell Kean's revised version to his colleagues as "the only game in town" and come out ahead for New Brunswick and its suburbs.

This account—Brer Rabbit and the briar patch brought up to date—is implicit in Cary Edwards's view of events. "We used the conditional veto successfully with sensitive issues. It was a way to get our agenda on the table. With some winks and some silent understandings, from time to time the Democrats would pass bills that they knew we were going to conditionally veto. That gave everybody the political posture they needed and allowed us to move issues forward to resolution. The legislators could do what they had to do, and we could do what we had to do." On occasion, localist diehards successfully resisted such maneuvering, as when Governor Kean was stymied in his efforts to impose statewide planning on New Jersey's overbuilt coastline. But in the case of the Fair Housing Act, Edwards notes, "the conditional veto was not aggressively fought."

The senate passed the governor's version on June 24, rejecting Senator Dorsey's attempts to attach his anti-*Mount Laurel* constitutional amendment to the bill. Senators Gerald Stockman and Wynona Lipman, who had sponsored the original legislation, voted no this time. While one of the major changes in the measure, granting suburbs the right to trade away half of their fair-share obligation, might well mean more housing for Newark, which Lipman represented, she couldn't bring herself to support what she labeled a "sham."

Three days later, after a debate lasting barely ten minutes, the assembly passed the measure. Camden assemblyman Wayne Bryant, who had backed the earlier measure, accused Governor Kean of "merely surrounding the cities" with his changes, producing "the epitome of plantation politics." But Bryant might as well have been talking to himself. The governor had done his political homework: although a number of Democrats turned against the bill, it won with a majority of yes votes coming from Republicans.

Days before the senate's June vote, 250 residents of the suburb of Denville, calling themselves Citizens Against *Mount Laurel*, journeyed to Trenton to hold a rally. Denville is the hub of Morris County, where resistance to the *Mount Laurel* decision had been fierce. The town had already spent two hundred thousand dollars defending itself against developers who wanted to build in their town, and these voters wanted to make their presence vivid. "Stop the Mount Laurel Horror Story," their signs read, and (spoofing the title of a then popular movie) "Whose Town Is It Anyway?" Their state senator cheered on his constituents: "We have got to stop it!"

In the months that followed, there were several attempts to revive Senator Dorsey's constitutional amendment. John Lynch, for one, was worried that Dorsey might prevail. "Maybe some of us were paranoid, but we saw the momentum building." Certainly the Democrats weren't winning over the voters; in the fall legislative elections, they were shellacked as Republicans took control of the assembly. Tom Kean was reelected in the biggest landslide in the state's history, and there was much talk of his being the vice presidential nominee on the 1988 GOP ticket.

The Council on Affordable Housing was soon up and running. The suburbs, sensing that the agency would go much easier on them than had the *Mount Laurel* judges, started filing plans with COAH to insulate themselves from the courts.

The big unknown remained the New Jersey Supreme Court. In *Mount Laurel II*, in 1983, the justices had given specific constitutional meaning to the idea of the "general welfare." Two years later, the Fair Housing Act rewrote—and substantially weakened—the judges' script. Ceilings on fair-share allocations and regional contribution agreements that allowed suburbs to buy their way out of much of their fair-share obligation—these were concepts very different from what the court had spelled out and what the *Mount Laurel* judges had required.

When ten townships, including Cranbury, petitioned Judge Serpentelli to transfer their pending cases to the new state agency, COAH, he refused most of the requests. To do otherwise, the judge ruled, would cause "manifest injustice," and the two other *Mount Laurel* judges denied similar transfer motions. Predictably, the Dorsey contingent in the state senate blew up—"the courts in New Jersey won't abide by the law"—and Governor Kean started murmuring once more about the need for a constitutional amendment. A referendum appeared on the 1985 ballot in 221 of the state's townships and five of its twenty-one counties, asking the legislature to submit to the voters a constitutional amendment "limiting the power of the courts, so that the courts cannot force municipalities to change their zoning laws to accommodate *Mount Laurel* housing." The referenda passed in every one of those jurisdictions, by an average margin of two to one.

This was the fractious political climate in which, in 1986, the Supreme Court delivered its third and final *Mount Laurel* decree. This time, the justices were being asked to pass judgment, not on the suburbs, but on the coordinate branches of the state government.

7

Can Bureaucrats
Build Houses?

The 1985 Fair Housing Act represented more than a legislative triumph of maneuvering and compromise. It also sent a blunt message to the high court: get out of exclusionary zoning. How the justices would respond was not so clear. The Supreme Court in its 1983 *Mount Laurel II* opinion had expressly invited the politicians to devise their own fair-share standard. But the statute crafted by these legislators collided with the spirit of the opinion and expressly rejected the most powerful of the court's remedies meant to enforce the municipalities' constitutional obligations.

One institution or the other had to give way. A few years earlier, during a similar standoff between New Jersey's legislators and the justices over the constitutionality of the state's school-finance provisions, the legislature blinked. "No thicket is too political for us," one of the justices boasted then; and in Trenton the politicians were concerned that the court might once again engage in some muscle flexing. But this time, it was the justices' turn to back down. On February 20, 1986, barely half a year after the passage of the Fair Housing Act, the Supreme Court unanimously upheld the new law. This case, formally known as *Hills Development v. Bernards Township*, was the last of the *Mount Laurel* trilogy—*Mount Laurel III*, it is commonly called. The opinion showed just how anxious the court was to remove itself from the affordable-housing business— anxious, too, that the furies stirred up by its earlier zoning decisions not drive Chief Justice Robert Wilentz from the bench.

And so, in the minds of many, the Supreme Court capitulated. Wilentz kept his seat, though just barely. And the Council on Affordable Housing, not the *Mount Laurel* courts, became the epicenter of statewide zoning and housing policy. Meanwhile, the national economy stumbled and the building boom drew to an end; across the Garden State there was very little construction of any kind. Courts can't build houses, the familiar criticism went. Now the question was whether COAH's bureaucrats could do any better.

The Retreat of the Justices

Robert Greenbaum, Esq., was entirely out of control in a court of law, and this marked a rarity on the order of a new ice age. Greenbaum is an avatar of his profession—a founder and first-named partner of one of the state's most prestigious law firms, a member of the New Jersey bar for nearly half a century who served as chair of both the land-use section of the state bar association and the local government law section of the American Bar Association. But the New Jersey Supreme Court had acted in *Mount Laurel III* in a manner Greenbaum regarded as unpardonable. Not only did it embrace the new Fair Housing Act as a substitute for its own constitutional creation (*Mount Laurel II*), glossing over all the consequential differences in approach; much more troubling, it effectively forced the *Mount Laurel* trial courts out of business. Judges Gibson, Serpentelli, and Skillman were ordered to transfer almost all their pending cases to the newly constituted Council on Affordable Housing.

Swept up in the fury of this retrenchment was Greenbaum's prior settlement, negotiated on behalf of a developer client, with West Windsor Township, a recalcitrant town that was attempting to ride the *Mount Laurel III* wave out of the courts and into the presumably friendlier confines of COAH. While the Supreme Court's transfer order did not apply directly to Greenbaum's case against West Windsor, the township's attorneys were attempting to convince Judge Serpentelli to refer the once all-but-closed matter to COAH anyway. Such a referral, the towns argued, would ensure that the settlement's terms were consistent with COAH's interpretation of the Fair Housing Act, and the statute made provision for the new agency to conduct just this kind of review.

To Greenbaum, however, the threatened referral to COAH would skewer his case. Gone would be Judge Serpentelli and his aggressive efforts to make the *Mount Laurel* doctrine a reality, to build actual low- and moderate-income units in the most resistant towns. Wasted, Greenbaum feared, would be those thousands of hours devoted to a case that had consumed him and brought on his ulcer. Now, in Serpentelli's ornate Toms River courtroom, the hard-fought settlement with West Windsor Township was about to be set aside. And, like so many other lawyers across the state, Greenbaum would have to fight anew in a strange forum, with unknown rules, all because of what the Supreme Court had done.

This, Greenbaum believed, was a Kafkaesque absurdity. Though he appreciated Serpentelli's situation—the justices in Trenton had transferred other cases to the new agency, and no one would question the judge's politely going along—Greenbaum's frustrations got the better of him. The Supreme Court's latest decision was "dishonest," he charged, a "political payoff" meant to ensure that Chief Justice Robert Wilentz could keep his seat on the bench. It was a betrayal of all the plaintiffs who had relied on the court's previous decision in *Mount Laurel II*, investing millions of dollars in hopes of getting affordable housing built—a betrayal, as well, of the court's own constitutional principles.

Leaning down from the bench, Serpentelli interrupted Greenbaum's tirade to remind him that he was speaking on the record and that he risked sabotaging his chances for a successful appeal or, more immediately, inviting a contempt citation. But the judge knew just how the lawyer felt. A few months earlier, shortly after passage of the Fair Housing Act, Serpentelli had ruled in several cases that, given how far those lawsuits had already come, transferring them to COAH would cause a "manifest injustice," the standard spelled out in the 1985 legislation to describe the circumstances when such a transfer was inappropriate. Now the Supreme Court had trashed those decisions, deflating Serpentelli, and he listened intently to the impassioned attorney before him.

There is a covenant between the bench and the bar, Robert Greenbaum argued. A lawyer has the right to rely on decisions of the Supreme Court, especially decisions based on constitutional law, which ideally should be fit for permanence. This is the stuff of homily, because without predictability there is no settled law at all, merely the whim of whoever wears the decider's robes.

Yet, as Greenbaum knew all too well, in a single amazing paragraph in *Mount Laurel III* the justices had abandoned this principle of doctrinal reliability. *Let the builder beware* became the court's newest message. "If there is any class of litigant that knows of the uncertainties of litigation, it is the builders. They . . . have walked the rough, uneven, unpredictable path through planning boards, boards of adjustments, permits, approvals, conditions, lawsuits, appeals, affirmances, reversals, and in between all of these, changes in both statutory and decisional law that can turn a case upside down. No builder with the slightest amount of experience could have relied on the remedies provided in *Mount Laurel II* in the sense of justifiably believing that they would not be changed. . . . If ever any doctrine and any remedy appeared susceptible to change, it was that decision and its remedy." As Judge Serpentelli balefully instructed Greenbaum, this language in *Mount Laurel III* made the attorney's argument a loser, and the judge was powerless to rule otherwise.

Serpentelli's sending of the West Windsor case to COAH "was probably the low point of my career as a lawyer," says Greenbaum. "The Supreme Court basically cut us off at the knees." That ruling gave the township more time—exactly the weapon it needed to keep up its fight against authorizing any housing for the poor. In the construction business, where mortgage rates, consumers' buying power, and property values are always in flux, timing is everything. Judge Serpentelli's refusal to force West Windsor to rezone, and the further delay caused by the proceeding before COAH, only inspired greater resistance by the township to any *Mount Laurel* enforcement. Eventually Greenbaum's developer-client went bankrupt when its lender's business was taken over by the Resolution Trust Corporation. Although another developer picked up the pieces, this fight with the well-to-do suburb continued everlastingly.

In *Mount Laurel III*, the New Jersey Supreme Court, which earlier had criticized the inaction of the political branches, now sounded almost delirious about the primacy of politics in housing and zoning. Writing for a unanimous court, Chief Justice Robert Wilentz emphasized how reluctantly the judiciary had intervened in the first place. "Enforcement of constitutional rights cannot await a supporting political consensus," as the court pointed out in *Mount Laurel II*, but now there was a new day and the eagerly awaited consensus was in hand.

Seemingly everyone was happy with the legislative solution, the opinion noted, including leading fair-housing experts, planners and lawyers who earlier had urged the court to action. The court quoted planner Alan Mallach, who figured in many of the fair-housing lawsuits, as praising the state for making "the first substantial commitment of general fund revenues to low income housing." (The court, disinclined to rain on its own parade, opted not to call attention to the title of the article from which this observation was extracted: "Blueprint for Delay: From *Mount Laurel* to Molehill"). Carl Bisgaier, who as an attorney with the Public Advocate had taken the lead in arguing the earlier *Mount Laurel* cases, and who had since moved on to become a developer-lawyer himself, delivered a more full-throated encomium, which the opinion also quoted. "The Act stands today as the nation's foremost state legislative effort to respond to the housing needs of low income persons."

Between the decree in *Mount Laurel II* and the legislation, there were differences in the details, the Supreme Court acknowledged, yet what mattered most was that the politicians had finally done *something*. "The basic explanation of today's decision is the Act—this substantial occupation of the field by the Governor and the Legislature. They have responded. . . . It is a response more than sufficient to trigger our 'readiness to defer.' " The justices had evidently learned from the ferocity of get-the-judge politics that wait and see was, after all, the more prudent judicial posture.

When the New Jersey legislature set up the Council on Affordable Housing, it was anxious to create an agency that it could control, a bureaucracy that would never do anything so disruptive to the lawmakers' suburban constituencies as the builder's remedies that the courts were issuing. For the future, COAH offered a fine solution—but still there remained the sticky matter of those cases, like historic Cranbury's, already in the courts. While legislation is ordinarily written to shape future events, not to reshape past ones, the suburbs were eager to be out from under the long judicial noses. From their point of view, turning *Mount Laurel* disputes over to the new agency would mean further delay—and probably a better deal, in terms of how much affordable housing they would have to accept.

Once the Supreme Court decided in *Mount Laurel III* that New

Jersey's Fair Housing Act was constitutional, it next had to determine how to handle all these pending lawsuits, some of which had been on the docket for more than a decade. Was the injustice that long delays and mounting costs would predictably visit upon builders, fair-housing advocates, and poor families serious enough—was it "manifest" enough, in the language of the statute—to keep these cases in court? The *Mount Laurel* trial judges decided in many instances that the answer was yes, and, while conservative legislators were vocally outraged by those rulings, calmer lawmakers pointed out that these judges were only behaving prudently.

Nonetheless, the Supreme Court overruled the trial courts, opting to terminate these cases. *Manifest injustice*: these two little words, inserted into the Fair Housing Act several months into the protracted legislative debate, became the crucial statutory text. Since the words themselves aren't crystal clear, the court had to divine what legal scholars refer to as the "intention" of the legislature. An early version of the act would have left the trial judges to manage almost all the *Mount Laurel*–type cases that had been filed at least sixty days before the statute went into effect; under that version, a transfer to COAH was appropriate only if it was evident that the agency could move faster than the courts to develop poor people's housing.

As the bill was being massaged in committee, however, the lawmakers substituted the "manifest injustice" requirement. The justices reasoned that, because of this change, the expectation of who would hear a pending case—court or COAH—was reversed. Almost every case should be sent on to the council, said the high court. Only in "the very narrowest, most extreme situation," one that produced "unforeseen and exceptional unfairness," would Serpentelli & Co. remain in charge. Despite those judges' view that undoing years of litigation would be patently unfair to the parties, such well-advanced cases—like Robert Greenbaum's never ending struggle against West Windsor—did not represent the kind of situation the legislators had in mind when they spoke of "manifest injustice," since a primary reason for the new law was "to get the courts out of the field [of affordable housing]."

True justice resided in the Fair Housing Act itself, the New Jersey Supreme Court decreed, indulging in the kind of wondrous word play that gives jurisprudence a bad name. "It would be ironic if the application of this Act, . . . so outstanding compared to the inactivity of other states, were to be characterized as 'manifest injustice' simply because . . . its remedy was not immediate; and ironic to label the inevitable initial delaying effect of this law, so manifestly just in its unprecedented attempt to provide lower income housing, as manifestly unjust in that very respect." In this rhetorical razzle-dazzle, the court seems to have forgotten that affordable housing involved not only legislative intentions but also constitutional rights, those brave pledges made just three years earlier in *Mount Laurel II*.

This judgment of the justices was more political and pragmatic than principled. The day after the decision, the *Philadelphia Inquirer* headline read: "New Jersey Supreme Court Hoists White Flag."

Even as the Supreme Court was hearing oral arguments on the Fair Housing Act, another time clock was ticking: the end of Chief Justice Robert Wilentz's seven-year term on the bench was only a few months away. The state constitution required that Wilentz either be reappointed and confirmed for a term that would end with mandatory retirement at his seventieth birthday, or else vacate his seat. Ever since the 1947 state constitutional revision, when Arthur Vanderbilt and his good-government allies cleaned up and depoliticized New Jersey's courts, gubernatorial renomination of judges with senate concurrence had been routine. Only a handful of judges had been removed from the bench in all those years, and always for financial peccadilloes; not once had a Supreme Court justice been rejected. But conservative legislators like Peter Garibaldi, the "go to jail" senator, and John Dorsey, still pushing his constitutional amendment to overturn *Mount Laurel II*, implored Governor Thomas Kean to find a new chief justice.

This was a high-stakes decision. Because Wilentz was fifty-nine years old, Kean's determination would influence the direction of the Supreme Court for more than a decade to come, and on ideological grounds there was reason to suspect that the governor would look elsewhere. The chief justice led a court described in a nationwide study as remarkable among state tribunals for its "confidently activist posture." For his part, the governor was inclined to the belief that judges, like children, should be seen more than heard, and he condemned the high court for "judicial activism at its worst." Kean particularly despised *Mount Laurel II*, the seminal ruling of Wilentz's tenure. "Infamous and incendiary," he called it, "social engineering on a scale never imagined by Marx or Engels." In two successive state-of-the-state speeches, the governor had converted a concern about affordable housing into a critique of judicial marauding.

"Get the judge" also looked like good partisan politics in 1986. Across the country in California, conservatives were mobilizing to oust Chief Justice Rose Bird, who was reviled for her near-perfect voting record to reverse death sentences, as well as two other liberal jurists appointed by former Democratic governor and perpetual presidential hopeful Jerry Brown. With little else to run on, Republican George Deukmejian campaigned for reelection as California's governor almost entirely on a pro-death-penalty, anti–Rose Bird platform. He won and she lost.

Yet other factors counted in Chief Justice Wilentz's favor, and these turned out to matter more to Governor Kean. For one thing, the pull of personal history makes a difference in New Jersey, a state that's almost as politically incestuous as the Hapsburg dynasty. A generation earlier,

Wilentz's father, the state's attorney general, had been a political friend of Kean's father, a longtime congressman; and, during the late 1960s, the governor and the chief justice were colleagues in the assembly. While the two men sat on opposite sides of the aisle, Kean especially admired Wilentz for his intelligence and his integrity. On one occasion, a stringent conflict-of-interest measure that prevented lawyer-legislators from appearing before state agencies for several years after they left office came up for an assembly vote. Although Wilentz knew the law would take business from his family's law firm, he voted for it anyway; and then, after the measure passed, he quit politics to resume his law practice.

"Here was belief in principle clearly triumphing over political ambition," Thomas Kean marveled, recounting the episode in his autobiography, *The Politics of Inclusion.* In the Wilentz affair, "principles over politics" ultimately became the governor's standard as well. While Kean delayed his announcement of the renomination, giving the anti-Wilentz forces a chance to build some momentum, eventually he submitted the renomination to the senate. "I always knew that, when the time came, I would reappoint the chief justice. The issue in my eyes was not *Mount Laurel* but judicial independence." Replacing Wilentz, he says, would have set a terrible standard. "I told [the opponents] that once you establish the precedent that you're going to throw a judge out just because you don't like the way that judge makes decisions, you totally compromise the integrity of the judicial system."

In this roiling political environment, the *Mount Laurel III* decision, with its obeisance to the new Fair Housing Act, was readily appreciated as a peace offering from the bench. The assembly speaker, Republican Charles Hardwick, lauded the chief justice for "properly reading the will of the people. I think he knew that reappointment was in jeopardy." Senator John Dorsey weighed in with the observation that "the justices are in fact sensitive to public opinion," while a senatorial colleague in the anti–*Mount Laurel* constitutional amendment drive opined: "I'm not so sure the outcome would have been so fortuitous if the tenure of Wilentz was not under review."

Despite the white flag of *Mount Laurel III,* and despite Governor Kean's subsequent renomination of Wilentz, the ouster of the chief justice remained a passion for GOP leaders. They organized a mass-mailing campaign, kicked off with letters to ten thousand party activists, aimed at pressuring wavering senators to vote against him. While *Mount Laurel* was the real source of their animus, it was unseemly to say so, since judges were theoretically immunized against partisan politics. But when the matter of Wilentz's out-of-state residence came to light, the antagonists seized on this more respectable issue to gather new support.

Press reports, which had it that the chief justice was living in Manhattan and commuting across the Hudson River to his New Jersey court, shocked this famously insecure state—the top jurist of New Jersey had actually taken up residence in the heart of the heart of enemy country. Although Wilentz dutifully explained that his wife's cancer treatments obliged the couple to live as close as possible to her hospital in New York City, this sad piece of personal history didn't stop the sniping. "Personal compassion finished a poor second to a parochial need to stand up and defend New Jersey," said Governor Kean. "Republicans who opposed Wilentz on ideological grounds now picked up allies in both parties who thought it was utterly embarrassing to have the state's chief judge live in another state."

On the night of July 31, 1986, when the Wilentz renomination came up for a vote, the governor was out of town—ironically enough, vacationing at his family's summer place on Fishers Island, just off the coast of Long Island in New York State. Wilentz phoned with the news that his nomination was in near fatal trouble. The vote tally stood at twenty to nineteen, one shy of the twenty-one votes needed for reappointment. The holdout senator was Les Laskin, who represented Cherry Hill, a town that had its own troubles with exclusionary-zoning litigation. Laskin demanded and got assurances from Wilentz that he would move back to New Jersey once his wife recovered and that, if a new measure requiring judges to live in-state became law, he would comply. (At least the legislator didn't insist that Mrs. Wilentz change hospitals.) After a three-hour recess, Senator Laskin descended the fence and voted aye. Both the chief justice's position and the continued independence of the judiciary were assured.

The New Jersey Supreme Court under Robert Wilentz's stewardship continued its forays into the fractious borderland of law and policy, notably in the territory of equitable public-school financing. There would also be new affordable-housing decisions testing the relationship between what COAH decided and what the *Mount Laurel* doctrine commanded. But in such cases the New Jersey Supreme Court after *Mount Laurel III* became a bit player, not the star performer.

Judicial Legitimacy and the Mount Laurel *Trilogy*

While the *Mount Laurel* cases resulted indirectly from a failure of political leadership in New Jersey, those rulings are the deliberate product of an activist Supreme Court, confident about its social judgments and its legal duty to undo terrible injustice. What transpired raises questions about the legitimacy of what the court did and, differently, about its ability to keep a reform agenda going.

The root sources of judicial intervention can be located in the New Jersey social landscape, in the intractable race and social-class conflict magnified by the ever growing economic and political importance of the suburbs. Also, in a state that lacks a center—"So you live in New Jersey; which exit off the turnpike?" runs the standard jibe—a longstanding commitment to local autonomy mostly kept the political branches quiescent. This institutionalized lethargy helped to fuel the court's involvement, as the justices filled a statewide political and policy vacuum.

But neither the doctrine outlawing exclusionary zoning nor the ambitious remedy the justices framed to enforce their rulings was predestined; neither demographic and social circumstance nor the state's constitution forced the justices' hand. Vital to the mix was the Supreme Court's own development of a strong, policy-minded perspective on lawmaking, concerning issues ranging from reapportionment and educational equity to reform of private liability law.

The zoning cases were the most ambitious, the most transparently political, and the most problematic of these judicial adventures. The constitutional right announced in *Mount Laurel I* had the flimsiest of support from the state constitution, since the "general welfare" means more or less whatever a majority of the justices says it means. By writing an opinion that sidestepped both federal constitutional law and state statutes, the high court sought to evade review—either on constitutional grounds, by the U.S. Supreme Court, or, for political reasons, by the coordinate branches of state government. The justices' hope was that the suburbs, if left alone, would go along with the decree; and so, as one member of the high court pointed out in a concurring opinion, the remedy in *Mount Laurel I* was deliberately vacuous. The anticipated dance of cooperation between court and community never occurred, though; instead, the Supreme Court's unsubtle political signal was greeted with pledges of resistance from suburbia. Since that 1975 decision, the justices have alternated between boldness and timidity. The New Jersey land-use cases from *Mount Laurel I* to the present send mixed if not irreconcilable signals.

"Practically every political decision winds up, sooner or later, as a legal decision," Alexis de Tocqueville observed more than a century and a half ago in *Democracy in America*, and this proposition is much truer now than it was then. The commonplace rationale for judicial activism, one that judges themselves are especially fond of reciting, is that courts have a duty to enforce constitutional rights and provide fitting remedies. Yet that justification begs all the interesting questions about whether amorphous constitutional language is best read as creating the sought-after right and how aggressive a court should become in righting a perceived wrong. A somewhat different argument for an activist judiciary is that such courts are vital if democracy itself is to run well. In the short term, the political process does not always reflect public values, this argument runs, and courts may be the best institution to prompt politicians into taking up important, if nettlesome, concerns. Access to the courts also gives voice to the least powerful, the effectively disenfranchised, in the halls of decision, and there are legal scholars who contend that courts, because of their political isolation, can best articulate public values.

As judicial skeptics see things, though, the courts' isolation from politics is no virtue but presents a central problem of legitimacy. The more a decree looks like a piece of legislation, the more political it comes to seem. Decisions like *Mount Laurel I* and *Mount Laurel II*, the critics say, really reflect the judges' political preferences rather than legally compelled decision making—why, then, do they deserve any respect? Activist courts are also faulted for lacking the expertise and political acumen necessary to decide complex social matters. To that concern about judicial effectiveness, however, there is an empirical answer: the New Jersey court showed considerable ingenuity in overcoming these impediments, especially when in *Mount Laurel II* it transformed advocates into consultants on law and policy. There is, as well, a fear that activist courts will deaden democratic institutions—that "Leave it to the judges" will become the legislative refrain, especially when the choices to be made are hard. The concern is plausible enough, yet when it came to zoning, the New Jersey courts didn't bury the politicians but instead brought them to life.

State courts have typically been more activist than their counterparts in the federal system, and such reformism has often been taken for granted. When the New Jersey justices rewrote the state's tort and contract laws, for instance, in a series of landmark cases that gave consumers vastly more power in bargaining with manufacturers, the legislators could have overruled the judges by writing new legislation but didn't do so. One reason that New Jersey's politicians have mainly acquiesced in judicial policy-making is that the justices stepped carefully when entering a new part of the policy forest. Frequently, as in the *Mount Laurel* cases and the school-finance litigation, the high court has given political actors time to adjust to the new doctrines, to devise politically acceptable outcomes, and to reclaim control over policy-making. Only when the coordinate branches—the legislature and the governor—balk has the court adopted a more aggressive stance; and then, by posing an unpalatable outcome, the court has forced a political response similar to the interim judicial solution. This pattern of interaction between justices and legislators was repeated in reapportionment and school finance as well as exclusionary zoning. For Chief Justice Joseph Weintraub, who presided over the high court during the 1960s and early 1970s, it represented a conscious strategy. The justices had to maintain a reputation for "unpredictable assertiveness," he said with remarkable candor, because the legislators would otherwise shrug off their decrees.

On pivotal policy matters, the judges have fared best when they could enlist powerful allies to their cause. The New Jersey court was able to rely on the U.S. Supreme Court in backing its stance on legislative reapportionment; in school finance, the justices could depend on politicians speaking for the interests of cities and public education. But when it came to zoning, such help was nowhere to be found: the U.S. Supreme Court refused to become what it derisively called a "super–zoning board" for the nation, and the most influential state politicians were adamantly opposed to "communistic" judicial intervention. The "fair share doctrine," as the New Jersey Supreme Court pointed out in its 1983 *Mount Laurel II* opinion, "does not arise from some theoretical analysis of our Constitution, but rather from the underlying concepts of fundamental fairness in the exercise of governmental power." The court may have concluded in the wake of the outrage that followed this decision that it had strayed too far from the Constitution and from shared public values.

In one respect, the 1985 Fair Housing Act and *Mount Laurel III* tell the story of how an isolated court was forced to admit defeat, since the legislation follows the court doctrine in form more than in fact. But under the circumstances, the fact that the Fair Housing Act codifies the constitutional concept of fair share is a remarkable accomplishment. As a nationwide study of state supreme courts points out: "Although the court's ruling was virulently attacked, its apparent threat to impose unacceptable changes in local zoning policies did motivate the New Jersey legislature to devise its own policy, which expressly recognized the state's responsibility to address the housing needs of the poor."

Meanwhile, the autonomy and integrity of New Jersey's high court survives intact, and this too is a triumph. In California, after popular fury against the state supreme court's anti-death-penalty decrees forced three justices off the bench in 1986, that tribunal was weakened to near impotence and its appointment process, already compromised by the nomination of Rose Bird despite her lack of qualifications, became an unashamedly political exercise. New Jersey's justices, by contrast, have continued to be legal innovators, and appointments to the Supreme Court still stress professional competence, not partisan politics.

Markets, Politics, and Rights

The *Mount Laurel* chronicle—the town history, the protracted litigation, the broader reverberations—also speaks to the complex relationship of markets, politics, and rights.

When the members of the Springville Action Council in Mount Laurel Township obtained an option on thirty-two acres of nearby land in 1968, they had to play the odds like any land developer. They faced the familiar uncertainties over whether they could obtain financing, whether they could afford construction and operating costs, and whether the rental price and occupancy rates of the built units would allow them, and their eventual funders, to break even over time. They hoped to obtain federal and state assistance to defray costs, but even those funds would eventually dry up. As local developer Richard Goodwin—who eventually went belly-up in Mount Laurel—could have told them, when you play the market, you win some and you lose some, and you have to protect yourself. Sometimes what you want from the world just isn't feasible—the market won't bear it. Of course, the inability of the Springville group even to emerge from the starting blocks came from what economists might call an insuperable "barrier to entry": their neighbors said no.

Ethel Lawrence and the other members of the Springville Action Council didn't count on being zoned out, but if they had faced facts at the beginning, they would have known that obtaining the necessary approvals wasn't a sure thing either. Local zoning boards are intensely political, governed more by under-the-table exchanges of favors than by anything logical. Though they clothe their decisions in the language of "the best interests of our citizens," minorities and the poor know what this means: "everybody but us." But the time was 1968, and the politics around race and poverty looked to be changing for the better. Besides, politics in a small town like Mount Laurel really boils down to problem solving among neighbors. Neighbors listen to reason, except perhaps when their fears are irrational. Unfortunately, the more irrational the fears concerning racial minorities and the poor, the greater political sway those fears have.

If the Springville group had objectively analyzed the market and weighed political realities, it might have thought better of its plans. But people like Ethel Lawrence don't plan their lives or chart their dreams upon probabilities and expected outcomes. The Springville Action Council was not a sophisticated syndicate, just a few townsfolk hoping to improve their station in life, and that of their children and grandchildren. Leave it to the Richard Goodwins of the world to understand how to leverage housing markets and pull strings with zoning boards. In planning their garden-apartment project, the people of Springville felt they were asserting only what they were entitled to—their legal rights, maybe even their constitutional rights. And so when their plans were rejected one after the other by Mount Laurel's politicians, they fought for those rights.

Markets, politics, and rights: each of these rules of decision operates, sometimes independently but more often in concert, to allocate the goods and assign the bads of society. It is convenient to pretend that buyers and sellers, politicians and voters, and lawyers, clients, and judges occupy divisible spheres; economics, political science, and law are regarded as distinct disciplines in academic discourse. But as hard as we practice separating them, these realms confound and collide with one another.

Economists like to think of the market as the natural state of things. The gospel of economic efficiency is offered as a sacrament for all social ills, as if scrawled on an ancient tablet in hieroglyphics. Social welfare is maximized when private individuals act individually to maximize their own happiness: allow people to bargain with each other freely, and optimal allocations will obtain, like magic. Prices set by freely bargaining individuals—rational actors—are the best indicators of the relative values of things. Winners will be the ones who tried hardest, and losers—the "lazy and quarrelsome" in economist Thornton Wilder's parlance—will deserve their status as bottom dwellers in society's tide pool.

Politics has its own claim to preordination. While bargaining is useful, some decisions simply cannot be struck effectively by buyers and sellers in small groups. Inevitably there are matters of broader community concern, like how to allocate commodities that cannot easily be owned (clean air, for instance), and how to defend the polity against foreign invaders. For such goods, representative voting and majority rule appear to be the best decision tools, even with their well-known frailties and manipulability. Voting may be necessary but not sufficient, however. Without reliable legal protections for private-property claims, Adam Smith's promise about how the invisible hand of private bargaining promotes the public good would never come true, and Hobbes's promise of a war of "all against all" might. As nascent free-market economies in Eastern Europe are discovering, political majorities must install property systems quickly and vigorously, lest private mobs set up their own. There are also the famous market failures—"externalities" like environmental degradation, economic "bads" that mount when those causing them don't have to pay recompense—and conventional theory holds that such harms can only be controlled through regulation engineered by majority-rule governments. So economists are on the right track, political scientists might argue, but it is "partisan mutual adjustment," bargaining through the vote, that is ultimately required for an orderly and happy society.

As economics and politics fight to a standoff for the theoretical high ground, the sphere of rights makes its own claim to transcendency. When American colonial sensibilities were crossed by King George's taxes, cries of basic unfairness were enshrined in Jefferson's "self-evident" logic. In his construction, and that of other Natural Law gospellers, the inalienability of the right to the pursuit of happiness derives from the Creator's having made it so. There are no arguments when it comes to such natural rights to equal treatment—they just are—and this verity permeates the claims motivating disadvantaged groups like the Springville Action Council in Mount Laurel. There is no why or wherefore; the status quo is just wrong and cannot persist. It is for the clever lawyers to find the right constitutional levers to pull—in this case, the "general welfare" language of New Jersey's constitution—but to the ordinary citizens deprived of them, rights are rights.

Yet in order to respond to such grievances, a court of law must do the dirtier work of staring down contrarian majorities. This is the constitutional enterprise, specifying claims that trump all political arguments. Yet inevitably, the constitution means, at most, only what the courts say it does. This arrangement is relativistic, transitory, and ineluctably human, but no better system for implementing inalienable rights has ever been found.

None of the *Mount Laurel* decisions declared a right to housing. Indeed, if Justice Hall or Chief Justice Wilentz had urged recognition of such a right, as growing out of the "general welfare" guarantee, neither could have garnered a majority on the bench. Instead, the court's response to the perceived problem of rights denied was to tinker with the politics and economics of the situation. The bare right constructed by the justices was perhaps "freedom from exclusionary zoning"; the remedy for its violation more directly benefited developers than the real victims, the poor and racial minorities.

Part of this mismatch between remedy and rights has to do with the nature of housing as a commodity. Housing is a complex and durable good; and to design market, political, or rights-based solutions to problems of inequitable distribution is decidedly tricky business. Actually, "housing" bundles together many different goods, including building materials, architectural design, interior and exterior space, land, landscape, views, climate, location, proximity to other desirable (and distance from undesirable) places, health and safety, and sense of *communitas*. The dimensions of each of these components can conflict, and different customers assess the relative importance of these goods differently. Thus there are as many reasons why a particular home will, or won't, seem appealing as there are potential occupants. This multifaceted nature of housing— and its status as a necessity—complicates efforts to allocate it through markets alone. Housing texts enumerate many of the perceived market failures and politically mediated efforts to resolve them. For many of these ills a central state apparatus dominates—rent control for urban lower classes, title-insurance requirements to prevent fraud, building and environmental standards for health and safety externalities. Not here, though. When it comes to our failure to house America's poor in the suburbs, though, economics proposes *and* disposes, while politics and rights play supporting roles, Rosencrantz and Guildenstern in this version of *Hamlet*.

Some of the things that give housing its value, like the quality of the cabinetry or the dimensions of the property, readily fit the framework of markets. It's logical for the biggest and most expensive homes, like big and expensive cars, to be priced beyond the means of all but the wealthiest. But this logic falters when basic minimums rather than luxuries are at play and, differently, when markets are tainted by bigotry. Private covenants or zoning ordinances that prevent minorities from purchasing or residing in a given neighborhood are intolerable as selling points on a real-estate broker's listing sheet, whatever the market preferences might be. Few towns were so lacking in subtlety in crafting their land-use laws as Mount Laurel. Most suburban zoning ordinances are couched in deceptively mild economic terms, like "ratables" and "property values," and bland cultural terms, like "health and safety" and "suburban tranquility." And judges dismantle legal barriers only to provide "realistic opportunities," not results: to do otherwise, even the boldest judges fear, would invite war on the courts and on the very idea of rights.

Politics, markets, and rights can also be thought of as rituals for settling conflict and establishing order—as the lid on the boiling societal kettle.

Political, economic, and justice institutions coexist uneasily in this country, frequently counteracting and contradicting one another. Sometimes this is by design: constitutional checks and balances become manifest in judicial parries and legislative and executive thrusts in stories like the Mount Laurel chronicles. At other times the institutional interplay becomes a free-for-all: win the vote, win the case, change the law, ride the market. At points in this history, the lines separating political, economic, and legal battles blur, as the issue heats up on multiple fronts simultaneously.

As the main events in this narrative shift arenas, the players' roles sometimes change. Ethel Lawrence was a community organizer who moved inside the political system when she actively sought the approvals and financing needed to build public housing. Her defining role would be as a plaintiff in a famous lawsuit, a human symbol of rights denied. Peter O'Connor started as a civil-rights litigator, then entered the Camden political arena, eventually becoming a nonprofit developer; his reputation will turn as much on the number of affordable housing units he builds as on the number of lawsuits he wins. Cary Edwards made his name as municipal attorney fighting zoning battles before he found himself a gladiator on the floor of the state assembly, then as Governor Kean's *Mount Laurel* man of the hour.

Rights issues such as those that permeate *Mount Laurel* usually emerge out of a concrete grievance, but politics, markets, and rights characterize problems differently. Problems in legal settings, whether political or judicial, are by definition adversarial; interests are aligned, allies and enemies identified, winners and losers tallied. Because markets are anonymous, such calculations are harder to construct. Market outcomes appear to be insulated from moral judgment: everyone is involved in economic exchange, after all, and the desire to better oneself is nearly universal. Yet since the market lacks a persona, it is also commonly regarded as responsible for the status quo, even as politics and law are conceptualized as methods to bring about change.

Each arena has its own rhythm and tempo. Elections occur at regular intervals, separated by several years, as gauges of popular preference, and policy-making is invariably shaped by both the election concluded and the one to come. In contrast with the episodic pace of politics, the market pulses steadily. Individual deals are too numerous and too quickly consummated to track, and so economists rely on statistical inferences to monitor gains and slowdowns. While the motions of the economy writ large, boom and bust as *tableaux vivants,* can only be intuited by participants, economic cycles dictate grand consequences.

Closer to politics than markets in their rhythm, courts are episodic in a more phenomenological sense. Rights-redefining lawsuits seem to occur like freaks of evolution, needing just the right chemistry to emerge from society's organic soup. Each ingredient in the mix—the people, the situations, the state of the law, the social context—is crucial. Sometimes one of the parties will stake out a position that encapsulates nascent social values; or a lawyer's advocacy starkly reveals what's at stake; or else a judge's testing of the virtues of claim and counterclaim confers gravity upon the outcome. Modest legal adjustments take place with marketlike regularity, since access to the courts is guaranteed, but tempestuous cases like *Mount Laurel* occur only with an almost magical confluence of people and facts, placed just so, that emboldens judges to try changing the world.

These differing tempos are accompanied by differing logics. Legislators typically make broad decisions, writing laws to apply to many situations. Lawsuits, by contrast, are initiated by particular claimants, and courts must determine whether they receive the specific relief sought. In practice, though, the ways in which courts solve problems more closely resembles the legislative process. Particularly at higher levels of the judiciary, the precedent-making impact of cases requires judges to reach, and to frame, decisions with a view toward their broader consequences.

By contrast, the observed allocation of wealth and structure of production are received wisdom in economics. The status quo is seen as representing aggregate social choice rather than particularized solutions to actual problems of distribution or inefficiency. Instead of revealing themselves through outcomes—the elections, statutes, and case reports that mark pivotal decisions in politics and law—markets as institutions of social choice manifest themselves in the process of exchange.

According to conventional economic theory, single transactions affect the world in imperceptible increments. Aggregate economic trends are produced through the offices of the familiar, if spectral, invisible hand. In idealized competitive markets, individual actors have no influence on who owns, or owes, anything. But reality is somewhat more complicated than the model: flesh-and-blood people, with real families and fortunes, experience real success and failure in everyday economic life. To the extent that economics simplifies society through its models, it ignores the consequences of winning and losing in the marketplace, and the felt effects of unequal income distribution. Whatever the theory suggests, the wealthy invariably have an easier time steering the aggregate than the poor, for whom the "margin" becomes not just an econometric construct but a state of being: this too is evident in the life details embedded in *Mount Laurel*.

The Council on Affordable Housing: Doing Good by Stealth

In the end, an administrative agency designed to draw upon politics, markets, *and* rights concerns—yet with the capacity to muzzle and sanitize the issue—was designated to manage the enterprise of affordable housing in New Jersey.

Legislatures and courts are often settings for high public drama, transfixing political crises and path-breaking, or at least curiosity-provoking, legal cases. Lawyers and lawmakers strut on the public stage; popular movies get made from these events; TV channels, Court-TV and C-SPAN, are given over to broadcasting from courtrooms and legislative chambers.

By sharp contrast, administrative agencies are almost always invisible to the public eye. There are no Robert Redfords playing the role of bureaucrat, no "Administrative TV" to broadcast Postal Council or Council on Affordable Housing meetings. Instead of the riveting courtroom story or the packed legislative hearing, agency business is carried out, usually through memos written in lead-weight prose by mandarins who worship the gods of regularity. "The routinization of charisma" is how the nineteenth-century sociologist Max Weber summarized the progression by which inspiration is tamed by rules and leaders are domesticated by bureaucrats. That phrase exactly captures how the Council on Affordable Housing has gone about its business.

From High Point in the north to southernmost Cape May, there was an almost audible sigh of relief among New Jersey politicians once the transfers of exclusionary-zoning cases out of the courts to COAH became a sure thing. Towns that had been anticipating frightening judicial decrees now had their reprieve, while communities that, in the manner of lawyer Henry Hill's baby harp seals, were cudgeled into settling lawsuits could begin the entire process again with the hope that COAH would reduce the amount of affordable housing for which they had to make room. Though no one knew for certain what the agency would do, surely it would be friendlier to municipal concerns than the courts had been. And because Governor Kean, the man who despised what the judges had done, had the power to appoint the nine council members, it was certain that this new agency would pay close attention to suburban sentiments.

The *Mount Laurel* doctrine produced for developers what in chess is called a "won game": the Supreme Court had already decided that the towns had to do something, and only the details of the remedy were left to the judges to decide. After the Fair Housing Act, however, the outcome for developers was much riskier. A township, whether already in litigation or not, could produce a housing plan, often one that whittled down its affordable-housing quotas to a fraction of what the *Mount Laurel* "consensus methodology" required. Regional contribution agreements (RCAs) allowed such a community to transfer up to half of its fair-share obligation, typically to a distressed city, for a modest cash outlay. Also, by counting housing for seniors and recent rehabilitations of dilapidated housing, a town could reduce still further the number of new units necessary to satisfy the quota.

"Kick and scream. Fight for every adjustment you feel is legitimate," COAH's first chair, Arthur Kondrup, urged suburbanites. To be sure, the agency's rules required towns to come up with plans more realistic than the sham rezoning ordinance drafted by Mount Laurel in the mid-1970s, ostensibly in response to the *Mount Laurel I* decision. But once the council approved a municipality's plan, it was effectively shielded from litigation.

A town that was poor or had little land to be developed could presume that it was unlikely to be sued and so choose to avoid the agency entirely; the Fair Housing Act offered that option. Even a community that knew it risked a lawsuit by not submitting a plan didn't really risk a lot. The *Mount Laurel* judges, Serpentelli and his kind, were gone, replaced by seventeen judges with less experience in, and perhaps less opposition to, exclusionary zoning. Any new legal complaint might well be transferred to COAH, as the Supreme Court so evidently preferred; and once such a transfer happened, almost any gesture of municipal cooperation would be rewarded by a grateful agency possessed of modest powers. It is little surprise, then, that if one adds up all the land rezoned for affordable housing, either in plans approved by COAH or in court orders, space has been set aside for no more than seventy-one thousand units, a figure less than half the agency's estimates of what New Jersey needs to do for its poorer citizens, which itself was half of what the consensus methodology required.

All of this sounds very dry and technical. All of it *is* very dry and technical, which is precisely the point—the creation of COAH neutered affordable housing as a political issue.

Life inside the council was almost entirely nonadversarial, and about as peaceful as a chapel on a weekday morning. There were seldom any reporters present, no Ethel Lawrences to lend their *gravitas*, when a municipality requested agency approval of its zoning laws. The most aggressive that COAH ever got was to request that a township revise and resubmit its plan, and that simply gave a town time to do more planning. At worst, COAH and the objecting town would enter into a mediation process provided for in the act. While those unhappy with a municipality's plan were legally entitled to make their concerns known to the council, few parties actually did so. With no builder's remedy—no guarantee that a particular parcel of land would be rezoned if a builder successfully challenged the legality of a zoning ordinance under the act—developers lost interest in COAH. The Public Advocate had handled some of the biggest *Mount Laurel* cases. But that department, its staff shrunk by Governor Kean, stayed out of the administrative process of reviewing plans on a town-by-town basis. Only when the council adopted broader rules did Stephen Eisdorfer, the indefatigable Public Advocate attorney, make an appearance. As for the activists, some, like Carl Bisgaier, became developers themselves; others, such as Roy Epps from the New Brunswick chapter of the Civic League (formerly the Urban League, plaintiff in the Middlesex County cases), generally found COAH less fertile ground than the courtroom to recount the misdeeds of the suburbs.

In short, there was a change in how official business was conducted after the Fair Housing Act became law—not least because the fate of the suburbs was being determined by bureaucratic, not judicial, personalities.

Those who decide cases in court are obliged to be neutral, and bias is a reason to disqualify a judge in a system of decision making that isn't supposed to be affected by the identity of the decider. But those who set policy under the Fair Housing Act operate under different rules of engagement: they are named by the governor to represent the viewpoints of specified interest groups. Where courts are supposed to act on principle, the more politically constituted agencies are expected to factor in political and marketplace concerns.

Of the nine council members, the law specifies that four must be local elected officials, one of them from a city (Governor Kean first selected Newark mayor Kenneth Gibson, a conspicuous absentee at COAH sessions). Three members are supposed to represent that loosest of all imaginable constituencies, "the public interest"; for these seats, Kean's initial picks included a well-to-do horse farmer and the public-affairs director at Johnson & Johnson, the pharmaceutical giant. The remaining two council seats are reserved for the state's housing finance officer and a builders' representative, who is supposed to be an expert in land-use and housing policy. While an activist like Peter O'Connor or Carl Bisgaier fits this job description, there wasn't a prayer that Governor Kean would appoint that kind of person. Instead, Kean named Ara Hovnanian, head of the firm of K. Hovnanian and Sons, one of the most prosperous developers of suburbia on the East Coast; and when Democrat Jim Florio became governor, he reappointed the developer to this seat.

As the one council member who really understood the issues, Hovnanian's voice has been the most influential. Although he stepped down from COAH in 1994, his replacement is the chief counsel of his construction company, who presumably speaks in the same cadences as his boss. The Hovnanian company name is synonymous with reasonably priced townhouse developments, pitched mainly to first-time home buyers, mostly in quickly growing outer suburbs of metropolitan areas from Massachusetts to Florida. These condominium communities have kept the American dream of home ownership alive for the straitened middle class; and in states like New Jersey, where the law has encouraged construction of affordable housing, they have provided for moderate-income households as well. The Hovnanians "are killers. Charming killers," says Rutgers University housing expert George Sternlieb. "These guys build essentially the same twelve-hundred-square-foot dumb house. If they build it in a luxury community, it's a hundred fifty thousand dollars. If they build it in a blue-collar community [where land costs less], it's eighty-five thousand—and that's probably fifteen or twenty grand less than the competition."

The Hovnanian family story is an American classic. Forty years ago, Kevork Hovnanian, an Armenian immigrant, fled from war-wracked Iran, bringing some capital with him (in Iran, he had been a prosperous builder of highways). Soon he was a participant in the suburban boom, building and selling houses, using his station wagon as an office to keep costs down. The strategy of undercutting the rest of the market while providing decent homes on a high-volume basis worked well. By the mid-1980s, at the zenith of New Jersey's building boom, the demand for a Hovnanian home was so great that would-be buyers camped out in front of sales trailers, sometimes for a solid week, just to make an offer. Down payments were so low and the firm's reputation so solid that buyers were willing to buy from blueprints, without even inspecting a model home; seven Hovnanian developments were sold out before the first home was completed. In 1986, when Ara Hovnanian was named to COAH, his family's firm had grown into the nation's second-biggest homebuilder in its class.

Developers like the Hovnanians represent a special breed. Show them acreage and they see, not great vistas or fragile ecosystems or settings where social crusades can be won, but instead places where people can live and money can be made. Their mission is to build; it's not suburbia but opportunity itself that excites their imaginations. "He could understand the value of places that should be kept open for ballfields, or jogging trails, or picnic spots—for human use," writes Joel Garreau in *Edge City*, describing a developer much like Hovnanian. "But the idea that land should be left untouched . . . because there should be reverence to an abstract notion of the land—well, that was beyond him. He was the bringer of civilization. . . . What did they have against the works of man?" Most of Hovnanian's developments are in the suburbs. But one of the firm's best-known projects, Society Hill, a mix of market-priced and subsidized condominiums that resembles a miniature Georgetown, is situated in a Newark neighborhood that's still digging out from the 1960s riots; and another development, equally successful, is located in the tired metropolis of Jersey City. Whether land should be maintained as a tamed preserve, with multiacre lots for the rich, or instead developed intensively for the less affluent is not a very interesting question to these developers. All that matters, says Hovnanian, speaking the language of a Wharton Business School graduate, is "what the market will bear. . . . What people don't realize is that builders are not responsible for growth. We are accommodating the growth. . . . We have already made the growth versus no-growth decision. We made that when we gave birth to the baby boom. The issue now is how to accommodate them."

The Hovnanians were quick to treat the 1983 *Mount Laurel II* decision, with its promise of builder's remedies, as a cash cow. Initially, many New Jersey communities resisted the prospect of hundreds of tract townhouses, out of the plausible concerns that their public schools would be overwhelmed, their sewage systems overburdened, their last patches of greenery plowed under. But once the flood of litigation began, the Hovnanians, successful developers who preferred soft-voiced persuasion to threats of litigation, looked to be the lesser of the seemingly inevitable evils that awaited these towns. That's why, as affordable-housing lawyer and Rutgers professor John Payne points out, "Hovnanian is responsible for the single largest number of housing units built under the *Mount Laurel* doctrine."

What Ara Hovnanian has accomplished, however, is leagues removed from the vision of lawyer-progressives like Peter O'Connor and Carl Bisgaier. The developer doesn't downplay the difference or apologize for what he is doing. "Our *Mount Laurel* homes, the 20 percent of every development we must set aside for low- and moderate-income families, sell for forty to fifty thousand dollars. These are still not affordable by welfare families or the poor. They are intended for working people—teachers, firemen, nurses."

This philosophy of expanding the availability of affordable housing—not to the poor, but only to moderate-income families, who constitute a larger portion of the state's population—has become COAH's philosophy as well. "Hovnanian is not going to push for increasing the financial commitment that developers will have to make, and the rest of the council defers to him," says planner-activist Alan Mallach. The limousine that ferried Hovnanian to all the COAH meetings, and that daily delivers him from his Manhattan residence to his firm's headquarters in Red Bank, land-use lawyer John Payne wryly notes, "could probably fit three low-income housing units in the backseat."

Although Ara Hovnanian understood well how housing markets

work, he was a political novice when he joined the council. At COAH, politics became the preserve of Arthur Kondrup, once mayor of Freehold Township, who was heading the Housing and Development Division of the state's Department of Community Affairs when Governor Kean appointed him chairman of the council. Kondrup was Kean's point man, and his mission could not have been clearer: make the fair-housing issue go away politically, and make life easier for the municipalities. "My job is to reduce the trauma," Kondrup stated, and at that he did well.

Like the governor, COAH's chairman wasn't interested in reinventing the suburbs. Instead, he saw the new legislation as a charter for old-fashioned urban renewal. "Many people read *Mount Laurel* to mean that we had to build a whole lot of houses in the suburbs. What the law said is, 'That's crazy. Let's build some of those houses where they are needed, in the cities, where they have been needed all along,' " Kondrup explained to a local reporter, rewriting the history of the litigation. He also labored to lower expectations. In the spring of 1986, when the new agency announced that, statewide, New Jersey needed 145,000 affordable new houses—a figure more than 100,000 lower than the number earlier arrived at by Judge Serpentelli's "consensus methodology" planners—Kondrup hastened to assure local officials that even this reduced figure was just a target, not a realistic goal.

To handle the daily operations of the new agency, Kondrup named Douglas Opalski the agency's first executive director. More Jersey politics: previously, Opalski had been a legislative aide to Senator John Lynch of New Brunswick, and then he became planning director of Middlesex County, which Senator Lynch also represents. The senator had been the pivotal legislative figure in manufacturing the political compromise on affordable housing; in his capacity as mayor of New Brunswick, he also was eager to extract money for urban construction from this new law. Now his alter ego was executive director of COAH, and the suspicion in Trenton was that this appointment had been arranged between Kean and Lynch even before Arthur Kondrup was appointed as head of COAH.

Emulating his new boss, Opalski spent a lot of time explaining why the council achieved so little. For one thing, he said, urbanites just don't want to venture into the suburbs. "They're worried about moving costs, dislocation, and the fear of being social pioneers." For another, he insisted, the agency's job was only to encourage "realistic opportunities," not to build housing.

After New Jersey's building boom ended in the late 1980s, Opalski had a new and more persuasive explanation for the state's do-little record on affordable housing: the real problem was the economy. As he told a *New York Times* reporter in 1990: "This isn't a perfect process, but it's the best we know. . . . It is an extraordinary thing that these homes are being built at all, because housing is essentially a market-driven process." That proposition was true enough as far as it went. Yet even under ideal market conditions, rental housing was needed for the significant numbers of poor families who couldn't be expected to scrape together even a modest downpayment on a home purchase. Affordable housing for the poor would have required pressing for public subsidies for private builders or rent subsidies for the indigent. While COAH flirted with requiring town plans to include rental housing, the agency backed off when the suburbs bristled.

In 1993, the second in command at COAH, Art Bernard, succeeded Opalski. Bernard's career at the agency had focused on generating the target figures for affordable housing. He has worked closely with the Rutgers University Center for Urban Policy Research, an institution known for its hostility to the courts' approach to zoning. The administrator and the academics have generated formulas for allocating to particular townships fair shares so complicated that neither local officials nor civil-rights groups can readily decode them.

The power of COAH resides substantially in its own obscurantism and fetishism for detail. As the housing activists and developers have learned, it's not worth spending the hours and hours required to get two more units, possibly ten, in a town plan that the agency approves.

There has been relatively little low- and moderate-income housing built in New Jersey since the Fair Housing Act was passed in 1985. According to a state report titled "The Math of *Mount Laurel*," by 1993 about 14,000 units of "*Mount Laurel* housing" had been or were being built, and of these just 8,000 represented completed new housing. Meanwhile, though, the official estimate of the state's unmet housing need became the incredible shrinking number.

The planners who gathered in 1984 in Judge Serpentelli's courtroom to devise a "consensus methodology" projected the statewide need at 240,000 units. Then, in 1987, COAH chopped this number by nearly 100,000, to 145,000. In 1993, the council slashed its estimate even more, to just 85,000. At this rate, even if not a single new unit gets built, the state should be prepared to announce a housing surplus as the millennium approaches. (This may sound absurd, but it isn't so far off the official mark. COAH predicted in 1987 that within six years' time 61,000 units would "filter down" to the poor, partly through what the analysts, indulging in a bit of unintended whimsy, called "spontaneous rehabilitation.")

These calculations tally decrepit homes, not poor people—buildings, not pocketbooks—and this is one reason why the estimates of need are so very low. Even as COAH claims that the state needs 83,000 more units, the state's Department of Community Affairs estimates that well over six hundred thousand New Jersey households presently pay more than 30 percent of what they earn on housing. That is a standard benchmark of what's affordable; and, since the *Mount Laurel* doctrine has more to do with poor people than tumbledown residences, it's also a better estimate of the size of the problem. When COAH systematically disregards the economic plight of so many state residents as it does, the agency is only making life easier for towns that want to keep out the poor.

Townships' fair-share numbers came crashing down as far and as fast as did the stock market after Black Monday of 1929. Princeton, which once had worried that Judge Serpentelli's order might result in housing that interfered with the view from its historic Revolutionary War battle-field, saw its fair-share calculation cut by nearly three-quarters, from 800 to 215. The village of Cranbury, a few miles down the road, had antici-pated having to make room for more than 800 units of affordable hous-ing, over 4,000 new units in all, a prospect that chilled the hearts and fired the political passions of residents who enlisted the deities of History on their side. But COAH's quota for Cranbury was less than a quarter of what the court planners had come up with, just 187 units, and even this comparatively modest number was more than double the final figure. By the time Cranbury had reduced its quota through rehabilitations and rentals, then paid the derelict city of Perth Amboy two million dollars to take half of its remaining obligation under a regional contribution agree-ment, and then authorized a project for senior citizens, that figure had dropped to a mere 40 units. There was more good news for the town: half of these units, COAH agreed, could be reserved for people with local ties, teachers, police officers, and firefighters, as well as the grown-up children and the retired parents of the current generation of Cranbury homeown-ers. Not a single poor person, it was confidently predicted, would move into Cranbury because of how it met its fair-housing obligations. Even Peter Garibaldi, the senator and mayor from nearby Monroe, whose demagogic "I'd go to jail" speeches were so reminiscent of George Wal-lace, expressed his pleasure at how life under COAH was turning out.

One explanation for these differences between judicial and adminis-trative numbers is that the methodology devised by Judge Serpentelli's cadre was necessarily soft. "Best guess" captures the flavor of this enter-prise better than "methodology," which smacks too much of science. As housing-law specialist John Payne of Rutgers Law School points out: "You can never remove the fair-share estimate from its political determi-nants. . . . That COAH could manipulate the numbers as easily as it did— with the assistance, I'm sorry to say, of the [Rutgers] Center for Urban Policy Research—suggests that the methodology is . . . so squishy that it doesn't guarantee objectivity. So long as one knows the outcome one wants, there are lots of defensible ways" to get there, and well-paid consul-tants, speaking with the imprimatur of the university, prepared to provide the road map.

Mostly, though, what has changed is the politics of affordable housing. The lower numbers are what a succession of governors, legislators, municipal leaders, and suburban voters wanted, and the agency has had little choice but to oblige. Flashes of administrative bravery have led only to being disciplined by the politicians. When, for instance, COAH approved a plan that included demolishing existing structures so that the built-up town of Fanwood, with almost no empty land, could nonetheless make room for some affordable housing, the press took notice: "Buildings Razed to Make Way for Low Income Housing," the headlines read, and the legislature leaped into action, overruling the council.

The Fanwood fiasco was COAH's coming of age, as council members and staffers acquired a sense of how the noisome politics of *Mount Laurel* could invade even their antiseptic sanctuary. From the other side, the pro-housing side, there has been little pressure to expand opportunities for the poor. While one appellate court overturned, as irrational, a COAH-made rule that no township could ever be required to provide for more than a thousand units of affordable housing, such decisions have been judicial rarities. The signal from the judges and the politicians has been that administrative activism is risky, passivity the safer course.

Across the state, regional contribution agreements have proven a popular way for communities like Cranbury, bent on preservation, to halve their affordable housing obligations. The cities are where the poor have historically congregated, and their tax bases are pitifully low. Consequently, cities remain desperate for any help with housing, and so they have fought for the crumbs.

New Brunswick had also pursued Cranbury's RCA allotment, for instance, but it was underbid by Perth Amboy. That outcome infuriated John Lynch, COAH's angel in the legislature, who is both New Brunswick's mayor and its state senator. But Lynch's hometown has done well in subsequent RCA deals—four of them to date, amounting to $7.65 million for 406 units, a fraction of the half a billion dollars the city has secured in the last twenty years (from local foundations and Rutgers University, among other sources) to try raising New Brunswick from the dying. Only Paterson and Newark, two bigger cities with even worse problems of blight, have done better with RCAs. Statewide, by 1994 seventy-five million dollars had flowed from suburbs to cities in thirty-nine regional contribution agreements. As a result, nearly 4,000 units will be built or, more typically, rebuilt.

To many economists, these regional contribution agreements make sense because the cities and the suburbs are getting what each wants: more housing for the former, no poor neighbors for the latter. Besides, as the pragmatists have contended, few poor city dwellers really wish to live in WASPish enclaves like Cranbury. Although the city-suburb deals haven't given municipalities enough money to construct new housing—a typical contribution runs to less than twenty-five thousand dollars a unit, less than half of what it would cost to build, but roughly the cost of rehabilitating, such a unit—the pocketful of dollars has meant, at least, that worn-out urban housing could be brought back to life. If the *Mount Laurel* doctrine and the legislation are seen as focusing on the production of affordable housing, RCAs are a critical aspect of the scheme.

But those who read *Mount Laurel* as a civil-rights case that stands for a vital constitutional principle see this commerce in a darker, more Faustian light. The RCAs have undermined one of the goals of the litigation, the racial and economic integration of the suburbs. Instead, city housing is being rebuilt, which, as Peter O'Connor and his colleagues in Camden predicted a generation earlier, will never solve the problems of the poor. As a study by the Princeton Urban and Regional Research Center concludes: "The Court is quite explicit about its intent to encourage the dispersion of some lower-income residents. . . . In fact the Court was really more concerned with economic integration than with housing provision, because if housing had been concerned, there would have been no reason to focus so heavily on construction in the suburbs."

Planner Alan Mallach lives with this tension between the realpolitik of RCAs, which means getting more housing for the poor under *any* circumstances, and the principled politics of racial justice. The onetime plaintiffs' expert witness in exclusionary-zoning litigation has become the housing director for Trenton, a city that plays daytime host to state-government officials who nightly scurry back to their suburbs. Trenton has learned to take advantage of regional contribution agreements, so far amounting to one and one-third million dollars, to underwrite some of its own housing. "As a Trenton official, I have an obligation to do whatever I can to make Trenton a better place," Mallach says. "That means taking RCA money. . . . But taking a step back, it gets more complicated."

For their part, officials in Mount Laurel Township, whose long-ago dispute with Ethel Lawrence and Peter O'Connor over thirty-six garden apartments set the affordable-housing issue in train, closely watched what COAH was doing and perceived the new fair-share quotas as an opportunity to exhume supposedly settled matters. These politicians had settled their case with the plaintiffs in 1985. But once the agency's numbers came out, they gave some thought to returning to court, so that the new, lower quota for their township could be substituted for the figure on which they had agreed. Ethel Lawrence was irate when she heard about this threat. "It's a stall, stall, stall tactic . . . and they're playing a very dirty game."

Whatever Happened to Race?

By and large, the state Supreme Court has distanced itself from these proceedings. In *Mount Laurel III*, the justices deferred to the legislature in authorizing regional contribution agreements, and deferred again when

COAH used out-of-date figures to calculate the state's overall need for affordable housing. Chief Justice Wilentz has not written another word on the topic.

But in 1990, the court gingerly returned to the fray. The justices held that, with COAH's guidance, municipalities could impose fees on developers to finance affordable housing. Then, three years later, the high court reversed a COAH regulation for the first time, and in doing so returned to the integrationist theme of *Mount Laurel.* The council could not permit a township to favor insiders by setting aside half its affordable-housing quota for people with local ties, the justices ruled, because such a preference "excludes from eligibility . . . members of the class for whose benefit the obligation to construct that housing was established" in the Fair Housing Act. The focus of the opinion was the *Mount Laurel* doctrine itself, as the court repeatedly pointed out how the state's constitution defined "general welfare" in regional, not town-specific, terms. If COAH sputters, another round of judicial intervention may be in the offing.

As the 1980s ended, even as the Council on Affordable Housing kept approving townships' plans and adopting regulations, the housing market in New Jersey collapsed. Although this downturn affected much of the nation, whenever the demand for new housing slows, developers cast about for someone to blame, and in New Jersey the council and the *Mount Laurel* doctrine came in for criticism. Too much bureaucracy and too many requirements, some builders were saying, meant less building.

It was ironic that those who had once relied so heavily on the *Mount Laurel* doctrine were now arrayed against it, but the situation was truly very different. The slothful economy and a cautious council gave townships a chance to plan for their futures, and for the first time many were facing up to their fair-share obligations. Affordable housing was now on the table in every negotiation for a zoning variance or other township-planning approval. Yet from the developers' perspective, subsidies had become even scarcer, since state money generated by the real-estate transfer tax had largely dried up as homes went unsold; costs were high; competition was tight, because houses built a few years earlier remained on the market; and profit margins had become microchip thin. For a suburb to insist on affordable housing in these circumstances jeopardized the enterprise; developers were better off looking elsewhere for opportunities to build. On all these matters, neither the courts nor COAH had a ready response.

To depend on builders' incentives as a way of providing poor families with housing, as *Mount Laurel II* and the Fair Housing Act both do, works well enough in prosperous times, because then it is possible to piggyback on developers' obvious incentives to build. In times of recession, though, these incentives disappear. If affordable housing really is a matter of the state's constitutional "general welfare," as the New Jersey

Supreme Court has twice said, then building such housing should not depend entirely on the vagaries of the market. Public dollars are needed too. In an era when helping the poor is derided as pork-barrel politics, it may require another court order, perhaps a decision that puts housing on a par, constitutionally, with public education, to prise open the treasury. Someday, perhaps, there will be a *Mount Laurel IV*.

Proceedings before the Council on Affordable Housing, attorney Stephen Eisdorfer observes, were as well choreographed as a medieval mystery play. Eisdorfer, who specialized in *Mount Laurel*–type matters for the Public Advocate, first in the courtroom and later in COAH hearings, recalls delivering the identical message in each of his appearances before the council. The redundancy, he felt, approached tedium. An effective *Mount Laurel* remedy must go beyond rewriting a zoning ordinance to compel the construction of housing, Eisdorfer kept saying. Moreover, *Mount Laurel* is not concerned only with housing but is also supposed to undo segregation. "*Mount Laurel* is about race."

For his part, COAH chairman Arthur Kondrup always delivered the same response. The amiable politician complimented the advocate for his refreshing—and surprising—presentations. The beat of a metronome, Eisdorfer knew, only surprises someone who has not become accustomed to it. That his arguments seemed perpetually to startle COAH members made him feel as if he were speaking to them in a language other than English—a language they had no hope of understanding; a language that New Jersey's governor, legislature, and well-to-do suburbanites, who had wound up the council members and then set them in motion, never really intended them to learn.

PART THREE
FORBIDDEN NEIGHBORS IN SUBURBIA

There are people who are attracted by the permanence of stone. They would like to be solid and impenetrable, they do not want change: for who knows what change might bring? . . . They have no wish to acquire ideas, they want them to be innate . . . they want to adopt a life . . . in which one never becomes anything else but what one already was.

Jean-Paul Sartre, *Portrait of an Anti-Semite*

The story is, really, the battle over who we are, how we got that way, where we're headed, what we value, a geography of the soul. . . . We shape our houses, then they shape us.

Tony Hiss, *The Experience of Place*

8

Virtual Housing

When he sat for an interview with a reporter from the *New York Times* one muggy day in the summer of 1993, Henry Cisneros was visibly frustrated. The secretary of housing and urban development—President Clinton's brightest Hispanic hope, policy wonk, *and* charismatic politician, the man with the matinee-idol looks who, as mayor of San Antonio, revitalized that city—had returned to government from self-imposed exile with an immodest ambition.

Cisneros intended to do no less than remap the social landscape to give racial minorities and poor people the chance for a decent life, yet at every turn he was being thwarted. Inside his bloated department, he was being stalled by a bureaucracy that had been slighted by every president since Richard Nixon, battered by revelations of mismanagement during the Reagan years, and so had come to exalt rules over results. Form is conventionally supposed to follow function, but at HUD form had *become* function. On those days when Cisneros the can-do manager cruised the corridors of his empty empire, what he mostly found were officials who fetishized paperwork in hopes of evading new accusations.

Nor were the external political signals any more promising. While a Democrat occupied the White House and Democrats controlled both houses of Congress, party unity did not translate into a government run from the center with parliamentary smoothness. On the contrary, the calculus of self-interest and business-as-usual reigned inside the beltway, together with a kind of moral stupor. Seemingly nothing could be accomplished—neither the simple justice of ending discrimination against gays in the military nor the more complex justice required to overhaul the nation's health-care system. With the president deeply engaged in the public business of finding his own center, the federal role in housing was nowhere to be spotted on the national agenda. The broader idea of revitalizing communities, with which Cisneros was concerned, seemed to have disappeared like Alice through the looking glass.

The Unmentionable Topic

The HUD secretary used his *New York Times* interview—one of the few occasions he has received national press attention for his policies, rather than his personal life—to talk about racism in the United States. Cisneros had a sweeping argument to make to the *Times* reporter, that racism was "a malignancy . . . the great Achilles' heel of our nation's future." More to the point, racism was a way of life that had been sustained by half a century of federal housing policy, shaped by a desire, as the HUD secretary phrased it, "to just put them on the other side of the tracks and keep them there." In coming to terms with the prevailing social disarray, Cisneros acknowledged that "questions of behavior and individual responsibility"—teen pregnancy, crime, drugs, family break-up—made a difference, as did social class, the prime culprit fingered by sociologist William Julius Wilson in his influential book *The Declining Significance of Race*. But all these explanations were subordinate to racism in the U.S. equation.

Race is not a matter of "diminishing significance," Cisneros said, for it occupies "the very core of the problems which confront America's urban areas." First, government had built the ghettos, and then it locked the gates. As sociologists Douglas Massey and Nancy Denton point out in *American Apartheid: Segregation and the Making of the Underclass*, "during the 1970s and 1980s, a word disappeared from the American vocabulary . . . segregation." Cisneros believed that Washington could make a start in opening these gates by bringing together blacks, whites, Latinos, and Asians—specifically, by tempting well-to-do suburbs like Mount Laurel with subsidies to underwrite affordable housing, as well as by delivering housing vouchers that poor people trapped in cities like Camden could use to rent their own suburban homes.

There were modest successes that the HUD secretary could report. Negotiations were under way to coax Detroit's suburbs into taking on a bigger share of subsidized housing, in a region whose central city appears beyond the possibility of rejuvenation. Newly introduced federal legislation proposed "community banks" to underwrite more affordable homes. Cisneros had reversed an earlier HUD decision to expand a public-housing development in Dallas because the plan concentrated too many poor people and minorities in a single place; and in a matter of months, a federal force would be sent to Plano, Texas, protecting black families who had dared move into what had been all-white public housing, only to be driven off, fearful for their lives.

Yet these steps barely traced out a beginning. "I'm not naive about how difficult this is. I know people tire of hearing of the role of race," Cisneros said, "and suburban settings don't want to accept public housing." The opinion polls bore out his contention. While black families mostly don't like living in ghettos—they'd prefer neighborhoods that are between a quarter and a half black—whites say they don't want to coexist with more than a handful of black families, 10 percent at most. The incompatibility of those desires means that a racially balanced community is almost inevitably a community in transition, on its way to becoming a ghetto.

When it comes to social policy, suburbanites regularly confuse race with hopeless poverty, turn impoverishment into a mark of Cain, and construct a conventional wisdom out of fearful tales. But the housing market is made up of builders, bankers, and brokers, not moral philosophers; it is driven by preferences and dollars, not visions of what's just. Seven out of eight white suburbanites have chosen to live in neighborhoods that are less than 1 percent black. The policymakers Cisneros decries, who promoted this version of apartheid, aren't about to reverse course—on the contrary, in the aftermath of the 1994 GOP landslide, leading Republicans proposed eliminating HUD entirely, and President Clinton considered a 33 percent budget cut.

A senior staffer with the National Housing Law Center, which helps attorneys to prepare lawsuits that are meant to open up housing opportunities for the poor, enthused that Henry Cisneros's 1993 proposals represented "the most important shift in [federal] housing policy in twenty-five years." Indeed, not for a quarter of a century has Washington paid the slightest attention to integrating the suburbs. What Secretary Cisneros had to say calls to mind the hopes of previous occupants of the HUD secretary's office—not the Reagan-era embarrassments, the cabinet member whom the president couldn't even recognize on sight and who later flirted with indictment, but able and ambitious black leaders such as Robert Weaver, the first HUD secretary and the first African American to hold any cabinet post, and Patricia Roberts Harris, who served under President Carter. Others, such as Republican presidential aspirants George Romney and Jack Kemp, used their cabinet position as a bully pulpit. "I believe that the greatest threat to this nation is the confrontation in our states and cities between the poor and minority groups, who are concentrated in great numbers in the central core of our cities, and the middle income and affluent families who live in the surrounding and separate communities. This confrontation is divisive. It is explosive. It must be resolved." *The greatest threat*: the words were George Romney's, but they could just as well have been Henry Cisneros's, so little had changed in the intervening years.

Does Anyone Have a Dream?

Each of the distinguished HUD secretaries who has served during the past three decades put forward a vision of a nation remade, structure and soul, by some combination of public beneficence and private initiative: Model Cities . . . public housing dispersed among neighborhoods, rather than concentrated in enclaves of poverty . . . urban restoration, not "Negro removal" . . . housing vouchers, which gave the poor freedom to rent where they pleased . . . private ownership of public housing. Although these visions differ from one another in their particulars, any one of them would mark a great advance over the present if brought fully to life.

Yet ever since Richard Nixon, decrying past federal blunders, declared a moratorium on federal housing aid in 1973, there has been little support from Washington for housing the poor. The last word, almost, came in the form of a syllogism from Daniel Moynihan, then President Nixon's amanuensis: "Any kind of threat situation will fail; the community will find some way either to evade or repudiate the threat. Government should not be in the business of failing; therefore it should not try threatening" as a way to open up the suburbs. As the *Wall Street Journal* reported, Nixon "draped the dreaded race-mixing shroud" over the effort to "move subsidized housing beyond city limits," and that was the end of that.

The explanation for these decades of federal inaction doesn't have much to do with the usual culprits, a failure of policy imagination or a misapprehension about the difficulties of implementing policy. Of course, government has made big mistakes in the name of promoting affordable housing. In the spring of 1994, Newark, New Jersey, literally blew up one of those mistakes when it leveled a public-housing project that in less than a lifetime had degenerated from shelter to menace. The earlier dynamiting of the Pruitt and Igoe towers in St. Louis—those massive blocks of public housing, one built for blacks and the other, across the street, for whites, deliberately demolished less than a single generation after they were built—remains vivid in the popular imagination as a symbol of how *not* to house the poor.

But no one is building Pruitt-Igoes now, or anything like them. When HUD Secretary Cisneros visited Chicago's notorious housing projects in 1994, he pronounced them "as close to the approaches to Hell as I have seen in America." If he had his way, Cisneros said, he'd blow them all sky high. Neighborhoods are no longer ripped down to be saved; skyscrapers are no longer constructed to warehouse the poor. Across the country, most of the subsidized housing that has been put up in the past decade looks more like country-club condos, or else like knockoffs of Georgetown townhouses, than like something the old Communist regimes in Eastern Europe would have built, and there are long waiting lists of families anxious to move in to these homes.

Bright ideas also abound for reinvigorating manageable-sized enclaves, with new housing built mainly by nonprofit groups and scattered inconspicuously among the old, providing more for the occupants than bricks and mortar, including job training, health clinics, neighborhood policing, nearby public schools operated as day-long centers for child minding as well as education. A number of those bright ideas are already written into law, but not one of them has ever received adequate financial support, and their present prospects are especially bleak.

"There is rarely one right solution to a complex social problem," writes historian Garry Wills, in an essay about the nature of urban blight.

"But when people want to solve the problem, even bad programs can be made to work. Their successful aspects are recognized and built on; their detrimental ones downplayed. . . . Besides, those anxious to address the problem do not rely on one approach, and then drop the whole matter if it fails. They keep pushing ahead with whatever tools are at hand.

"Conversely, even a good program will fail if people do not really want a problem to disappear. Why were so many good intentions and mobilized resources so quickly dropped in dealing with poverty as it affects blacks? The answer is not in the conceptual details of this or that program. The answer is racism."

A generation ago, housing economist Anthony Downs wrote a book titled *Opening up the Suburbs*. Downs envisioned a coalition of profit-motivated builders and construction workers, overtaxed homeowners and the ill-housed poor in the cities, suburb-bound corporations wanting to assure a supply of housing for their employees, liberal-opinion leaders and suburban malcontents. "They could muster great political strength if they organized effectively behind key dispersal policies," he believed. But there is no such coalition and probably never will be—indeed, even to talk about "dispersal" or "opening up the suburbs" invites political suicide.

Most people, including most of the suburbanites whom Henry Cisneros hopes to persuade, are pretty satisfied with things as they are and wish only for more of the same. New houses have gotten bigger and bigger, averaging over two thousand square feet in 1990, and consequently less affordable, even as families have become ever smaller. More communities, and not just the wealthiest either, are building electrified fences and posting security patrols to keep outsiders away. "Edge cities" are rising, invented landscapes economically and socially independent of the older metropolises.

What truly terrifies suburbanites is the idea of a future imposed from outside, whether it be a fair-share future of the kind the New Jersey Supreme Court contemplated in its first two *Mount Laurel* rulings or the racially integrated future upon which HUD Secretary Cisneros futilely pinned his hopes. When they hear terms like *public housing,* they do not imagine country-club condos for the less well off, because such successes never figure on the nightly TV news. Instead, they envision the worst urban nightmares transported to their backyards, South Central Los Angeles visited on Orange County, Camden in Bedminster. They see the graffiti on the wall, an end to a way of life that is already under siege from other quarters.

A quarter of a century ago in Mount Laurel, the black congregation of Jacob's Chapel A.M.E. Church bluntly was told that they had effectively been priced out of their hometown and that the township would take no steps to ease their plight. But the engine of economics grinds on impersonally, continually creating new haves and have-lesses. Since 1980, the cost of housing has risen two and a half times faster than earnings, and not only the poor have been affected. Some housing economists argue that, with relatively few people still living in dilapidated dwellings, the real issue is redistributing income, not developing shelter. In fact, neither is happening: little affordable housing is being built, and the gap between rich and poor has widened. As a consequence, those capacious homes in suburbs like Mount Laurel are priced out of the reach of many of the *children* of the homeowners whose interests town officials had protected, who are now ready to plant their own suburban roots.

The dream persists of "a suburban innocence . . . where the everyday creates a sense of protective closure." The reality, though, is more menacing, marked by the suburban scourges of our time, drug dealers and drive-by shootings, contract killings and gang rapes in communities that fantasized they were Edenic in their innocence. If it wasn't for the highways, people say, these intrusions wouldn't have happened, forgetting that the highways are what made these towns burgeon in the first place. The unlocked front door is a barely remembered custom of the past. Now public schools are installing metal detectors to spot weapons, and some school buses have hidden cameras to monitor the young for signs of trouble.

Unlike these menaces of macroeconomics and modernism, more shadowy and elusive, what gets called "public housing" poses a tangible threat that the embattled residents can hope to stop. In *Cities without Suburbs*, a book published to considerable attention in 1993, David Rusk urged nothing less than doing away with the suburbs, folding the city and its surrounding towns into a single metropolis. Such communities, Rusk points out, "elastic" cities like Houston and Albuquerque (of which he was mayor), have consistently been economic winners with strong growth records and resilient industries. They have also been less racially segregated places than "inelastic" cities like Detroit or Camden, which are separated by a *cordon sanitaire* from the suburbs. The suburbs themselves also benefit from being part of this healthier economic mix, Rusk argues, and so it is foolish to rebuild the Camdens—to create urban tax havens, "enterprise zones," as a way of attracting businesses—since "bad communities defeat good programs."

Though this is interesting stuff for the policy maven, it's simply not going to happen. During the past two generations, even as some inner suburbs like Evanston, adjacent to Chicago, and White Plains, outside New York City, have witnessed an influx of blacks, the outer precincts have fought off every effort to prise them open, whether initiated by judges, politicians, or developers, whether laced with requirements or sweetened with incentives. As suburbanites' political power keeps growing—in 1992, for the first time, they cast the majority of votes in a presidential election—

the lines between city and suburb, sometimes approximating apartheid, seem likely to sharpen.

The story in New Jersey might well have turned out differently, for the state was poised on the brink of a future in which communities would be committed to the principle of fair shares for the well off and the poor alike. But then the justices and the politicians—critically, Governor Thomas Kean and Chief Justice Robert Wilentz—drew back from that bold new conception of the commonweal.

As governor, Thomas Kean said that he believed in helping to house the poor, as long as they remained in urban areas and didn't move to suburbia. When the sweeping 1983 *Mount Laurel II* court decree was handed down, with its push for social intermixing, he derided it as "communistic." But Kean killed neither the *Mount Laurel* concept nor its judicial messenger. Instead, he transformed the court's housing-plus-integration message into a more modest housing initiative that has helped people of moderate means and the cities. After leaving Trenton in 1989, Kean became a university president in the familiar manner of politicians-in-waiting. He hoped for much more—for the vice-presidential nomination on George Bush's 1988 ticket, for a position in the bipartisan cabinet Bill Clinton promised four years later—and his political ambitions have remained alive through the Clinton presidency.

In 1990, President Bush appointed Kean to chair the federal Advisory Commission on Regulatory Barriers to Affordable Housing, one of those consolation-prize positions that fill up ex-politicians' days. The former governor used this occasion to position himself as a leading voice in the more liberal, *Politics of Inclusion* wing of his national party, pushing a commission's report that recommended wholesale revisions in the country's zoning laws. "Millions of Americans are priced out of buying or renting the kind of housing they otherwise could afford, were it not for a web of government regulations." That sentiment, which suggested opening up the suburbs, might have been penned by Robert Wilentz.

While in recent years the U.S. Supreme Court has been mainly a voice for reaction, Chief Justice Wilentz and the New Jersey Supreme Court have remained committed to promoting equality. Education, not housing, has become the focus of judicial attention, as it was a generation ago. When the state was brought to court, it defended a financing system that shortchanged the cities by arguing that students in benighted districts like Camden "simply cannot benefit from the kind of vastly superior course offerings found in the richer districts," and that the "education currently offered in these poorer . . . districts is tailored to the students' present need." This argument is reminiscent of the discredited proposition, put forward in the affordable-housing litigation, that poor families were really better off staying in the cities because they were unfit for suburban life, and the Supreme Court was having none of it. In 1991, the justices demanded that the state boost the school budgets of desperate cities like Newark and Camden. The state moved to close the gap, but in 1994 the court demanded more: "substantial equivalence" among all school districts.

Even broader universes of injustice were on the mind of Chief Justice Wilentz, who took up this theme in an emotional speech at Rutgers Law School's 1990 commencement. The message was less a judge's than a martyred black preacher's proclaiming his famous dream. "New Jersey today, like much of this country, is a collection of islands," Wilentz declared, "white islands and black islands, not happy with each other at all, potentially hostile, a black and Hispanic population overwhelmingly and disastrously poor, a white population trying to have ends meet, not having it easy at all.

"Our separateness is frightening. The problem is deep, severe, crippling to a good society, and we are a good society. The separateness of our society is horrible, and it is not getting better. We must not become blind to it. We must see it and we must deal with it. Not in order to become rich, not in order to become safe, not even to be fair—although all of that—but to be a happy society, at home with each other, at ease with each other, friends and neighbors, not enemies: not at arm's length but hand in hand.

"The causes are complex but at this point in our history we don't need to fix blame. There is enough to go around for all of us. *We need to fix society."*

Such calls to rebuild Jerusalem are out of fashion these days, when the very idea of our being a "good society," a city on a hill, commands little credence. Compassion, once a byword, has become a political liability. In 1994, for the first time since opinion polls started measuring such things, a majority of whites stated that equal rights have been pushed too far; black Americans have done well enough, nearly six whites in ten believed, and public support for social welfare programs has fallen precipitously. Yet it is vital that the idealists keep talking the talk, whether they are wearing judges' black robes like Robert Wilentz or pinstriped suits and power ties like Henry Cisneros. It is important, too, that the structures with which to reimagine the nation's communities—court rulings like *Mount Laurel*, administrative machinery, and grants programs—be encoded into the law, to be relied upon in more public-minded times.

"In no other country in the world," Alexis de Tocqueville pointed out a century and a half ago in *Democracy in America*, "has the principle of association been more successfully used or applied to a greater multitude of objects than in America. . . . *When help was needed, [Americans] hardly ever failed to give each other trusty support"* (emphasis added). If the Republic is going to change—to recognize that help is needed and to respond in a "trusty" manner—neither messianic leaders nor new institutional structures will be enough. Real change, if it happens, will mainly take place town by town: in cities like Camden, made less phantasmagorical block by block, and in suburbs like Mount Laurel that come to accept more than token numbers of poor families who share their hopes for the future. In such places, amazingly enough, people who dream of sheetrock—people like Peter O'Connor and Ethel Lawrence—are still at work.

9

House of Dreams

The fates of Mount Laurel and Camden, so intimately joined in the years leading up to the landmark litigation that bears the suburb's name, have remained linked in the decades since. Even as the city has continued its free fall, becoming the region's dumping grounds, the suburb has grown and prospered.

In this apparently inexorable process, all the court rulings appeared irrelevant and all the visionaries' hopes seemed doomed to remain on the drawing boards. Yet very recently a historic preservation project turned one Camden neighborhood into a place where people might actually want to live. That project also generated some of the funds that might make housing for poor families a bricks-and-glass reality in Mount Laurel.

Camden: "God Would Scream"

Camden literally passed through the fires during the 1960s, but to the indefatigable optimists who inhabited the city, subsequent years offered hope for yet another revival. There was talk of major new construction, brave talk even of being the next Baltimore. Some housing for poor families was in fact constructed, and, more recently, a Baltimore-style aquarium opened in a bid for tourists. Politics changed too, as the dispossessed took charge of city hall.

None of this, however, is remotely sufficient to rewrite a script that was, and still is, being written elsewhere—by indifferent if not hostile lawmakers in Trenton who have starved the city; by company executives who have talked of city renewal while planning their own getaways; and by intractably hostile suburbanites who have been willing to give the city only their garbage.

In the early 1970s, as Camden was digging itself out of the riot-caused rubble, the first promising news had to do with the end of a lawsuit. The blockbuster case brought against the city by Peter O'Connor and the Legal Services office in 1970, which had halted all urban-renewal construction—the litigation that some people believed had done in the city—was settled two years later. With that agreement, development could finally go forward, this time taking into account the needs of the poor.

There was also good news on the political front: Angelo Errichetti, who for years had run the Democratic Party from the back rooms, was elected mayor in 1973. The onetime Camden High football star worked his way up the party ladder as a good old boy; during the 1960s, as longtime mayor Alfred Pierce lost his interest in running things and started spending all his days on the links, Errichetti became the man to see. He backed Joe Nardi, a young lawyer, to succeed Pierce as mayor, but once in office Nardi was overwhelmed, a gentle man unsuited for the times who couldn't cope with the race riots and the urban-renewal lawsuit. Unceremoniously, Errichetti pushed aside his protégé to take over city hall himself. A few years later, he expanded his political portfolio by getting elected to the state senate as well, and he quickly became one of the people to see in Trenton as well as in Camden.

Errichetti had his own wish list for the city, which included a middle-income community along the Delaware River facing the Philadelphia skyline, a three-hundred-acre port with a new neighborhood growing up alongside, a thirty-five-million-dollar city hall–shopping mall complex that would revive downtown, a Veterans Administration hospital, and block-by-block rehabilitation of Camden's neighborhoods through city homesteading. Yet as so often has happened in Camden, few of these hopes were ever realized.

The real innovation was in how Camden was run, as local politics began to reflect the changing racial and ethnic character of the city. "I inherited a place where the minorities were in an uproar," Errichetti says. "When you go through a social revolution and you have cities aflame, whose fault is that? When the revolution was over, I recognized the change. It was no longer a city of all white people." The old-line politicians were eased out, and in their place Errichetti appointed leaders of the Black People's Unity Movement (BPUM) and of Puerto Rican neighborhood organizations, people who until then had known city hall only when they were filing lawsuits or organizing protests. One of BPUM's founders, Randy Primas, whose family had lived in Camden for four generations, was picked as deputy mayor, and in 1981 he succeeded Errichetti as mayor. Errichetti's administrative assistant and director of community development came from the Puerto Rican community, as did members of the city's zoning board and of the housing authority. The mayor, who began his career in the Tammany Hall tradition of boss politics, recreated himself as an ethnic John Lindsay.

Equally remarkable was the identity of Mayor Errichetti's top policy aide: Peter O'Connor. The two men had started off badly—"that dirtball," Errichetti called O'Connor, and the insult was returned in kind—yet during the negotiations to settle the 1970 lawsuit they had come to see past their differences in style, to appreciate each other's talent for getting things done. The outsiders had become the insiders in Camden by the mid-1970s, a transition that would recur with more or less strain in scores of cities. "I intend to put this city back on the map as the industrial hub of all New

Jersey," declared Mayor Errichetti, who still fantasized that a countywide government would come to the rescue of Camden.

These were brave words, brave thoughts too, but beyond the symbolism it was not evident that changing the type of people who ran Camden could have much impact on the life of a dying place. The last of the big stores, Lits Department Store, shut down, and so did the now derelict Walt Whitman Hotel, that marvel of an age when the Ben Franklin Bridge, its span dedicated by a president, was still new. Migration to the suburbs was unceasing. Three-quarters of Camden County's population lived in the suburbs in 1975, and Cherry Hill, much of which was farmland a generation earlier, had nearly as many residents as Camden itself.

On a crisp November Sunday in 1991, Campbell Soup razed its old manufacturing plant in downtown Camden. So expertly placed were the explosives that in a matter of seconds the six-story buildings were reduced to rubble. Four red-and-white Campbell Soup cans, each about twenty-five feet high, Warholesque icons that had decorated the main building for generations, fell gracelessly to earth and were crushed upon impact. No one among the corporate strategists at Campbell had paused to think of the sentimental value, the *kitsch* value, of those trademark cans.

Camden's state assembly member, Wayne Bryant, an African American whose family has lived in the city for several generations, had no time for sentimentality. "The manufacturing era is dying," he said. "We're now bringing in high-tech jobs, preparing for the future." So far, though, the promise of new jobs is just another in the litany of promises that has been Camden's lot, for Camden is not Silicon Valley East but Salvage City. The Campbell Soup factory was the last major manufacturing operation in town. Now the city's chief industry is collecting scrap like those oversized soup cans, more than a million tons each year, sending it away to make something else in some other place.

Even in broadest daylight, Camden looks like the set for a post-apocalypse film, *Terminator* come to New Jersey. Chiseled into the granite walls of city hall, those fine lines about the virtues of *civitas* lifted from native son Walt Whitman's *Leaves of Grass* mock the urban enterprise. "No legacy is so rich as honesty," says the north face; on the opposite side of the building, unnoticed by the petitioners who daily enter that building to seek some official favor, the text reads: "In a dream I saw a city invincible." Attached to the base of city hall is a shack, grandiosely named Ye Olde Shoe Shine Parlor, which does a brisk business.

Across the road, adjacent to the Hall of Justice, is the city jail. At night the wives and mothers and lovers of the prisoners come to the street below, to communicate in a kind of Morse code with those who are incarcerated. A state prison was built in downtown Camden early in the 1980s, and so was a county jail. Although some things, like the prison and the

jailhouse, are up-to-date in Camden, almost none of them herald a rebirth. A sewage-treatment plant in the city, built during the last decade,
processes the fifty-five million gallons of waste generated daily by inhabitants throughout Camden County. It replaced forty-six local treatment
plants, which were shut down when suburbanites voiced concerns about
environmental degradation in their own towns. The city also houses a
facility that burns all the trash from the suburbs, fifteen hundred tons a
day. On a typical working day, 127 trucks drive through Camden bound
for the incinerator, and when the wind is blowing the wrong way the
stench is everywhere.

Sewage, trash, and prisoners—who are regarded as human debris
in the blunt political calculus of the unwanted—do not describe the future that Camden had in mind for itself. Every one of these deals represents the terrible price the city has been forced to pay for its annual
handout from the state. Each demonstrates the city's underlying and
irresolvable problem—while local needs are crushing, the perpetually
shrinking local tax base generates barely a sixth of the city's operating
budget, even though the property-tax rate is the highest in the state. All
these miseries, the sewer plant and the trash-burning plant and the two
jails, were inflicted on Camden by cold calculation: the state needed to
locate unwanted activities somewhere, and the city had no choice.

The 1970 lawsuit challenging the city's urban-renewal plan was intended to make low-income housing part of the grandiose plans being
bandied about. But another harsh irony is that, for almost a quarter of a
century, low-income housing was the *only* housing that got built. On the
waterfront where the 1960s moguls envisioned City Centre stands River-
view, which provides apartments for seniors of modest means. The complex is framed with barbed wire to protect its elderly occupants from all
that lies outside, and next door, Mickle Tower, which houses a hundred
poor families, is similarly defended. A few blocks away is Royal Court,
built as part of the settlement agreement in the Camden Coalition's 1970
lawsuit. When it opened in the mid-1970s, it too was supposed to deliver
home ownership to the poor, but that never came to pass. Even though
there is a two-year wait for public housing in Camden, just a handful of
Royal Court's ninety-three units are occupied; the buildings are mostly
covered with slapped-on plywood, ready for the wrecker's ball.

Royal Court squats at the entrance to the latest version of the Camden
dream, a revival of the waterfront, patterned after Harbor Place in Baltimore and run by the Cooper Ferry Development Corporation. City officials like former mayor Randy Primas hope that Camden's rebirth will
begin here and spread in concentric circles to reach the rest of the city.
Primas looks at North Camden, which never recovered after the Ben Franklin Bridge opened in 1926, and takes solace from the fact that "thirty years
ago, Baltimore was worse than North Camden is today." Cooper Ferry's

director is also an optimist. "In the past, Camden would get its act together, then a recession or a riot would hit and the players would go home. But this development is recession proof. When prosperity comes, Camden will be ready." But others, like the director of the regional port authority, have a less bright-eyed vision. "Camden is like a doughnut. Everything worthwhile is on the edges, and the center is hollow."

Grass and trees have been planted at harbor's edge, and brick walkways and plazas have been laid to form a park. A marina has been constructed, an enclosed circle of water designed to house pleasure boats, and its history offers a microcosm of what makes Camden's future so problematic. The marina was not built because of any obvious need but because federal funds were available, and it never opened. For a time, there were hopes that a Hyatt Hotel would occupy the site and operate the marina, as a 1990s version of the Walt Whitman Hotel, pride of South Jersey, but Hyatt pulled out; there was talk of a hotel and conference center, talk as well of a sports arena to lure the pro-hockey and basketball teams from Philadelphia, but no money. Barely a hundred yards away, forming an unsightly backdrop to the marina and a new twenty-five-thousand-seat waterfront amphitheater, the SONY–Blockbuster Waterfront Entertainment Centre, there stands a mountain of refuse collected by the regional port authority, an agency with its own, ruder agenda for the city.

The centerpiece of the new waterfront project is an idea lifted from Baltimore, a state-of-the-art aquarium, the country's second biggest, which opened in 1992. But Camden is no Baltimore; after an early flurry of interest, attendance has dropped well below projections, and the aquarium has had to cut back its hours of operation. Even when the crowds come, the impact on the local economy has been virtually nil. Tourists speed across the Ben Franklin Bridge directly to the aquarium, or else they take the ferry from Philadelphia, which after a forty-year hiatus started operations soon after the aquarium opened. Yet once these tourists have had their fill of pretty fish, they depart just as quickly, and almost none of them ever set foot downtown. Unlike those visitors who walked across the Ben Franklin Bridge on the day it opened nearly seventy years ago to marvel at the city they had reached—"almost like Philadelphia, only it's cleaner"—the new day-trippers have no reason to realize they have ever been to Camden at all. The waterfront project is merely a display of "gold fillings in a mouthful of decay."

On almost every conceivable index of human grief in the United States, Camden figures prominently. More violent crime was recorded in Camden in 1975 than in any other city of its size in the entire nation, a title that this city has held onto during almost all the years since—among New Jersey cities, only Newark annually records more murders and rapes, and Newark is three times bigger. Local police describe Camden as a serious contender for "the title of auto-theft champion of the United States." Its drive-by "drugstores" are a mecca for South Jersey, the Camden County prosecutor reports, and Philadelphia's dealers sometimes buy their heroin and crack there as well. Abandoned houses have been turned into shooting galleries. When the parishioners at Holy Name Church organized a protest against the drug traffic, they became targets of shotgun blasts and exploding hand grenades, vengeance wreaked by one of the thirty or forty gangs that have carved up the city.

During the early 1990s, the night before Halloween—Mischief Night, as it is locally known—became an occasion for arson and mayhem on a level not seen in Camden since the race riots a generation earlier. On Mischief Night 1991, 133 fire calls were recorded and forty-nine buildings were torched, and each year since it has taken a massive effort by police and ordinary citizens to keep such wholesale destruction from becoming the city's latest dread tradition. The police chief's rallying cry suggests not Main Street U.S.A. but a war zone: "No retreat, no surrender."

Camden has grown poorer in recent years—national reporters on the misery beat call it "Welfare City"—and smaller. A city whose population once exceeded 120,000 has lost nearly a third of its residents since 1970, and now Camden numbers barely more than 80,000 inhabitants, almost 70 percent of whom are either children or elderly. Unlike Philadelphia or New York or Boston, which have their pockets of misery, nearly all of Camden is unstable, for there is no longer a discernible middle class. Per-capita income, barely a third of nearby Cherry Hill's, falls 15 percent below Newark's, and in 1990 fewer than a hundred households in the entire city reported incomes above $50,000. Unemployment is twice the national average, a figure that understates the problem, since a disproportionate number of people in this depressed city have given up looking for jobs and have become statistically invisible. The average property value in 1990 was $25,000, compared with the statewide average of $200,000—all the property in Camden is worth less than one prime piece of Atlantic City real estate.

"With increasing poverty, new conditions come into being that recall nineteenth-century slum life," a *New York Times* reporter notes. "Firefighters tell of seeing things, while extinguishing fires, that people do not have time [or perhaps the desire] to hide: Using candles for light and kerosene or kitchen stoves for warmth." In a city where three-quarters of the population depends on some kind of public assistance to get by, Mother's Day is any day when the welfare checks arrive. The infant mortality rate, twenty in a thousand, is nearly twice the national average, more like Karachi or Cairo than Cherry Hill. The incidence of child poverty is the highest in the country: more than three children in five live below the poverty line, a rate that is more than five times higher than the national average. *Savage Inequalities,* Jonathan Kozol's indictment of urban schools, takes special aim at Camden and its overcrowded, malnourished schools, where almost one child in two quits before graduation.

"The five minute drive from Cherry Hill to Camden," Kozol writes, "is like a journey between different worlds." One black teacher with whom he talked, who had just moved his family out of Camden after his house was broken into and stripped, was resigned to what was happening to the city. "I'm not angry. What did I expect? Rats packed tight in a cage destroy each other. I got out. I do not plan to be destroyed."

These problems were partly masked during the 1970s when the city got away with spending beyond its means. But that tactic has obvious shortcomings, and when Angelo Errichetti stepped down as mayor in 1981, having been swept up in the FBI's elaborate sting operation known as ABSCAM, Camden was on the verge of bankruptcy. The city nearly doubled the property-tax rate that year, which, while helping to solve the immediate fiscal problem, undermined its longer-term economic prospects. As the state Supreme Court pointed out in *Abbott v. Burke*, a lawsuit that challenged inequities in financing New Jersey's public schools, there are no tolerable choices. "Either Camden does not raise taxes and faces long-term problems with the city's infrastructure or Camden raises taxes and faces loss of businesses and homeowners, as well as adversely affecting the ability of those who remain to pay their tax bills."

To every great need, city officials respond by saying that there simply is not enough money. Entire blocks are caving in because the antiquated sewers have deteriorated, and on some blocks there are no curbs, for the city has made a habit of cheaply repaving its collapsing streets rather than rebuilding them. The once elegant public library, built at the turn of the century with the support of financier Andrew Carnegie, has been so neglected that it is now beyond repair and must come down. Although mounds of trash line the streets and fill the vacant lots, the city can't afford to haul them all away. When *Time* magazine ran a story about Camden in 1992, it titled the piece "Who Could Live Here?" and the implicit answer was plain—only people with nowhere else to go.

Against all odds, there are still those who remain hopeful of saving the city. In recent years, BPUM, which organized protests during the 1960s, made itself over into an economic development organization, BPUM Impact Corporation, which tried and failed with the city's only Chicken George franchise and has since sought to launch an industrial park. Eight nonprofit organizations have taken on the Sisyphean task of restoring decayed houses and providing new homes to poor families. Each of these nonprofit operations—some, like Heart of Camden and Camden Lutheran Housing, organized by local churches; others, like the North Camden Land Trust, run by neighborhood groups—has the best of intentions, and each has touched those who, engaged in reconstructing the houses, have remade themselves. Yet each counts its successes only by the handful.

The result of these collaborative efforts, together with the occasional individual venture into housing rehabilitation, is a crazy quilt that only an urban pioneer could cherish. On one block of the North Camden street once known as Doctors' Row, after its prosperous turn-of-the-century occupants, four red-brick buildings with gabled roofs have been brought back to life by the North Camden Land Trust. Families have moved into these rehabilitated apartments, and, while some buildings are beyond saving, others will be renovated if the money can be found. On the very next block, though, only a couple of homes are even worth considering for restoration. A few houses have been pulled down, leaving the street looking gap toothed, and grass grows waist-high in the trash-filled lots where buildings once stood.

One step forward, two steps back: during the 1960s, a Philadelphia builder rehabilitated some of these very same homes, and others besides, with money from RCA and Campbell Soup, but in less than a generation the buildings were allowed to slip back into decay. Two haiku by Nicholas Virgilio, Camden's contemporary poet laureate, mourn the progression: "the old neighborhood / falling to the wrecking ball: names in the sidewalk" and "the old neighborhood / with fresh paint and new faces: / the whores up the street."

Camden's wreckage is also human. In the summer of 1994, Luis Galindez, the thirty-one-year-old administrator of the North Camden Land Trust, was found in his apartment, stabbed to death. The previous autumn, this street kid who had started out squatting in an abandoned home, then became a community leader, the onetime drug user who had cleaned up his act, was invited to Washington to attend Vice President Al Gore's announcement of community-bank housing legislation. "There was," a mourner said, "something about the rehabilitation of his life and the rehabilitation of the neighborhood that was interwoven," and there is as well a connection between this death and the fragility of the neighborhood.

More than 1,200 abandoned and derelict houses have been torn down in the past decade, not for some new city-in-the-city scheme but because they are unfit to be restored, and hundreds have been lit up by the fires that are almost a fixture on the city skyline. There remain standing thousands of vacant and dangerously dilapidated houses that the city cannot afford to demolish. The streets where shoppers used to promenade are lined with empty storefronts, in a city that has many more unoccupied stores than going concerns. Every single theater in Camden has been boarded up or ripped down for a parking lot. The only thriving legal businesses are the 200 liquor stores and bars and the 180 gambling establishments. Display windows in some shops are covered with scrap metal, old doors, plywood, mismatched and rusting gates, as if barricaded against a hurricane, while other buildings have been gutted and their insides exposed to the elements.

There are stores that have burned to cinder and ash, stores that are breaking up and falling down. On one such building is a sign that is itself fading: "We Call Camden to Life."

Nonetheless, the believers see hints of progress amid the rubble. The nonprofit housing groups promise to triple their output, to five hundred units a year, by the beginning of the twenty-first century. There was a flurry of talk about a "Camden Initiative" that news accounts, ever boosterish, described as a "massive public-private effort to construct houses, boost business, improve police protection and education." Although the specifics are new, the idea that there is money to be made in remaking Camden has been voiced countless times before. More meaningful if less cheering is the fact that when Campbell stopped production at its Camden plant in 1989, 940 manufacturing jobs moved away to Paris, Texas, and the company since has backed out of a commitment to build its new headquarters on the Camden waterfront.

None of these grandiose plans matter very much, writes *Courier-Post* reporter Kevin Riordan in a richly detailed series of articles on the city's future. What's truly important are the neighborhoods where there is a new store, a freshly renovated row house, a corner where the drug dealers have been driven away, "the slow suturing of something wounded, but very much alive." A less kind observer sees Camden entirely differently, as a place that in its devastation resembles Dresden after the firebombing.

"I think of Camden as having three great resources—its people, its river, and Walt Whitman, in that order," says Michael Doyle, the priest at Sacred Heart Church, and for a quarter of a century, Doyle himself has been a great resource. The diocese banished the rebellious priest to Camden in the sixties as punishment for his antiwar protests, then handed him a Gothic pile of a church with a handful of parishioners and $4.68 in the bank. He has made that church, situated between the trash burner and the sewage plant, into a thriving community.

Doyle is no apologist for his "city of broken wings." Appearing in 1984 on *60 Minutes,* he infuriated the town's image polishers, who still wince at the religious imagery he used to such devastating effect. "When God saw Jerusalem, the Bible says, he wept—but if God came to Camden he would scream!" Yet Doyle has been able to accomplish something, albeit in miniature, that no one else in this part of the world has pulled off at all—he has constructed a human bridge that connects the suburbs and the city. Every Sunday, a hundred or more worshippers drive in from the surrounding communities to worship at Sacred Heart alongside the parishioners who live in the impoverished neighborhood.

"There's something about coming to a place where you expect nothing," says Doyle. "It's a chance to connect with something that is broken."

But because these connections are private and intimate, not open and public, they cannot substitute for an enriched sense of civic responsibility. Speaking of the sewage plant and trash-burning plant and the rest, the priest says: "We're a graveyard for everyone else's problems, and there is a feeling that this is somehow acceptable because those who live here are poor. What I have to say to the suburbs is this. 'You've got your foot on our neck. That's why we can't stand up.'

"On Ash Wednesday, I'd like to get dirt from Camden, put it on the foreheads of society, and say 'Think!' "

Site Specific

Michael Doyle shares Peter O'Connor's dream of opening up the suburbs. "I would like America to put up yellow ribbons and welcome 5 percent of the poor to affordable housing in the suburbs." Five percent hardly sounds utopian—in fact, it approximates how the law of the state has been interpreted by the courts in the *Mount Laurel* cases and by the state's Council on Affordable Housing as applying to a typical suburb—but so far reality has fallen far short of this standard.

Suburbs want to pay the cities to take over their legal duty to house the poor, and all the momentum is on their side. The state's Fair Housing Act authorizes these regional contribution agreements; city officials like these arrangements, since they keep their political base intact and bring in some revenue; and the state Supreme Court has approved them. But a familiar figure, Peter O'Connor, has devised a strategy that draws on federal and state resources to encourage the shared social responsibility that regional contribution agreements kill off.

While Fair Share Housing Development, Inc., the organization that Peter O'Connor founded, has spent the past fifteen years translating the rubric of fair share into real housing in the suburbs—housing for seniors in Salem County; housing for poor families in Gloucester County, adjacent to Camden—O'Connor has never left the city behind. In 1980, Fair Share Housing took over the biggest housing project built as part of the Camden Coalition settlement. The 402-unit enterprise called Northgate was in trouble then, but now the buildings are as graffiti free and the grounds as coifed as any ordinary condo complex. A twenty-two-story high-rise, the tallest building in Camden, houses the elderly; garden apartments provide homes for poor families; adjacent sits a state-of-the-art playground built with funds hustled from the state. The townhouses a block away had mostly been abandoned, but these handsome buildings are also being renovated through O'Connor's initiative. "Twenty years from now this street could be a little Paris boulevard," he says—"if you stretch your imagination."

In the fall of 1994, after years of trying, O'Connor finally finished restoring a row of once grand nineteenth-century homes that borders Cooper Hospital, converting them into sixty-four apartments for people who work in the neighborhood and so expanding the livable parts of Camden. In what is called Cooper Plaza, all but eleven of those apartments will be rented to low- and moderate-income families. There were many times during the protracted process when it seemed certain that someone—the city, the state, or HUD—would pull the plug on Cooper Plaza. O'Connor had to get approval from seventeen separate agencies, each with its own mission and timetable. "The financing has been convoluted," says Randy Primas, who went from being Camden's mayor to heading the state Department of Community Affairs under Democratic governor Jim Florio. "The cards are so stacked against anyone trying to find housing money for the poor that there really is no other way."

Through some financial wizardry, the benefits of this enterprise may reach beyond Camden and connect the city to Mount Laurel. Financial support partly comes from New Jersey's Balanced Housing Program, which generates funds from a tax imposed on all real-estate sales. (The fund itself is an outgrowth of the legislation that followed *Mount Laurel II*, and since almost all home sales these days are in the suburbs, their residents are making a modest contribution to housing the poor.) Nonprofit corporations like Fair Share Housing are provided a "developer's fee" and, in this case, O'Connor negotiated the maximum fee allowed by law: 20 percent of the project, or $1.6 million. This money, plus some of the tax credits for the private investors—historic-restoration credits, low-income-housing credits, more than Cooper Plaza required—is going to another good cause. It is being used to help finance the construction of housing that is planned for Mount Laurel Township.

When that moment—long awaited in some quarters, long dreaded in others—finally happens, the relationship between this "broken-winged" city and its anxious, hostile suburban neighbor will have come full circle. A successful effort to turn Camden from a hellhole into a place where people want to live will also contribute to the democratization of Mount Laurel. This seems entirely fitting, since the prosperity of that well-planned suburb has been largely purchased at the expense of the city.

Mount Laurel: Yellow Ribbons in Suburbia?

In 1984 in Mount Laurel, a year after the New Jersey Supreme Court's decision in *Mount Laurel II*, developer Roger Davis finally got to build Tricia Meadows, the manufactured homes that were supposed to provide affordable housing. And in Rancocas Woods, the neighborhood where the first of the township's developments sprang up in the 1950s, one apartment building dedicated specifically to affordable housing was opened.

On the surface, it seemed as though the town had turned around—that the idea of fair share had come to life—but the reality was otherwise. The progression to Tricia Meadows was hardly smooth. First the *Mount Laurel* trial court judge, Alexander Wood, had to order the recalcitrant township to grant a building permit, and then the town refused to process the application, claiming that there wasn't sufficient sewerage capacity. Only when Wood, the mild-mannered Quaker, finally lost his patience and decreed that Mount Laurel could accept no other building permit applications until Tricia Meadows was approved did the sewer district manage to increase its capacity and authorize the project. In fact, the 460-unit development, a fifth of which was designated for poor and moderate-income families, proved not to be the trailer park eyesore that fretful town-council members had expected. The trailers are double width, about the size of a normal home, and they have been dressed up in all sorts of ways, including a *faux* log cabin. Homes in Tricia Meadows designated as "affordable" sell for upwards of forty thousand dollars, and rentals there run five hundred dollars a month. This is within reach for families with moderate incomes, but not for the poor.

In Renaissance Homes, located in Rancocas Woods, all the condominiums in Building 15 are designated for low- and moderate-income households. Yet while everyone who lives in that building may technically qualify, they certainly aren't the people whom housing activists had in mind. Like the rest of the Renaissance Homes residents, they are at least fifty-five years old—"safe seniors," as they are called, no drain on township resources and no threat to anyone. Most are widows living on fixed pensions, who sold their bigger family homes, paying the below-market price for their apartments in cash. All are white.

The developer could have recruited more widely—from the waiting lists for Northgate, for instance, the impeccably maintained complex that Fair Share Housing operates in downtown Camden—but neither the builder nor the other residents nor the politicians in Mount Laurel wanted that to happen. This is how matters stand, not only in the township but also in most New Jersey communities where affordable housing has been built to satisfy a judge or COAH. Developers and town officials tacitly agree to make what amounts to a gift to the kinds of families who will blend in nicely, rather than inviting the poor, black families of Camden—inviting "them"—into "our town." The beneficiaries of this largesse have mainly been retirees with modest paper income but significant assets and young families who can rely on their parents for help with the down payment on their first home. The forty-something generation, which predominates in these suburbs, has been able to use *Mount Laurel* to underwrite housing for its grown-up children as well as for its aging parents.

"Suburbs appear to exist because their inhabitants want neither the isolation of the open countryside nor the anonymity of the city," argues planner J. B. Jackson in *Landscapes*. "What they seem to prefer is a small-scale society where happiness comes (or is supposed to come) from conformity to a generally accepted set of traditions and not from the pursuit of individual freedom." In March 1994, in a quiet Mount Laurel complex occupied mostly by seniors, a forty-three-year-old white woman, at home with her seventy-one-year-old mother-in-law while her husband was away, called 911 in hysterics. A black man had viciously attacked them, she said, smashing her over the head with a hammer, stabbing and beating her mother-in-law.

This was exactly what many white Mount Laurel residents had dreaded would happen—the reason why, years ago, they had turned down the request of Ethel Lawrence and her neighbors to build housing for poor families in Springville, and why they kept resisting all these years. But as the police asked more and more questions, the women's tale came to look suspicious. When a neighbor reported having heard the women screaming at one other, it was unmasked as a hoax; the injuries had really been caused when the wife, taking offense at her mother-in-law's jibes about her husband, launched an attack.

Such stories have become a staple of our time. In Boston a few years ago, Charles Stuart concocted the chilling account of a black man who shot and murdered Stuart's pregnant wife, a crime that Stuart had actually committed himself. A white woman in Philadelphia accused three black men of killing her children when she herself had murdered them. In the summer of 1994, a white Los Angeles man killed his wife and laid the blame on a black man. That fall, the nation was transfixed by the tale of a black man who supposedly kidnapped and drove off with the two young sons of Susan Smith in her red Mazda compact.

In each of these cases, as in Mount Laurel, the racial accusations were lies. There was no black brutalizer; the accuser was in fact the perpetrator. Yet seemingly nothing can keep such lurid narratives from becoming immediately plausible in the white middle-class imagination, so deep and familiar and readily reinforced are the underlying racial beliefs, so prevalent is this debased and dehumanized image of African Americans. Until suburbanites see firsthand that violence and drugs aren't the baggage that all poor and black people bring with them, strategies of exclusion, like the story of Building 15 in Mount Laurel's Renaissance Homes, will remain the order of the day. As New Jersey senator Bill Bradley said, in clear and candid language so rarely heard on the floor of the U.S. Senate, "Race is an explosive on the tongues of men."

Across the country, more and more black families have migrated to the suburbs, driven by the same concerns that earlier led to the white exodus—better schools for their children, safer and more pleasant lives. Many of them have found themselves living in communities that, like

Willingboro in New Jersey, have become largely nonwhite in composition, as whites, recreating the racial pattern set earlier in the cities, have moved out. Yet there are some towns whose residents span the divides of race and class. Over time, perhaps, the inhabitants of places like Ramblewood and the newer, fancier enclaves in Mount Laurel will cease to demonize those who are living in affordable housing a few blocks away—families who, regardless of their bank balances, share an understanding of what "our town" signifies.

    Perhaps.

In March 1985, it seemed that the push for genuine affordable housing in Mount Laurel Township was finally coming to a successful end. Nearly twenty years after Ethel Lawrence and her mother, Mary Robinson, Reverend Stuart Wood and the Springville Action Council first proposed building garden apartments for thirty-six poor families in the wrong-side-of-the-tracks part of town, two trials and two Supreme Court opinions later, township officials signed an agreement with Peter O'Connor, the founder, and Ethel Lawrence, the president of Fair Share Housing, the nonprofit housing organization run by Peter O'Connor.

    The New Jersey Supreme Court's 1983 decision in *Mount Laurel II* made a settlement in the township possible—a change in the local political climate made it happen. The politicians who carried on the fight against affordable housing were long gone, and the current generation of elected officials was more inclined to bargain than to fight. Bill Haines used the money he made from selling his farm to the developers to buy himself a peach farm in a part of New Jersey still untouched by development. In 1993, Haines, who had been elected to the state senate, was in the news again, this time facing fines for violating pesticide regulations on his farm and providing his migrant workers with unsanitary toilets.

    On the other side of the table, Ethel Lawrence's side, only Peter O'Connor remained from the trio of Camden Regional Legal Services attorneys who had talked through the case with Ethel Lawrence in her living room, so many years ago. Carl Bisgaier, stung financially by a failed foray into development in the village of Cranbury, had opened his own law office. Ken Meiser had also left the Public Advocate and maintained a modest private practice; when the job of town counsel opened up in Cherry Hill, he grabbed it. But for O'Connor, who was now both a nonprofit-housing developer and a lawyer, seeing Ethel Lawrence's dream through to completion had grown into an obsession. The two of them, lawyer and client, spent lots of time together, as O'Connor became almost a member of the family, and when Ethel Lawrence showed up in Jacob's Chapel with Peter O'Connor in tow, members of the congregation twittered that she had found herself a young beau.

What propelled this settlement was a legal blunder committed by the township. In 1984, Mount Laurel's planning board modified the plans for a five-thousand-unit planned development known as Larchmont. That was its mistake. Until then, Larchmont had not been part of the court case, because its approval predated the judicial decision. The unintended—and, to township officials, the horrifying—consequence of the planning board's action was to bring the entire project under the ambit of *Mount Laurel II*, obliging the developer to set aside 20 percent of its units for affordable housing. Peter O'Connor pounced at the news, but instead of going to court and so prolonging the litigation, a compromise was reached. O'Connor offered grudging praise for the local politicians. "At least there was a desire to solve a problem," he told reporters after the deal was made. "Prior to that, no one would even talk."

The agreement was signed in the Atlantic City courtroom of Judge L. Anthony Gibson, who had been assigned to the case as one of the state's *Mount Laurel* judges after the 1983 decision in *Mount Laurel II*. The particulars of the deal involved complicated swaps of land claims in the existing developments for $3.3 million paid to Fair Share Housing, as well as a rewritten zoning ordinance to allow for low- and moderate-income homes. Although, under the agreement, 950 new units of affordable housing could potentially be built throughout the township, Mount Laurel officials contemplated that the money O'Connor was getting would pay for just 40 units—only 4 more than the Springville Action Council had sought a generation earlier.

Characteristically, though, Peter O'Connor wasn't satisfied with such modest prospects; he had something much more ambitious in mind. Equally in character, Ethel Lawrence also hoped that all the years of waiting could produce more housing. O'Connor borrowed from the commercial developer's bag of tricks, spending the cash settlement to buy up parcels, using front men to conceal the purchases, while the township displayed the behavior of a sitting duck. By the time Mount Laurel figured out what was happening, O'Connor had assembled 122 acres—enough property, he figured, to build 255 rental units, more than six times what the township contemplated in the 1985 settlement agreement.

This revelation prompted Mount Laurel to drag O'Connor back to Judge Gibson's court in 1989. The township complained that his land speculating violated the terms of their deal—complained, as well, that in acting both as developer and lawyer, O'Connor was wearing one hat too many. "His lawyering was masterful," the township's attorney told local reporters, "but he is now an administrator and perhaps shouldn't even be involved in this nonprofit group that's supposed to be implementing housing in Mount Laurel Township."

While the town eventually dropped its objections, other pitfalls kept opening up. The financial plans, always seat-of-the-pants, at times resembled an improvisational con game. Paying for the Mount Laurel project depended partly on securing the tax write-offs generated by Cooper Plaza, the Camden historic-preservation undertaking. This use of urban restoration to help finance suburban integration was also O'Connor's innovation, and a clever one, but when construction was delayed in Camden, the State of New Jersey, a major backer, threatened to pull out. That chain of events temporarily derailed O'Connor's plans for Mount Laurel.

As if all these troubles weren't enough, two local landowners, including the Quaker matriarch of the town, took Fair Share Housing to court. This new lawsuit was designed to stop the nonprofit corporation from building on one of the parcels it had purchased, ten acres situated not far from Jacob's Chapel. In 1985, when the settlement was signed, the best land in Mount Laurel Township had already been bought by developers or had become impossibly expensive. There were developments like Holiday Village, designed for seniors, and Laurel Knoll, where the houses run in the $250,000 range. The only property that Fair Share Housing could afford was more swampy acreage.

The neighbors' complaint raised questions about the adequacy of the proposed drainage system reminiscent of objections posed by the township engineers who critiqued the Springville Action Council's plans in the late 1960s. One of the plaintiffs, Betty Ransome, owned a nursery business across the street from the project. Environmentalism, not exclusion, was her motivation, she maintained. "If any other builder had submitted that plan, I would have fought it. The township's planning board is intimidated because of all the litigation. People want the *Mount Laurel* case out of their hair. No one is looking down the road fifteen or twenty years." But the other plaintiff, octogenarian Alice Rudderow, whose Quaker ancestors had lived in Mount Laurel for more than two centuries, was less an environmentalist than an opportunist in this litigation. Years before, Rudderow had sold off all but a couple of acres of the family's farm to developers. "I used the water business," she admits, as a rationale to block the housing.

In this perpetual struggle, Fair Share Housing, presided over by Ethel Lawrence and propelled by Peter O'Connor, has also had its share of successes. The biggest triumph was the announcement in 1994 that the AFL-CIO's Housing Investment Trust would help finance 255 rental apartments in Mount Laurel. By then, the money earned from restoring the Cooper Plaza buildings in Camden was about to be deposited in the bank. The nonprofit group also struck a deal with the federal Department of Housing and Urban Development, authorizing the use of housing vouchers—a small part of HUD Secretary Henry Cisneros's integrationist vision realized.

On June 24, 1994, nine years after signing the first agreement with Mount Laurel Township, Peter O'Connor, Ethel Lawrence, and township officials were again in Judge Gibson's courtroom. On this occasion, O'Connor agreed to sell off a thirty-acre parcel to a developer who planned to build quarter-million-dollar homes there. Skittish officials were concerned that if Fair Share built on this particular property, the value of the pricey adjacent homes would fall, and O'Connor didn't press the matter, since he still had enough land to build on. The judge also turned over the environmental issues raised by Betty Ransome's lawsuit to a court-appointed master.

But no one in Ethel Lawrence's camp was ready to uncork the champagne, to dig that first shovelful of earth that marks the ground breaking. The 1995 cutbacks in HUD's budget threatened not only the promised federal help but also the AFL-CIO investment, which was contingent on HUD support; that news sent Peter O'Connor scrambling for funds once again. It was also possible that new obstacles would be posed locally, for this was the experience elsewhere. In the aptly named Los Angeles enclave of Hidden Hills, residents rose up against a plan to build forty-eight apartments for seniors. The elderly, they complained, "will attract gangs and dope." A national plan to scatter a handful of poor families in better neighborhoods, launched in 1994, was scuttled when residents loudly protested even before any of the families were moved. Peter O'Connor's experience in other New Jersey communities was much the same. In Salem Township, near the Delaware border, it took seven and a half years to get all the approvals needed to build housing for the poor, and those apartments were to be occupied by seniors. It took even longer to open fifty units of affordable rental housing in Gloucester. In Salem, race and taxes were the issues, while in Gloucester, the problem had simply been race. Why, O'Connor mused, should anyone anticipate that, in Mount Laurel of all places, things would be any easier?

Before the millennium, the first tenants will be moving into handsome new homes in Mount Laurel. For some of the poorest families in the Republic, among them the children and grandchildren of the plaintiffs in the 1971 lawsuit, this housing will represent the promised land, after so many years in the desert. Fittingly, it will be named after Ethel Lawrence and her mother, Mary Robinson.

Rich and Poor Folk in the Hereafter

On May 2, 1985, the day that the deal between Fair Share Housing and the town was approved, Ethel Lawrence was, as always, in Judge Gibson's Atlantic City courtroom to witness the event. Afterwards, the judge took the time to commend her for her tenacity. "It was an effort that would have discouraged most people, caused those less committed to fall by the wayside." Nine years later, in the spring of 1994, she was talking with state officials as they toured the sites where the new housing would be built.

But Ethel Gertrude Robinson Lawrence would not live to see those homes spring up on the landscape. On July 19, 1994, at the age of sixty-eight, she died of cancer at her home on Elbo Lane—the very same day, as it happens, that thirty-one-year-old Luis Galindez, the spirit behind the North Camden Land Trust campaign to restore houses in that derelict part of the city, was murdered in his bed. Just six months later, in January 1995, Ethel's mother and fellow community activist, Mary Robinson, passed away as well.

Ethel Lawrence never became nearly so famous as Rosa Parks, the black seamstress whose refusal to give up her seat to a white man on a Montgomery, Alabama, bus marked a milestone in the modern civil-rights movement. But, like Rosa Parks, she lived in an exemplary way that others would describe in the language of politics. It was a life defined by values that Americans, when surveyed, say are what really counts—a sense of personal responsibility, faith in God, respect for others, love for her family, commitment to community and country.

After the first *Mount Laurel* trial court decision in 1972, reporters began coming around to interview her, first from the local papers, then from the big-city dailies and TV stations. "I was her bodyguard, her Rock of Gibraltar," the late Mary Robinson proudly said of her daughter, "she was educated, she was the spokesman." That attention won her new respect from skeptical members of the Jacob's Chapel congregation. Yet when some of her old associates in the local Democratic Party were named as defendants in the lawsuit, they sniped at her, called her an egotist and a troublemaker, wrote cranky letters in the local paper. This was hardly the worst of it. There were hate mail and obscene calls, and one time a whispery caller threatened that her house would be burned down—after that she kept her porch light turned on through the night. Sometimes people would drive by and shout, "Nigger"; sometimes they splattered eggs on her front door. Once they fired a shot at her bedroom window. She carried on.

The Jacob's Chapel congregation has shrunk from nearly a hundred members a quarter of a century ago to about half that size, as old parishioners have died off and no one has replaced them. Years ago, simple economics pushed three of Ethel Lawrence's church sisters, her aunts Emma and Laura and her cousin Betty, out of Mount Laurel and into Camden. They had always wanted to return, but they are all dead. Her mother, Mary Robinson, used to say: "I was born here and I want to die here. They can bury me in Jacob's Chapel cemetery." For the last several years of her life Mary suffered from Alzheimer's disease and lived in a nursing home, largely unaware of her surroundings. A few years ago on Mother's Day, Ethel Lawrence took her mother to church, and while Mary didn't recognize most of the people, she remembered all the words to all the hymns.

There was always a crisis in Ethel Lawrence's extended family to claim her attention—one of her children was diagnosed with lupus, another was out of work—and always a neighbor or friend's kin who needed her help. Those nine children are all grown, and she was a grandmother twenty-five times over when she died.

Her daughter Ruth, after serving in the army, returned home for a while, to work nights in the local hospital and live next door to her mother. Clayton Lawrence, a marine sergeant on the front lines during the fighting in Kuwait, will be the first, he says, to sign up for affordable housing in Mount Laurel. Renee, Ethel's youngest child, was the first member of the family to finish college and became an officer with a title company. Some of Ethel's children, like Frances and Renee, are settled into their own suburban lives. Others, like Frances's twin brother, Frank, a salesman for a company that sells technical equipment, want to come home. Mary Smith, Ethel Lawrence's niece and a plaintiff in the 1971 lawsuit, was living in Springville with her infant daughter in an unheated chicken coop when the case was filed. Long ago she gave up her own hopes of moving back to Mount Laurel; she lives in Moorestown, which, unlike Mount Laurel, refurbished decent housing for a number of poor families in the heart of the village. Maybe there will be some place in Mount Laurel for her daughter, who is fast approaching thirty.

"They're tough, that generation," says Mary Smith, talking about her aunt. "I watched her bury her husband and then, in the space of little more than a year, put three brothers in the ground. 'She's not going to make it,' I thought, yet somehow she kept going."

"I got a little stronger as I went along," said Ethel Lawrence, and she never complained through all the twists and turns of a case that most of the time seemed to be a lost cause. The event that disturbed her most occurred in 1990, when the lawsuit alleging drainage problems with one of the Mount Laurel parcels was filed. It wasn't the case itself that troubled her so much as the fact that Alice Rudderow, the Quaker matron, was a plaintiff. "What she did to our housing shocked me," Ethel Lawrence said. "She had saved a little piece of property she hadn't sold [to the developers, which is what gave her grounds to litigate]. She's fighting the hardest battle against us. I went over there to explain the project, but it didn't do any good. That hurt me personally more than anything." It represented a betrayal of the unwritten codes that whites and blacks in Mount Laurel had lived by in years past. "When we were children, her children used to play with us," she added, believing that such a fact from half a century ago should still carry moral weight.

Ethel Lawrence never knew what it meant to feel sorry for herself. "The people that I feel sorry for are the powers-that-be in Mount Laurel. They tell you they're Christian people, but they don't want to deal with poor people on earth. They're going to have a hard time in the hereafter.

There's poor people in heaven and poor people in hell. God meant for us to live in harmony on earth, or else he'd have made rich and poor communities in the hereafter." Perhaps she's right, although a sadder reading of the account of how long, how fiercely, and how successfully the Township of Mount Laurel fought against housing the poor would conclude that there must be Laurel Knolls and Ramblewoods for the souls of the rich, Springville chicken coops for the souls of the poor, gated communities even in heaven.

Chronology

YEAR	CAMDEN AND MOUNT LAUREL	NEW JERSEY COURTS
1924	Walt Whitman Hotel opens in Camden.	
1926	Benjamin Franklin Bridge, connecting Camden and Philadelphia, opens.	
1944		
1947	Holly Department Store opens in Camden.	New Jersey constitution amended, creating a more independent and centralized court system and giving the governor a conditional veto.
1948		Constitutional reformer Arthur Vanderbilt becomes chief justice of the revitalized Supreme Court.
1950	Rutgers University's Camden campus opens. Population: Camden, 124,555; Mount Laurel, 2,800.	
1951		
1952	Mount Laurel exit from New Jersey Turnpike opens. Ferry service between Camden and Philadelphia ceases.	*Lionshead Lake v. Wayne*: Supreme Court upholds exclusionary zoning ordinance setting minimum floor size; court holds "general welfare" requirement refers only to a town's current residents.

NEW JERSEY LAND USE POLICY & POLITICS	THE WORLD BEYOND NEW JERSEY
	Just 114,000 homes built nationwide.
	Gunnar Myrdal's *An American Dilemma: The Negro Problem and Modern Democracy* published.
	William J. Levitt starts construction on first Levittown, on Long Island, New York.
	1,692,000 homes built nationwide, nearly 15 times the number in 1944.
	Levitt builds second Levittown, in Bucks County, Pennsylvania.
New Jersey Turnpike completed, connecting northeastern and southwestern New Jersey and creating New York–Philadelphia development corridor.	

(*continued*)

YEAR	CAMDEN AND MOUNT LAUREL	NEW JERSEY COURTS
1953	First Lady Mamie Eisenhower christens the *Nautilus,* the nation's first nuclear-powered submarine, at its launching from the Camden shipyards.	
1954		
1955	RCA introduces color television and enjoys first billion-dollar year. Mount Laurel's first housing development, Rancocas Woods, marks the beginning of suburban development there.	
1956		Supreme Court Justice William Brennan elevated to U.S. Supreme Court by President Eisenhower.
1957		Joseph Weintraub becomes chief justice of the Supreme Court.
1960	Population: Camden, 117,159; Mount Laurel, 5,250.	
1961	Enclosed Cherry Hill Mall opens, one of the first suburban malls in the nation.	

NEW JERSEY LAND USE POLICY & POLITICS	THE WORLD BEYOND NEW JERSEY
	Brown v. Board of Education [Brown]: U.S. Supreme Court unanimously holds that racial segregation in public schools violates the Equal Protection Clause of the U.S. Constition.
Garden State Parkway, traversing the entire east side of the state, from Cape May to the New York State Thruway, completed.	*Brown v. Board of Education [Brown II]*: U.S. Supreme Court unanimously holds public schools must remedy school desegregation "with all deliberate speed."
	Charles Abrams publishes *Forbidden Neighbors,* decrying American apartheid.
Richard J. Hughes (D) elected governor.	

(*continued*)

YEAR	CAMDEN AND MOUNT LAUREL	NEW JERSEY COURTS
1962	Ramblewood housing development opens in Mount Laurel.	*Vickers v. Gloucester.* Supreme Court upholds zoning ordinance excluding trailer parks; Justice Frederick Hall dissents, arguing the law is unconstitutionally exclusionary.
1964		
1965	Camden's historic Stanley Theatre, opened in the 1920s, closes.	
1966		Supreme Court signals departure from *Lionshead Lake* decision in two decisions on regional needs. *Kunzler v. Hoffman* upholds variance for construction of a mental hospital, while *Roman Catholic Diocese, Newark v. Ho-Ho-Kus* urges municipalities to consider regional education needs "with due concern for values which transcend municipal lines."
1967	Mount Laurel approves four planned unit developments totaling 10,000 housing units. Springville Action Council founded in Mount Laurel. New York Shipbuilding Company closes Camden yard.	

NEW JERSEY LAND USE POLICY & POLITICS	THE WORLD BEYOND NEW JERSEY
Expressway connecting Philadelphia and Atlantic City completed.	
	Federal Civil Rights Act enacted.
Governor Hughes reelected, and Democrats win both houses of the legislature.	Watts riot in Los Angeles kills 33 and causes nearly $100 million property losses.
The legislature adopts first statewide tax (3% on sales).	Federal Legal Services program established.
Newark riots kill 26 and cause $10 million property losses.	

(*continued*)

YEAR	CAMDEN AND MOUNT LAUREL	NEW JERSEY COURTS
1968	State Department of Community Affairs grants Springville Action Council $6,000 to develop 36 units of affordable housing in Mount Laurel.	
1969	Allegations of police brutality spark Camden riots killing two policemen, injuring scores of black citizens, and burning dozens of buildings.	
1970	Lawyers from Camden Regional Legal Services, Peter O'Connor and Carl Bisgaier, file *Camden Coalition* suit, stopping highway-construction and urban-renewal projects then bulldozing Camden neighborhoods.	*DeSimone v. Greater Englewood Housing Corp.*: Supreme Court upholds variance for low-income housing. Justice Hall's opinion for the unanimous court states that "general welfare" requires land-use planning and zoning to accommodate all segments of the population.
	Population: Camden, 102,551; Mount Laurel, 11,221.	
	Mount Laurel's Larchmont development, featuring luxury housing opens.	
	Mount Laurel Township committeeman tells Jacob's Chapel congregation the township will not permit construction of 36 garden apartments, declaring "If you folks can't afford to live in our town, then you'll just have to leave."	

NEW JERSEY LAND USE POLICY & POLITICS	THE WORLD BEYOND NEW JERSEY
Governor's Select Commission on Civil Disorder warns "suburban residents must understand that the future of their communities is inextricably linked to the fate of the city, instead of harboring the illusion that they can maintain invisible walls or continue to run away."	Rev. Martin Luther King Jr. assassinated. Kerner Commission report decries "two Americas, black and white, separate and unequal." George Romney begins his tenure as federal housing secretary, over-seeing largest low-income housing subsidy program in U.S. history.
William Cahill (R) is elected governor, and Republicans win both houses of the legislature.	
The legislature raises sales tax to 5%.	
Governor Cahill, in state-of-the-state speech, decries exclusionary zoning and urges suburbs to allow more affordable housing.	

(*continued*)

YEAR	CAMDEN AND MOUNT LAUREL	NEW JERSEY COURTS
1971	Following Camden prosecutor's refusal to charge police brutality in a beating incident, five days of rioting burns numerous city blocks.	Coalition of fair-housing plaintiffs files administrative complaint before state civil-rights agency against suburban Mahwah Township, challenging its zoning as racially discriminatory. Agency rejects case for lack of jurisdiction. Plaintiffs appeal.
		Mount Laurel I begins: Camden Regional Legal Services sues Township of Mount Laurel, charging its zoning is unconstitutionally exclusionary.
		Developer Allan-Deane Corp. sues Township of Bedminster, challenging minimum-lot-size and single-family-residence restrictions.
		Oakwood-at-Madison v. Madison: for the first time in New Jersey, a trial judge declares an exclusionary ordinance—which requires large-lot zoning and minimum floor area, sets aside a small amount of land for apartments, and sharply limits the number of bedrooms in apartments—violative of the state zoning law. Madison's zoning must be amended to meet a "fair proportion . . . [of] the housing needs of its own population and of the region."

NEW JERSEY LAND USE POLICY & POLITICS	THE WORLD BEYOND NEW JERSEY
	James v. Valtierra: U.S. Supreme Court upholds California's public referendum requirement for proposed public-housing projects.

(*continued*)

YEAR	CAMDEN AND MOUNT LAUREL	NEW JERSEY COURTS
1972	Under *Camden Coalition* settlement city reserves several hundred units of new housing for poor families.	After trial in *Mount Laurel I,* Superior Court Judge Edward Martino declares zoning prohibition against affordable housing unconstitutional "economic discrimination."
		In *Mahwah* case, appeals court upholds civil-rights agency's refusal to take jurisdiction, forcing a lawsuit in the courts.
		Rutgers v. Piluso: in opinion by Justice Hall, Supreme Court unanimously permits Rutgers University to override local zoning limit on married-student housing, emphasizing that "fiscal zoning" is a "legally dubious stratagem" and "clearly not a legitimate local interest."
1973	Angelo Errichetti elected mayor of Camden.	Supreme Court hears arguments in *Oakwood-at-Madison* and *Mount Laurel I*; reargument later ordered.
		Robinson v. Cahill: Supreme Court unanimously holds state's finance system for public schools unconstitutional and orders legislative reforms.
1974	Mickle Tower and Royal Court housing projects open in Camden.	Richard Hughes, former Democratic governor, becomes chief justice.
		Supreme Court hears second round of arguments in *Oakwood-at-Madison* and *Mount Laurel I.*

NEW JERSEY LAND USE POLICY & POLITICS	THE WORLD BEYOND NEW JERSEY
Governor Cahill requests county housing plans based on state guidelines.	
Governor Cahill defeated in Republican primary. Brendan Byrne (D) elected governor, and Democrats take over state senate and assembly.	*San Antonio Independent School District v. Rodriguez*: U.S. Supreme Court holds states not constitutionally required to equalize financing of public schools. President Nixon imposes moratorium on federal subsidies for low-income housing construction.
New Jersey Department of Public Advocate established.	Norman Williams publishes his multivolume treatise, *American Land Planning Law*, dedicated to Justice Frederick Hall—"the most distinguished judge of our time in this field of law." President Nixon resigns; Gerald Ford (R) takes office.

(*continued*)

YEAR	CAMDEN AND MOUNT LAUREL	NEW JERSEY COURTS
		Oakwood-at-Madison: on remand trial court invalidates amendments to Madison's zoning ordinances.
		Urban League of Greater New Brunswick files suit against 23 towns in Middlesex County, claiming exclusionary zoning.
1975	More violent crime recorded in Camden than in any other city its size in the nation.	*Mount Laurel I*: Supreme Court establishes state constitutional obligation to provide realistic opportunity for construction of affordable housing constituting "fair share" of regional need. A month later, the opinion's author, Justice Hall, retires. Supreme Court denies township's request for rehearing. Later Judge Martino denies township's request for additional time to comply, calling it a "deliberate stall."
		U.S. Supreme Court denies Mount Laurel's petition for certiorari.

NEW JERSEY LAND USE POLICY & POLITICS	THE WORLD BEYOND NEW JERSEY

Governor Byrne, in state-of-the-state address, warns of the harmful effects of exclusionary zoning on the state's economy and citizenry.

Warth v. Seldin: U.S. Supreme Court holds urban residents cannot challenge suburban zoning laws under the Constitution.

Senator Martin Greenberg (D), Governor Byrne's former law partner, introduces housing legislation requiring towns to observe Department of Community Affairs zoning guidelines.

The federal government razes Pruitt-Igoe, the first public-housing project ever demolished, just 15 years after construction.

Governor Byrne proposes legislation establishing guidelines for compliance with *Mount Laurel I.*

Legislature defeats Byrne proposal for state income tax; voters reject $100 million bond issues for housing.

Numerous mayors, led by Mount Laurel's Joe Alvarez, seek constitutional amendment overruling *Mount Laurel I* and giving Department of Community Affairs, not the courts, authority over zoning matters.

(*continued*)

YEAR	CAMDEN AND MOUNT LAUREL	NEW JERSEY COURTS
1976		Mount Laurel amends zoning dedicating 23 acres of swampy, unusable land for low-income housing.
		Public Advocate renews *Mount Laurel* suit alleging "pattern and practice of economic discrimination."
		Judge Martino withdraws from *Mount Laurel* case due to pending retirement and ill health. Case reassigned to the reluctant Alexander Wood III.
		Developer Roger Davis files own suit charging that Mount Laurel improperly refused permit for 590-unit mobile-home park.
		In re Karen Quinlan: Supreme Court's "right-to-die" decision is first in nation recognizing parents' constitutional right to withdraw life support from incapacitated child.
1977		*Oakwood-at-Madison:* in split decision Supreme Court dilutes *Mount Laurel I* by prohibiting judicial calculation of numerical "fair share"; "good faith" zoning by towns will satisfy constitutional obligation. Yet court authorizes use of "builder's remedies" against towns in special circumstances.

NEW JERSEY LAND USE POLICY & POLITICS	THE WORLD BEYOND NEW JERSEY
Governor Byrne's Executive Order 35 requires preparation of state low-income housing allocation plan. Byrne aims to allow certain state and federal aid only to those towns permitting low-income housing.	Jimmy Carter (D) elected president.
In school-finance crisis, legislature adopts state income tax after Supreme Court closes public schools for one week.	
Senator Greenberg proposes state master plan and voluntary certification of local zoning. Proposal fails to emerge from committee.	*Village of Arlington Heights v. Metropolitan Development Corp.*: The U.S. Supreme Court holds zoning is constitutionally valid unless plaintiffs show intent to discriminate.
Governor Byrne (D) is reelected.	

(continued)

YEAR	CAMDEN AND MOUNT LAUREL	NEW JERSEY COURTS
		Pascack Ass'n v. Washington and *Fobe Associates v. Demarest*: Supreme Court further limits *Mount Laurel I,* restricting its application to "developing" areas. *Washington* majority states courts are "not suited to the role of an ad hoc super zoning legislature, particularly in the area of adjusting claims for satisfaction by individual municipalities of regional needs."
1978	Riverview Tower apartments, privately operated for seniors and the disabled, open in Camden.	Trial in *Mount Laurel II*: relying on *Washington* Judge Wood dismisses suit, finding township complied with *Mount Laurel I* with its new zoning for low-income housing. Yet he grants relief to Roger Davis, allowing construction of the mobile-home park.
		Public Advocate sues 27 municipalities in Morris County, claiming exclusionary zoning.
1979		*Home Builders v. Berlin*: Supreme Court declares minimum floor-size requirement invalid.
		Robert Wilentz, former assemblyman and son of a former state attorney general, appointed chief justice.

NEW JERSEY LAND USE
POLICY & POLITICS

THE WORLD BEYOND
NEW JERSEY

Senator Greenberg's balanced-
housing bill passes senate but dies
in assembly committee chaired by
Cary Edwards, later counsel and
attorney general under Governor
Thomas Kean.

(continued)

YEAR	CAMDEN AND MOUNT LAUREL	NEW JERSEY COURTS
1980	Population: Camden, 84,910; Mount Laurel, 17,614. Peter O'Connor's Fair Shair Housing Development Corporation opens Northgate Apartments in Camden, a refurbished affordable-housing project once part of the *Camden Coalition* settlement. I-676, a highway that bulldozed Camden housing in its path, is completed.	Signaling its desire to re-examine *Mount Laurel* issues, Supreme Court grants hearing in six exclusionary-zoning cases, including *Mount Laurel, Mahwah,* and *Urban League.* Judge Wood invalidates Lumberton ordinance restricting residential development on 60% of its land to two-acre minimum lot size. Supreme Court hears 18 hours of oral argument over three days in *Mount Laurel II* cases, asking the lawyers to address 24 written questions prepared by the court.
1981	Randy Primas replaces Angelo Errichetti, becoming Camden's first black mayor.	
1982		
1983		*Mount Laurel II*: 25 months after oral argument Supreme Court unanimously reaffirms *Mount Laurel I,* instructing lower courts to devise numerical fair-share formula, sanctioning builder's remedies against towns refusing to rezone properly, and later designating three special *Mount Laurel* judges, Eugene Serpentelli, L. Anthony Gibson, and Stephen Skillman.

NEW JERSEY LAND USE POLICY & POLITICS	THE WORLD BEYOND NEW JERSEY
Constitutional amendment prohibiting judicial and executive interference in local zoning decisions introduced in assembly but never enacted.	Ronald Reagan (R) elected president, promising to reduce federal spending on housing.
With narrowest margin in modern state history (2,000 votes), Thomas Kean (R) is elected governor.	
Governor Kean rescinds Byrne's Executive Order 35, thereby stopping preparation of state plan for fair-share housing allocation.	Mortgage interest rates, rising for several years, hit 17%.
Senator John Dorsey (R), lawyer for some Morris County towns, asks Governor Kean to order Public Advocate to drop Morris County suit.	
Republican legislators renew call for constitutional amendment removing courts from zoning arena.	
Governor Kean refuses to update State Development Guide Plan as requested by Supreme Court in *Mount Laurel II.*	

(*continued*)

YEAR	CAMDEN AND MOUNT LAUREL	NEW JERSEY COURTS
		When Mount Laurel sewer district stalls Roger Davis's application, Judge Wood enjoins all further permits; sewer district immediately grants permit to Davis.
		Mount Laurel amends zoning, requiring new housing developments larger than 10 units to set aside 20% for affordable housing.
1984		With *Mount Laurel II* builder's remedies available, 61 new suits filed against towns in first year after decision; of these, 57 suits are by developers, 2 by Public Advocate (including *Mount Laurel* case), and 2 by civil-rights groups.
		Judge Gibson authorizes construction of 460-unit mobile-home park in Mount Laurel; 92 units set aside for lower-income families.
		AMG Realty v. Warren: Judge Serpentelli assigns Warren (population 9,805 and 3,000 homes) fair share of 946 affordable housing units, using a "consensus methodology" formula later adopted in other *Mount Laurel* cases.

NEW JERSEY LAND USE POLICY & POLITICS	THE WORLD BEYOND NEW JERSEY

Study by Rutgers Center for Urban Policy Research, funded by municipalities and builders, claims *Mount Laurel II* will require 300,000 lower-income units by the year 2000.

Governor Kean, in state-of-the-state address, calls *Mount Laurell II* "undesirable intrusion on the home rule principle," later adding that it is "communistic."

President Reagan reelected in landslide.

Senator Gerald Stockman (D) proposes legislation creating state planning commission. Senate Republicans propose similar bill with 18-month moratorium on new *Mount Laurel* cases. Officials from 40 towns meet to endorse moratorium. Senator Stockman's bill passes the senate.

Mayor/Senator Peter Garibaldi (R) says Monroe Township will not rezone in 90 days to permit 774 lower-income units.

Senator Dorsey proposes constitutional amendment to limit court jurisdiction over zoning challenges.

(*continued*)

YEAR	CAMDEN AND MOUNT LAUREL	NEW JERSEY COURTS
		Public Advocate announces it has settled all its zoning suits, except *Mount Laurel* case. All remaining suits are by private developers.
		Judge Serpentelli assigns historic village of Cranbury (population of 1,927 and 720 homes) fair share of 816 affordable-housing units.
1985	Camden's Riverfront State Prison completed.	140 *Mount Laurel II* lawsuits pending.
		Twenty-three towns hire counsel to seek reconsideration of *Mount Laurel II* and stay of Cranbury order in Supreme Court. Court refuses. With progress on adoption of state Fair Housing Act, the towns drop their appeal to the U.S. Supreme Court. Legal bill for aborted effort totals $250,000.
		Allan-Deane Corp. v. Bedminster. 14 years after it was filed, Judge Serpentelli approves settlement of the first exclusionary-zoning case.
		Mount Laurel case: town settles, agreeing to rezone for 950 lower-income units; two developers agree to contribute $3.3 million to Peter O'Connor's Fair Share Housing Development, Inc. Judge Gibson approves settlement.

NEW JERSEY LAND USE
POLICY & POLITICS

Senator Wynona Lipman (D)
introduces bill establishing
administrative agency to review
exclusionary-zoning claims and
$100 million subsidy program for
affordable housing in suburbs.

Numerous municipal officials
pledge to finance federal suit
challenging constitutionality of
Mount Laurel II.

Governor Kean refuses to support
fair-housing bill if it subsidizes
affordable housing.

Senate passes the Fair Housing
Act, including $25 million fund
for housing. Assembly Democrats
pass fair-housing bill over
Republican opposition; bill
includes 12-month moratorium on
new suits.

Governor Kean conditionally
vetoes Fair Housing Act, objecting
to the subsidy program and
demanding increase, from 33% to
50%, in proportion of the fair-
share burden towns can transfer to
one another under regional
contribution agreements.

Senate and assembly enact a new
Fair Housing Act meeting Kean's
objections; Senators Lipman and
Stockman vote no.

(continued)

YEAR	CAMDEN AND MOUNT LAUREL	NEW JERSEY COURTS
		After state Fair Housing Act creates Council on Affordable Housing (COAH), Judge Skillman refuses to transfer three Morris County cases to the new agency. Judge Serpentelli also refuses to transfer several townships' cases in the *Urban League* lawsuit to COAH.
		Supreme Court, on its own motion, grants hearing on challenges to Fair Housing Act's constitutionality under *Mount Laurel II* and lower courts' refusal to transfer pending cases to COAH.
1986		*Hills Development v. Bernards [Mount Laurel III]*: Supreme Court unanimously upholds the constitutionality of Fair Housing Act and requires transfer of virtually every pending case to COAH.

| NEW JERSEY LAND USE POLICY & POLITICS | THE WORLD BEYOND NEW JERSEY |

Kean signs Fair Housing Act, codifying but significantly weakening *Mount Laurel II,* creating Council on Affordable Housing (COAH), and establishing administrative process to set fair shares and to determine municipal compliance. COAH members are appointed and staff hired.

Republican senators again seek constitutional amendment to strip courts of all authority over zoning.

Legislature adopts State Planning Act, creating state planning commission for land-use planning.

Governor Kean is reelected by largest margin in state history. Republicans win control of the assembly. Two hundred twenty-one municipalities vote in nonbinding referenda, by an average margin of two to one, in favor of constitutional amendment curtailing judicial power over local zoning matters.

Assembly Republicans again propose constitutional amendment to strip state courts of jurisdiction over zoning challenges; senate Democrats table the proposal.

California voters reject Chief Justice Rose Bird and two other justices of the California Supreme Court for failure to carry out death penalty.

COAH reduces estimate of statewide affordable-housing need dramatically, stating overall need is 145,707 units, about half that estimated under the "consensus methodology" used by the *Mount Laurel* judges.

(*continued*)

YEAR	CAMDEN AND MOUNT LAUREL	NEW JERSEY COURTS
1987	Camden city sewage-treatment plant upgrade completed. Plant begins operation as a county facility, accepting sewage from other towns.	
1988	County jail opens in Camden.	

NEW JERSEY LAND USE POLICY & POLITICS	THE WORLD BEYOND NEW JERSEY

Over protests within his party, Governor Kean reappoints Chief Justice Wilentz for new term, arguing for an independent judiciary. By a single vote, state senate confirms Chief Justice Wilentz for a second term.

Only 225 of state's 567 towns meet COAH deadline to submit a letter of intent to comply with fair-housing quotas. Only 130 towns submit required housing plans; many are unacceptable.

Republican legislators propose bill to cut fair-share quotas in half.

Over 100 municipalities fail to file fair-housing plans with COAH.

Robert Bork, President Reagan's nominee for the U.S. Supreme Court, denied confirmation by the Senate.

COAH places, 1,000-unit ceiling on the number of lower-income housing units required in any town over next six years; cap is later overturned in court. COAH certifies the first municipal-housing elements, thereby insulating those towns against exclusionary-zoning claims.

COAH approves the first regional contribution agreement (RCA), as Tewksbury pays Perth Amboy $1.2 million to assume 45-unit affordable-housing obligation. Several other RCAs are quickly negotiated.

George Bush (R) elected president.

COAH grants housing certification to 47 towns.

(*continued*)

YEAR	CAMDEN AND MOUNT LAUREL	NEW JERSEY COURTS
1989	Campbell Soup Co. stops production at its Camden plant, eliminating over 900 jobs.	*Urban League*: Supreme Court denies attorney fees to public-interest groups.
1990	Population: Camden, 82,492; Mount Laurel, 30,270. Camden's median income is $9,285; city has 25% unemployment; 57% of residents live in poverty; and 75% receive some form of public assistance.	*Holmdel Builders v. Holmdel*: Supreme Court allows towns to impose developer fees to subsidize lower-income housing, but only if COAH issues regulations governing such fees. *Calton Homes v. COAH*: appeals court voids COAH's 1,000-unit cap as violation of Fair Housing Act. *Abbott v. Burke*: Supreme Court again invalidates school-funding plan for failing to ensure substantial equality among districts or to provide for the special needs of cities.
1991	Campbell Soup Co. razes its nearly century-old manufacturing plant in Camden. "Mischief Night" fires destroy 49 buildings in Camden.	
1992	The second-largest aquarium in the nation opens on the Camden waterfront, as does a new marina.	

NEW JERSEY LAND USE POLICY & POLITICS	THE WORLD BEYOND NEW JERSEY
Slowdown in construction industry further reduces incentives for builders to pursue exclusionary-zoning claims.	
James Florio (D) is elected governor, after Kean declines to run for third term, hoping for a Washington post.	
COAH approves regional contribution agreements totaling $60 million for construction or rehabilitation of 2,900 housing units in urban areas.	President Bush appoints former governor Kean to head the federal Advisory Commission on Regulatory Barriers to Affordable Housing.
	HUD Secretary Jack Kemp proposes giving more lower-income tenants vouchers and allowing them to manage and even acquire housing projects.
COAH grants zoning certification to 117 municipalities.	
	Bill Clinton (D) elected president vowing new Democratic agenda.

(continued)

YEAR	CAMDEN AND MOUNT LAUREL	NEW JERSEY COURTS
	Time magazine publishes an article about Camden entitled "Who Could Live Here?"	
	Ferry service between Camden and Philadelphia resumes after a 40-year absence.	
1993		*In re Substantive Certification Filed by the Township of Warren*: after COAH certified plan granting affordable-housing occupancy preferences to local residents and workers, Supreme Court declares the ordinance invalid under *Mount Laurel II* and Fair Housing Act.
1994	Peter O'Connor's Fair Share Housing Development, Inc. completes the Cooper Plaza project, replacing historic Camden homes with 64 apartments, 53 of which are reserved for lower-income families.	*Abbott v. Burke*: a unanimous Supreme Court declares unconstitutional Quality Education Act adopted after 1990 court decision.
	The AFL-CIO Housing Investment Trust announces investment in 255 lower-income apartments in Mount Laurel.	
	Ethel Lawrence dies of cancer at the age of 68; on the same day Luis Galindez, North Camden housing organizer, is murdered at the age of 31.	

NEW JERSEY LAND USE POLICY & POLITICS	THE WORLD BEYOND NEW JERSEY
Christine Todd Whitman (R) is elected governor after defeating Cary Edwards in the primary.	New HUD Secretary Henry Cisneros decries racial isolation in U.S. cities and suburbs.
COAH lowers estimate of statewide affordable-housing need from 145,000 to 85,000.	
Since 1986, COAH has approved 39 RCAs involving $75 million and commitments to construct or rehabilitate 4,000 urban housing units.	
	Newark razes high-rise public-housing projects as unlivable.

Notes

1 Shades of Fear—*Mount Laurel* and Beyond

(1–2) "The day was unseasonably warm . . ." Our account of the events in Jacob's Chapel is based upon our interviews with the late Ethel Lawrence in 1991 and 1992.

(3) "*Mount Laurel* became . . . the *Brown v. Board of Education* of exclusionary zoning": see Richard Kluger, *Simple Justice* (New York: Knopf, 1976), and J. Anthony Lukas, *Common Ground* (New York: Knopf, 1985), which place the seminal race cases in broader social perspective.

(4) "apartheid American style": see Gunnar Myrdal, *An American Dilemma: The Negro Problem and Modern Democracy* (New York: Harper, 1944); Charles Abrams, *Forbidden Neighbors: A Study of Prejudice in Housing* (New York: Harper, 1955); Robert Reich, "Secession of the Successful: Retreat of the American Elite," *New York Times Magazine* 140 (January 20, 1991): 16; Douglas Massey and Nancy Denton, *American Apartheid: Segregation and the Making of the Underclass* (Cambridge: Harvard University Press, 1993).

(4) "Variations on what happened in Mount Laurel . . . ": see Jonathan Rieder, *Canarsie: The Jews and Italians of Brooklyn against Liberalism* (Cambridge: Harvard University Press, 1985); Joel Garreau, *Edge City: Life on the New Frontier* (New York: Doubleday, 1991); Ron Powers, *Far from Home: Life and Loss in Two American Towns* (New York: Random House, 1991); David Rieff, *Los Angeles: Capital of the Third World* (New York: Simon and Schuster, 1991); Anthony Downs, *New Visions for Metropolitan America* (Washington, D.C.: Brookings Institution, 1994).

(4–5) "The Republicans' 'Contract with America,' . . . a declaration of class warfare": for a provocative and thoughtful discussion of contemporary U.S. politics, see E. J. Dionne Jr., *Why Americans Hate Politics* (New York: Simon and Schuster, 1991).

(5) " 'two societies, one black and the other white . . .' ": for the Kerner Commission's report, see U.S. National Advisory Commission on Civil Disorders, *Report of the National Advisory Commission on Civil Disorders* (New York: Bantam, 1968).

(5) "Reverend Martin Luther King Jr. . . . his last book": Martin Luther King Jr., *Where Do We Go from Here: Chaos or Community?* (New York: Bantam, 1968).

(6) "Gary Orfield, a leading student of U.S. race relations": the quotation is from Gary Orfield and Carol Ashkinaze, *The Closing Door: Conservative Policy and Black Opportunity* (Chicago: University of Chicago Press, 1991), p. 3. For the conservative critique, see Charles Murray, *Losing Ground* (New York: Basic, 1984); see also Richard Herrnstein and Charles Murray, *The Bell Curve* (New York: Free Press, 1994).

(6) "innermost ring of suburbs . . . has witnessed an influx of blacks": John Kain, "Black Suburbanization in the Eighties: A New Beginning or a False Hope?" in *American Domestic Priorities: An Economic Appraisal,* ed. John Quigley and Daniel Rubinfeld (Berkeley: University of California Press, 1985).

(6) "to assume responsibility for those whom they deliberately left behind": see generally Rieder (1985); Katherine Newman, *Declining Fortunes: The Withering of the American Dream* (New York: Basic, 1993).

(7) "something more than the pioneering spirit was at work": see Newman (1993).

(7) "black families spend more on housing": John Kain, "The Influence of Race and Income on Racial Segregation and Policy," in *Desegregation, Race, and Federal Policies,* ed. John Goering (Chapel Hill: University of North Carolina Press, 1986).

(8) "[racial zoning] was outlawed by the U.S. Supreme Court": *Buchanan v. Warley,* 245 U.S. 60 (1917); see generally Richard Babcock, *The Zoning Game* (Madison: University of Wisconsin Press, 1969).

(8) "suburban politicians insist . . . the housing market . . . causes segregated schools": see *Milliken v. Bradley,* 418 U.S. 717 (1974); see also Charles Lawrence, "Segregation 'Misunderstood': The *Milliken* Decision Revisited," *University of San Francisco Law Review* 12, no. 1 (Fall 1977): 15–56.

(8) " 'edge cities' . . . attract business and industry": see Garreau (1991).

(8) " 'spatial mismatch' ": John Kasarda, "Urban Change and Minority Opportunities," in *The New Urban Reality,* ed. Paul Peterson (Washington, D.C.: Brookings Institution, 1985), pp. 33–67; see generally William Julius Wilson, *The Truly Disadvantaged: The Inner City, the Underclass, and Public Policy* (Chicago: University of Chicago Press, 1987).

(8–9) "relationships between residential segregation and [education, housing, jobs, and income]": see Orfield and Ashkinaze (1991), p. 12.

(9) "so familiar as to sound like a recital of the facts of life": the point has been reiterated for years, see U.S. Commission on Civil Rights, *Racial Isolation in the Public Schools* (Washington, D.C.: U.S. Government Printing Office, 1968); without effect; see Orfield and Ashkinaze (1991).

(10) "questions about judicial activism and political authority": see Donald Horowitz, *The Courts and Social Policy* (Washington, D.C.: Brookings Institution, 1977); compare Gerald Rosenberg, *The Hollow Hope: Can Courts Bring About Social Change?* (Chicago: University of Chicago Press, 1991).

2 Camden: A City Doomed by Design

(15) "a wall of separation between city and suburb": see Paul Peterson, *City Limits* (Chicago: University of Chicago Press, 1981).

(15) " 'the story of Camden has been obscured by that of Philadelphia' ": see Jeffrey Dorwart and Philip English Mackey, *Camden County, New Jersey, 1616–1976: A Narrative History* (Camden: Camden County Cultural and Heritage Commission, 1976).

(16) "the newest Baltimore, complete with its own aquarium": This chapter draws on newspaper accounts and unpublished documents, including historical essays prepared by undergraduates at Rutgers University in Camden, on file at the Camden County Historical Society, as well as on interviews with participants and knowledgeable observers. We list all the individuals with whom we spoke in a "Sources" section at the end of this volume.

(16) "Camden . . . was doomed by design": see Daniel Lazare, "Collapse of a City: Growth and Decay of Camden, New Jersey," *Dissent* 38, no. 2 (Spring 1991): 267–275; see generally John R. Logan and Harvey Molotch, *Urban Fortunes: The Political Economy of Place* (Berkeley: University of California Press, 1987).

(16) "[Camden's] undoing . . . mostly the work of outsiders": see Richard Muth,

"Urban Residential Land and Housing Markets," in *Issues in Urban Economics,* ed. Harvey Perloff and Lowden Wingo Jr. (Baltimore: Johns Hopkins University Press, 1968), p. 285.

(16) " 'Our highly urbanized country has chosen to have powerless cities' ": Gerald Frug, "The City as a Legal Concept," *Harvard Law Review* 93, no. 6 (April 1980): 1057–1154; see also Carol Rose, "Planning and Dealing: Piecemeal Land Controls as a Problem of Local Legitimacy," *California Law Review* 71, no. 3 (May 1983): 837–912. The playing surface has been tilted against traditional cities for such a long time, Jane Jacobs writes in *The Death and Life of Great American Cities* (New York: Modern Library, 1993), "the wonder is that any downtowns survive."

(17) " 'Ye most invitingst place to settle by' ": This historical account draws mainly on Dorwart and Mackey (1976). Of interest also are Lorenzo Fisler, *A Local History of Camden* (Camden: Francis A. Cassedy, 1858); George Prowell, *The History of Camden County, New Jersey* (Philadelphia: L. J. Richards, 1886); Charles Boyer, *The Span of a Century: A Chronological History of the City of Camden* (Camden: Camden Centennial Anniversary Committee, 1928); Paul Cranston, *Camden County, 1681–1931* (Camden: Camden Chamber of Commerce, 1931); A. Charles Corotis and James O'Neill, *Camden County Centennial, 1844–1944* (Camden: Board of Chosen Freeholders, 1944).

(17) "Barely a half century later, the Lenni Lenape were mostly gone": This era is described in John Pomfret, *The Province of West New Jersey, 1609–1702* (Princeton, N.J.: Princeton University Press, 1956); John Pomfret, *The New Jersey Proprietors and Their Lands, 1664–1776* (Princeton, N.J.: D. Van Nostrand, 1964); John Pomfret, *Colonial New Jersey* (New York: Scribner's, 1973).

(17) " 'pleasing uniformity of decent competence' ": Hector St. Jean Crevecoeur is quoted in Gwendolyn Wright, *Building the Dream: A Social History of Housing in America* (New York: Pantheon, 1981), p. 15.

(18) "The city's centennial history . . . celebrating this urban coming of age": see Prowell (1886). Mrs. Frances Trollope was less kind. "The great defect of the [American] houses is their extreme uniformity—when you have seen one, you have seen all" (ibid.).

(18) "Victor Talking Machine Company . . . built its first factory [in Camden]": Corporate histories for Camden companies include *50 Years: New York Shipbuilding Corporation, Camden, New Jersey* (Camden: New York Shipbuilding, 1949); B. L. Aldridge, *The Victor Talking Machine Company* (Camden: RCA Sales Corp., 1964).

(18) "Walt Whitman . . . the bard of democracy": see Henry Chupack, "Walt Whitman in Camden: The Formation of a Literary Circle" (Ph.D. diss., Columbia University, 1952).

(18) "[in 1820] there were still slaves on the local census rolls": see William Cooper, *The Attitude of the Society of Friends towards Slavery* (Camden: Camden County Historical Society, 1929); Simeon Moss, "The Persistence of Slavery and Involuntary Servitude in a Free State (1685–1866)," *Journal of Negro History* 32, no. 3 (July 1950): 289–314.

(18) "the Underground Railroad ferried hundreds of escaped slaves through Camden": for Underground Railroad history generally, see Larry Gara, *The Liberty Line: The Legend of the Underground Railroad* (Lexington: University of Kentucky Press, 1967).

(19) "[South Jersey's] white citizens were hostile to civil rights for former slaves": see Kent Allan Peterson, "New Jersey Politics and National Policy-Making, 1865–68" (Ph.D. diss., Princeton University, 1970).

(19) "[the] city's politicians gave the concerns of ordinary Camdenites short shrift": For a discussion of a very different brand of U.S. politics in this era, see Richard Hofstadter, *The Age of Reform* (New York: Vintage, 1955).

(19) "Independence Day 1926 . . . a decisive moment": This section draws on George Blyn, "The Delaware River Bridge: How It Helped/Hurt Its Hinterland," (n.d.); *City of Camden in New Jersey: A Great City Becoming Better* (Camden: Courier-Post, 1927, booklet); Dorwart and Mackey (1976); Walter Andariese, *History of the Benjamin Franklin Bridge* (Philadelphia: Delaware River Port Authority, 1981).

(21) " 'the aristocracy of Camden moved to Haddonfield' ": quoted in Blyn (n.d.).

(22) " 'Every Loyal American Knows What KKK Stands For' ": see Nancy Mac-Lean, *Behind the Mask of Chivalry: The Making of the Second Ku Klux Klan* (New York: Oxford University Press, 1994).

(22) " 'No principle [gives suburbanites] power to stop the progress and development of the city' ": quoted in Kenneth Jackson, *Crabgrass Frontier: The Suburbanization of the United States* (New York: Oxford University Press, 1985). On urbanization generally, see Sam Bass Warner Jr., *The Private City: Philadelphia in Three Periods of Its Growth* (Philadelphia: University of Pennsylvania Press, 1968); Allen M. Wakstein, ed., *The Urbanization of America: An Historic Anthology* (Boston: Houghton Mifflin, 1970); Sam Bass Warner Jr., *The Urban Wilderness: A History of the American City* (New York: Harper and Row, 1972); Sam Bass Warner Jr., *Streetcar Suburbs: The Process of Growth in Boston (1870–1900)*, 2d ed. (Cambridge: Harvard University Press, 1978). For a general discussion of this period in U.S. culture, see Robert Wiebe, *The Search for Order, 1877–1920* (New York: Hill and Wang, 1967).

(23) "A 1940 article in the *National Municipal Review*": quoted in Lazare (1991), as is historian Edna Haycock's observation contained in our subsequent paragraph.

(23) " 'the abandonment of the city, its abandonment as a blunder' ": Henry Ford is quoted in Lewis Mumford, *The City in History: Its Origins, Its Transformations, and Its Prospects* (New York: Harcourt Brace and World, 1961).

(24) " 'pent-up housing demands . . . unleashed with a vengeance outside the city after 1945' ": Peter Muller, "The Changing Economic Geography of the Restructured Metropolis," in *Economic Geography*, ed. James Wheeler and Peter Muller (New York: Wiley, 1981), pp. 161–162.

(24) " 'away from all the noise and dust' ": the Persian nobleman's missive is quoted in C. Leonard Woolley, *Ur of the Chaldees* (Ithaca, N.Y.: Cornell University Press, 1982). A more general observation pertains: "The places where we spend our time affect the people we are and can become. These places have an impact on our sense of self, our sense of safety, the kind of work we get done, the ways we interact with other people, even our ability to function as citizens in a democracy." Tony Hiss, *The Experience of Place* (New York: Knopf, 1990), p. xi.

(24) "suburbanization in the United States accelerated to . . . a stampede": on suburbanization generally, see Jackson (1985); Robert Fishman, *Bourgeois Utopias: The Rise and Fall of Suburbia* (New York: Basic, 1987); Joel Garreau, *Edge City: Life on the New Frontier* (New York: Doubleday, 1991).

(25) " 'If you seek the monuments of the bourgeoisie . . . go to the suburbs' ": Fishman (1987), p. 4.

(25) "The suburbs were 'a cultural creation . . .' ": ibid., p. 8.

(25) "The suburban home . . . 'a public symbol of achievement . . .' ": Herbert Gans, *The Levittowners: Ways of Life and Politics in a New Suburban Community* (New York: Pantheon, 1967). See also William Dobriner, *Class in Suburbia* (Englewood Cliffs, N.J.: Prentice-Hall, 1963).

(25) " 'No man who owns his own house . . . can be a Communist' ": William Levitt is quoted in Jackson (1985). President Calvin Coolidge had said much the same thing a generation earlier: "No greater contribution could be made to the stability of the nation and the advancement of its ideals, than to make it a nation of homeowning families" (ibid., p. 362).

(25) "reality was sacrificed to the pleasure principle": Mumford (1961), p. 494.

(25) "suburbanization proved to be . . . a powerful mind-set": Constance Perlin, *Everything in Its Place: Social Order and Land Use in America* (Princeton, N.J.: Princeton University Press, 1977).

(25) " 'the quintessential physical achievement of the United States' ": Jackson (1985).

(25) "Families hoping to finance a home in the city . . . had a harder time": see James Q. Wilson, ed., *Urban Renewal: The Record and the Controversy* (Cambridge: MIT Press, 1966); Michael Danielson, *The Politics of Exclusion* (New York: Columbia University Press, 1976); Nathan Glazer, "The Bias of American Housing Policy," in *Housing Urban America,* ed. Jon Pynoos, Robert Schafer, and Chester W. Hartman (New York: Aldine, 1980), pp. 428–430; Katharine Bradbury, Anthony Downs, and Kenneth Small, *Urban Decline and the Future of American Cities* (Washington, D.C.: Brookings Institution, 1982); Jacobs (1993).

(26) "With the New Deal . . . federal involvement in housing increased": Charles Abrams, *Forbidden Neighbors: A Study of Prejudice in Housing* (New York: Harper, 1955); Mark Gelfand, *A Nation of Cities: The Federal Government and Urban America, 1933–1965* (New York: Oxford University Press, 1975).

(26) " 'Salvation by bricks' ": Jacobs (1993), p. 114; see also Dorothy Rosenman, *A Million Homes a Year* (New York: Harcourt Brace, 1945); Peter Rossi and Robert Dentler, *The Politics of Urban Renewal: The Chicago Findings* (New York: Free Press, 1961).

(26) " 'culled from the Nuremberg laws' ": Abrams (1955).

(27) "the ferry company . . . closed down completely": Harold Cox, *The Road from Upper Darby—The Story of the Market Street Subway-Elevated* (New York: Electrical Railroaders Association, 1967); Robert Sechler, "Speed Lines to City and Suburbs: A Summary of Rapid Transit Development in Metropolitan Philadelphia from 1879 to 1974" (n.d., MS).

(28) "the idea of a city within a city was deeply flawed": Martha Derthick, *New Towns-in-Town* (Washington, D.C.: Urban Institute, 1972).

(30) "quiescence was replaced by civic interest": Robert Dahl, *Who Governs? Democracy and Power in an American City* (New Haven: Yale University Press, 1961); Michael Lipsky, *Protest in City Politics: Rent Strikes, Housing, and the Power of the Poor* (Chicago: Rand McNally, 1970); Sidney Verba and Norman Nie, *Participation in America: Political Democracy and Social Equality* (New York: Harper and

Row, 1972); Richard Cole, *Citizen Participation and the Urban Policy Process* (Lexington, Mass.: Lexington Books, 1974).

(30) "Griesmann's vivid account": Steven Leleiko and Donald Griesmann, "Camden, New Jersey: A Report Requested by the United States Department of Housing and Urban Development, 1967" (1967, MS).

(31) "Between 1964 and 1967, nearly fifty cities were split open": Jewel Bellush and Stephen David, eds., *Race and Politics in New York City: Five Studies in Policy-Making* (New York: Praeger, 1971); Edward Banfield, *The Unheavenly City Revisited* (Boston: Little, Brown, 1974).

(31) "[Camden] was indistinguishable from Harlem or Watts": William Gamson, *Power and Discontent* (Homewood, Ill.: Dorsey, 1968); Susan Fainstein and Norman Fainstein, *Urban Political Movements: The Search for Power by Minority Groups in American Cities* (Englewood Cliffs, N.J.: Prentice-Hall, 1974).

(32) "*Brown v. Board of Education*": 347 U.S. 483 (1954).

3 Mount Laurel: A Suburb at Odds

(35) "Mount Laurel residents regularly tell a self-deprecating story . . .": This chapter draws on newspaper accounts and unpublished documents on file at the Burlington County Historical Society, as well as on interviews with participants and knowledgeable observers. Interviews are listed in our "Sources" section at the end of this volume. Some interviews quoted in the text are taken from Marianne Oross, "The Examination of the Social, Political, and Economic Conditions Associated with Exclusionary Practices in Mount Laurel, New Jersey" (Ed.D. diss., Rutgers University, 1989). Although Oross does not identify interviewees by name, their identities are readily inferred from the contextual material Oross provides and from separate interviews that we conducted, and so all interviewees are fully identified in this chapter.

(36) "the kind of place that urban planners, meaning no compliment, call a slurb": see Joel Garreau, *Edge City: Life on the New Frontier* (New York: Doubleday, 1991).

(36) "Communities create their own myths, 'an imparted sense of the story of themselves as characters in a drama' ": Ron Powers, *Far from Home: Life and Loss in Two American Towns* (New York: Random House, 1991), p. 62.

(36) "the radical transformation took place in the brief span of a single generation": the early history of Mount Laurel Township is drawn from E. M. Woodward and J. F. Hageman, *History of Burlington and Mercer Counties* (Philadelphia: Lippincott, 1883); Barbara Picken and Gail Greenberg, *Mount Laurel: A Centennial History* (Burlington, N.J.: Burlington County Historical Society, 1972); and Wiliam McMahon, *South Jersey Towns: History and Legend* (New Brunswick, N.J.: Rutgers University Press, 1973). Later statistical material is drawn from *Mount Laurel Guide and Directory* (n.d., pamphlet) and from Complaint, *Southern Burlington County NAACP v. Township of Mount Laurel,* Burlington County Superior Court, 1971.

(36) "Nathan Haines, the 'fighting Quaker' . . .": see William Baker, *The Itinerary of General Washington* (Philadelphia: Lippincott, 1892).

(37) "and as late as 1950 its population stood at just two thousand eight hundred": Mount Laurel residents have generally been more mindful of pragmatic present needs than of the emblems of the past. During the 1940s, the cave where the

Evanses spent their first winter was filled in, without even a nod to the claims of history, by parents fearful for their children's safety. The fine Quaker center built in 1760, Evesham Meeting House, now stands largely disused and in disrepair; Quakers who live in Mount Laurel mostly attend the Moorestown meeting. The Darnell House, one of the town's oldest buildings, survives only because a developer preserved it to lend some class to a mammoth suburban housing complex.

(38) "PUDs are large-scale, self-contained communities within a community": see Gwendolyn Wright, *Building the Dream: A Social History of Housing in America* (New York: Pantheon, 1981); Delores Hayden, *Redesigning the American Dream: The Future of Housing, Work, and Family Life* (New York: Norton, 1984).

(38) "a growth rate more than three times that of the rest of surrounding Burlington County": for the economic theory underlying Mount Laurel's actions, see Charles Tiebout, "A Pure Theory of Local Expenditures," *Journal of Political Economy* 64 (October 1956): 416–424.

(39) "the American classic *Our Town*": Thornton Wilder, *Our Town: A Play in Three Acts* (New York: Coward McCann, 1938).

(40) "*If you people can't afford to live in our town, then you'll just have to leave*": the sentiment is hardly unique to Mount Laurel. A developer in the suburbanizing town of Kent, Connecticut, notes: "There are people who are saying, 'Our children don't have a place to live in Kent.' *Well, so what?* . . . There is no God-given right, simply because you're born in a town, that you should stay in that town. *If* you can't afford it, *if* your parents can't afford to buy you or give you a piece of land . . . you *may* have to go to an adjoining town where the jobs are and work your way back!" Powers (1991), p. 238.

(40) "Quakers brought the first African Americans to Burlington County . . .": Ernest Lyght, *Path of Freedom: The Black Presence in New Jersey's Burlington County, 1659–1900* (Cherry Hill, N.J.: E and E, 1978).

(43) " 'You mean Jewtown,' they say . . .": The historical account of Springville is largely drawn from Oross (1989).

(46) " 'a willingness to exclude whatever men and to ignore whatever events threaten the fulfillment of that hunger' ": Kenneth Lockridge, *A New England Town: The First Hundred Years* (New York: Norton, 1970), p. 169; see generally Christopher Lasch, *Haven in a Heartless World: The Family Besieged* (New York: Basic, 1977).

(48) "Planning and zoning have figured centrally in this political warfare": see generally Eugene Lee, *The Politics of Nonpartisanship* (Berkeley: University of California Press, 1960); Frank Michelman, "Political Markets and Community Self-Determination: Competing Judicial Models of Local Government Efficiency," *Indiana Law Journal* 53, no. 2 (1977–1978), pp. 145–206; Paul Peterson, *City Limits* (Chicago: University of Chicago Press, 1981).

(49) "deeper questions of political identity—how can we best control our destiny?": see Peterson (1981).

(51) " 'We can solve a housing problem or we can try to solve a racial problem . . . but we cannot combine the two' ": William Levitt is quoted in Kenneth Jackson, *Crabgrass Frontier: The Suburbanization of the United States* (New York: Oxford University Press, 1985), p. 242.

(51) "Willingboro remained a verdant and tidy place": see William Dobriner, *Class*

in Suburbia (Englewood Cliffs, N.J.: Prentice-Hall, 1963); Herbert Gans, *The Levittowners: Ways of Life and Politics in a New Suburban Community* (New York: Pantheon, 1967).

(53) "The only principles that drove the propertied classes . . . were efficiency and security": the quotation that follows is from Gerald Marzorati, "From Tocqueville to Perotville: The Call-In Show Has Replaced the Town Square," *New York Times,* June 28, 1992, p. E17.

(53) " 'They were naive. . . . They should have hired a good engineer,' adds the township's engineer": Planners routinely identify with their fellow middle-class citizens. The planners who assisted the Springville community group, like the lawyers who would later take their case to court, were a phenomenon of the activist 1960s. See Harvey Moskowitz and Carl Lindbloom, *The Illustrated Book of Development Definitions* (New Brunswick, N.J.: Center for Urban Policy Research, Rutgers University, 1981).

(53) " 'newcomers in Ramblewood didn't want poor people in Mount Laurel' ": The new residents weren't shy about expressing their hostility toward the old ways. Consider the story of Mattie and Herb Robinson, kin to Ethel Lawrence and longtime residents of Mount Laurel, who used to raise hens behind their house for eggs, just as many of the old-time families did. One day the Robinsons heard angry squawking, and when they investigated they found several teenagers from Ramblewood inside the henhouse beating their hens with sticks. While Herb Robinson held the boys, Mattie called the police. To their chagrin, the officers told them that they'd have to let the boys go and couldn't press charges—indeed, the Robinsons might get in trouble themselves for having laid hands on the youngsters. A few years later, the township council passed an ordinance banning all farm animals from its backyards.

(55) "[poor residents'] cause might arouse more sympathy than a lawsuit designed mainly to let in poor and black outsiders": see Peter O'Connor, "Suburban Housing for the Poor: The Untried Solution for the Cities," *Church and Society* 69, no. 1 (September–October 1978): 39–46.

(57) "an increase in the density of building, with more units, and hence bigger profits": see generally Robert Schafer, *The Suburbanization of Multifamily Housing* (Lexington, Mass.: Lexington Books, 1974); Barry Schwartz, ed., *The Changing Face of the Suburbs* (Chicago: University of Chicago Press, 1976).

4 Simple Justice

(61) "trilogy of *Mount Laurel* cases": *Southern Burlington County NAACP v. Township of Mount Laurel,* 67 N.J. 151, 336 A.2d 713, *appeal dismissed and cert. denied,* 423 U.S. 808 (1975) ("*Mount Laurel I*"); *Southern Burlington County NAACP v. Township of Mount Laurel,* 92 N.J. 158, 456 A.2d 390 (1983) ("*Mount Laurel II*"); and *Hills Dev. Co. v. Township of Bernards,* 103 N.J. 1, 510 A.2d 621 (1986) ("*Mount Laurel III*").

(61) "the U.S. Supreme Court first announced . . . municipalities could tell landowners how their land could . . . be used": *Village of Euclid v. Ambler Realty Co.,* 272 U.S. 365 (1926). See generally Richard Babcock and Fred Bosselman, *Exclusionary Zoning: Land Use Regulation and Housing in the 1970s* (New York: Praeger, 1973).

(62) "*James v. Valtierra*": 402 U.S. 137 (1971).

(62) " 'state decisions [based on state law] . . . are not even reviewable by, the Supreme Court of the United States' ": William Brennan, "State Constitutions and the Protection of Individual Rights," *Harvard Law Review* 90, no. 3 (January 1977): 489–504; see also Mary Cornelia Porter, "State Supreme Courts and the Legacy of the Warren Court: Some Old Inquiries for a New Situation," *Publius* 8, no. 4 (Fall 1978): 55–74.

(63) "[New Jersey's] tribunals 'the nation's worst' ": "New Jersey Goes to the Head of the Class," *Journal of the American Judicature Society* 31 (1948): 131. See also G. Alan Tarr and Mary Cornelia Aldis Porter, *State Supreme Courts in State and Nation* (New Haven: Yale University Press, 1988).

(63) " 'If you want to see the old common law in all its picturesque formality . . .' ": D. W. Brogan, *The English People* (New York: Knopf, 1943), p. 108.

(63) "the governor appointed Frank Hague Jr. . . . to 'please his daddy,' the governor admitted": see generally Dayton McKean, *The Boss: The Hague Machine in Action* (Boston: Houghton Mifflin, 1940); Richard Conners, *A Cycle of Power: The Career of Jersey City Mayor Frank Hague* (Metuchen, N.J.: Scarecrow, 1971).

(63) "a remarkable lawyer and politician named Arthur Vanderbilt": see generally Eugene Gerhart, *Arthur T. Vanderbilt: The Compleat Counsellor* (Albany, N.Y.: Q. Corp., 1980); Arthur Vanderbilt II, *Changing Law: A Biography of Arthur T. Vanderbilt* (New Brunswick, N.J.: Rutgers University Press, 1976).

(64) "The reformers . . . learned how to maneuver within smoke-filled rooms": Henry Glick and Kenneth Vines, *State Court Systems* (Englewood Cliffs, N.J.: Prentice-Hall, 1973), p. 16.

(64) "the New Jersey legislature had no power to veto court-made rules": *Winberry v. Salisbury*, 5 N.J. 240, 74 A.2d 406, *cert. denied.*, 340 U.S. 877 (1950). Some state legislators, angry at the justices, wanted to adopt a constitutional amendment restricting the court's rule-making powers, but they abandoned the idea when the bar and the press backed the court. Tarr and Porter (1988), p. 194.

(64) "The Supreme Court has 'creative responsibility for making law' ": Joseph Weintraub, "Justice Frederick W. Hall: A Tribute," *Rutgers Law Review* 29, no. 3 (Spring 1976): 499–501.

(65) "New Jersey's Supreme Court justices have been more openly political": Glick and Vines (1973), p. 64. See also Henry Glick, *Supreme Courts in State Politics: An Investigation of the Judicial Role* (New York: Basic, 1971).

(65) "Judicial innovation was the byword in New Jersey": John Pittenger, "The Courts," in *The Political State of New Jersey,* ed. Gerald Pomper (New Brunswick, N.J.: Rutgers University Press, 1986), pp. 160–179. On the New Jersey Supreme Court's place in the context of high courts nationally, see generally Robert Kagan, Bliss Cartwright, Lawrence M. Friedman, and Stanton Wheeler, "The Evolution of State Supreme Courts," *Michigan Law Review* 76, no. 6 (May 1978): 961–1005; Lawrence Friedman, Robert Kagan, Bliss Cartwright, and Stanton Wheeler, "State Supreme Courts: A Century of Style and Citation," *Stanford Law Review* 33, no. 5 (May 1981): 773–818; Dennis Coyle, *Property Rights and the Constitution: Shaping Society through Land Use Regulation* (Albany: SUNY Press, 1993), ch. 4 [comparison with Pennsylvania].

(65) "a policymaker acting in parallel with the governor and the legislature": see Stanley Friedelbaum, "Constitutional Law and Judicial Policy Making," in *Politics in New Jersey,* ed. Richard Lehne and Alan Rosenthal, rev. ed. (New Brunswick,

N.J.: Rutgers University Press, 1979); Lawrence Baum and Bradley Canon, "State Supreme Courts as Activists: New Doctrines in the Law of Torts," in *State Supreme Courts: Policymakers in the Federal System,* ed. Mary Cornelia Porter and G. Alan Tarr (Westport, Conn.: Greenwood, 1982), pp. 97–99; Tarr and Porter (1988), pp. 203–204.

(65) "*Lionshead Lake*": *Lionshead Lake, Inc. v. Township of Wayne,* 10 N.J. 165 (1952), *appeal dismissed for want of a substantial federal question,* 344 U.S. 919 (1953).

(65) "*Vickers*": *Vickers v. Township Committee of Gloucester Township,* 37 N.J. 232 (1962), *cert. denied,* 371 U.S. 233 (1963)

(66) "anyone else is perceived as a stranger outside the gates": Babcock and Bosselman (1973).

(66) " 'If and when conditions change . . . alterations in zoning restrictions . . . need not be long delayed' ": *Pierro v. Baxendale,* 20 N.J. 17 (1955).

(66) " 'Regional needs' matter, said the justices in 1966": *Kunzler v. Hoffman,* 48 N.J. 277 (1966); see also *Roman Catholic Diocese of Newark v. Ho-Ho-Kus Borough,* 47 N.J. 211 (1966).

(66) "A more critical ruling four years later involved the town of Englewood": *DeSimone v. Greater Englewood Housing Corp. No. 1,* 56 N.J. 428 (1970).

(67) " 'fiscal zoning' . . . [a] 'legally dubious strategem' ": *Rutgers University v. Piluso,* 60 N.J. 142 (1972).

(67) "Mount Laurel Township's best and only justification . . . ": see generally Mary Mann, *The Right to Housing: Constitutional Issues and Remedies in Exclusionary Zoning* (New York: Praeger, 1976).

(67) "A bookshelf's worth of academic commentary . . . sided with the *Mount Laurel* litigators": see, e.g., Norman Williams, "Zoning and Housing Policies," *Journal of Housing* 10, no. 3 (March 1953): 94–95; Charles Haar, "Zoning for Minimum Standards: The Wayne Township Case," *Harvard Law Review* 66, no. 6 (April 1953): 1051–1063; Norman Williams, "Planning Law and Democratic Living," *Law and Contemporary Problems* 20, no. 2 (Spring 1953): 317–350; Richard Babcock, *The Zoning Game: Municipal Practices and Policies* (Madison: University of Wisconsin Press, 1966); Norman Williams and Edward Wacks, "Segregation of Residential Areas along Economic Lines: Lionshead Lake Revisited," *Wisconsin Law Review* 1969, no. 3 (1969): 827–847; Lawrence Sager, "Tight Little Islands: Exclusionary Zoning, Equal Protection, and the Indigent," *Stanford Law Review* 21, no. 4 (April 1969): 767–800.

(68) "Norman Williams ruefully describes . . . 'badly thought-out cases' ": Norman Williams, "The Background and Significance of *Mount Laurel II,*" *Washington University Journal of Urban and Contemporary Law* 26 (1984): 3–23.

(70) "persons behind the tight-fitting masks of the law": see generally John Noonan, *Persons and Masks of the Law: Cardozo, Holmes, Jefferson, and Wythe as Makers of the Masks* (New York: Farrar, Straus, and Giroux, 1976).

(72) "the four-day trial in March 1972": our account of the *Mount Laurel* trial relies on documents generated by the parties, interviews with many of the participants, and interviews quoted in Marianne Oross, "The Examination of the Social, Political, and Economic Conditions Associated with Exclusionary Practices in Mount Laurel, New Jersey" (Ed.D. diss., Rutgers University, 1989).

(73) "[a Detroit judge's] novel legal conclusion . . . overturned by a bare majority of the Burger Court": the Detroit schools case decided by the high court is *Milliken*

v. Bradley, 418 U.S. 717 (1974). Two preceding trial court decisions are reported in *Bradley v. Milliken*, 338 F.Supp. 582 (E.D.Mich. 1971) and 345 F.Supp. 914 (E.D.Mich. 1972); the intermediate appellate decision is reported in *Bradley v. Milliken*, 484 F.2d 215 (6th Cir. 1973).

(77) "unanimous judgment in the *Mount Laurel* case": *Southern Burlington County NAACP v. Township of Mount Laurel*, 67 N.J. 151, 336 A.2d 713, *appeal dismissed and cert. denied*, 423 U.S. 808 (1975).

(78) "Weintraub had acquired a reputation for precociousness": on Weintraub generally, see Milton D. Cornford, "Joseph Weintraub: Reminiscences," *New Jersey Law Journal* 96 (1973): 1205; John Francis, "Joseph Weintraub—A Judge for All Seasons," *Cornell Law Review* 59, no. 2 (January 1974): 186–196; John Schupper, "Chief Justice Weintraub and the Role of the Judiciary," *Rutgers-Camden Law Journal* 5, no. 3 (Spring 1974): 413–417; John Francis, "Chief Justice Joseph Weintraub: A Tribute," *Rutgers Law Review* 30, no. 3 (Spring 1977): 479–481.

(80) "*Village of Belle Terre v. Boraas*": 416 U.S. 1 (1974).

(80) " 'The single-family home' . . . a place of 'blessings,' a 'sanctuary,' language that 'connotes the sacred' ": see Constance Perin, *Everything in Its Place: Social Order and Land Use in America* (Princeton, N.J.: Princeton University Press, 1977), p. 48.

(81) "neither poor city residents nor civil-rights–minded suburbanites could challenge . . .": *Warth v. Seldin*, 422 U.S. 490 (1975).

5 The Schoolmaster Court

In addition to cited sources, this chapter draws on newspaper accounts and our own interviews for certain facts and quotations.

(83) "[Home] symbolizes a 'haven in a heartless world' ": see Christopher Lasch, *Haven in a Heartless World: The Family Besieged* (New York: Basic, 1977).

(83) " 'failure to pay a single [mortgage] installment may bring foreclosure, eviction, and despair' ": Charles Abrams, *Forbidden Neighbors: A Study of Prejudice in Housing* (New York: Harper, 1955), pp. 137–138; see also Robert Bellah et al., *Habits of the Heart: Individualism and Commitment in American Life* (Berkeley: University of California Press, 1985).

(83) "Such fears . . . can evoke panic and worse": see Richard Hofstadter, *The Paranoid Style in American Politics* (New York: Knopf, 1965).

(83) " 'revolution in land . . . to put small holdings into the hands of the rank and file' ": Abrams (1955), p. 3.

(83) "Government would manage this distribution of land while otherwise staying clear": testifying before the House Select Committee on Lobbying Activities in 1950, Herbert Nelson, executive vice president of the National Association of Real Estate Boards, put this laissez-faire view succinctly: "I do not oppose government intervention in housing. I only believe that the powers of government should be used to assist private enterprise." Ibid., p. 154.

(83–84) "our people should live in their own homes": President Hoover is quoted in ibid., p. 147.

(85) "observers, both supporters and critics of Hall's opinion, were more skeptical yet": the quotations in this paragraph are drawn from: Frederick W. Hall, "An Orientation to Mount Laurel," in *After Mount Laurel: The New Suburban Zoning,*

ed. Jerome Rose and Robert Rothman (New Brunswick, N.J.: Center for Urban Policy Research, Rutgers University, 1977), pp. 3–13; Richard Lehne, "Revenue and Expenditure Politics," in *Politics in New Jersey*, ed. Richard Lehne and Alan Rosenthal, rev. ed. (New Brunswick, N.J.: Eagleton Institute of Politics, Rutgers University, 1979), quoting Sternlieb and Williams; Jerome Rose, "The *Mount Laurel* Decision: Is It Based on Wishful Thinking?" *Real Estate Law Journal* 4, no. 1 (Summer 1975): 61–70.

(85) "Carl Bisgaier predicted that the 'landmark' decision would 'finally open the suburbs to the poor' ": for the Bisgaier quotation and others in this chapter, we draw on newspaper accounts, unpublished materials, and interviews with knowledgeable sources. Interviews are listed in our "Sources" section at the end of this volume.

(89) "*Madison*, the same lawsuit that the justices had planned to hear": Ultimately the Supreme Court of New Jersey decided *Oakwood at Madison, Inc. v. Township of Madison*, 72 N.J. 481 (1977).

(89) "Two other zoning cases . . . added to this sense of disorderly retreat": *Pascack Assn. Ltd. v. Mayor and Council of the Township of Washington*, 74 N.J. 470 (1977); *Fobe Associates v. Mayor and Council of the Borough of Demarest*, 74 N.J. 519 (1977).

(90–91) "Yale Rabin . . . called [Mount Laurel's] ordinance a '*negative* fair share plan' ": Professor Rabin later referred to these practices as "expulsive zoning." Yale Rabin, "Expulsive Zoning: The Inequitable Legacy of Euclid," in *Zoning and the American Dream: Promises Still to Keep*, ed. Charles Haar and Jerold Kayden (Chicago: Planners Press, American Planning Assoc., 1987), pp. 101–121.

(93) " 'The experience of the 1947 [judicial] reform is so strong . . . that it still moves us substantially in New Jersey' ": Chief Justice Wilentz is quoted in Peter Buchsbaum, "The Courts: The 1947 'Revolution,' " *New Jersey Reporter*, November 1982, p. 33.

(93) "Wilentz *fils* followed his father to the state legislature . . .": "Reconstructing New Jersey, A Guide to the State Supreme Court—The Wilentz Years: 1979–1991," *New Jersey Law Journal* 130 [supp.] (February 17, 1992): 10 et seq.

(94) "the high court overturned that school-funding arrangement": *Robinson v. Cahill*, 62 N.J. 473, 303 A.2d 273 (1973).

(94) "the crusade left the judges weary, their reservoir of goodwill . . . practically empty": see Richard Lehne, *The Quest for Justice: The Politics of School Finance Reform* (New York: Longman, 1978); Norman Williams and Tatyana Doughty, "Studies in Legal Realism: *Mount Laurel*, *Belle Terre*, and *Berman*," *Rutgers Law Review* 29, no. 1 (Fall 1975): 73–109.

(94) "In the last days of 1979 . . . the court decided to tackle exclusionary zoning once more": John Payne, "Housing Rights and Remedies: A 'Legislative' History of *Mount Laurel II*," *Seton Hall Law Review* 14, no. 4 (1984): 889–943.

(96) "how one might anticipate the 'practical effect' of a decision . . . ; in *Mount Laurel II*, the justices asked for similar advice": this wasn't the first time that New Jersey's high court had departed from customary practice to improve the process of decision making. A decade earlier, Chief Justice Weintraub occasionally invited counsel and their experts for informal talks in complex cases, as a way of showing the advocates "from the open discussion that the justices now comprehended the issues presented for decision." Weintraub saw his innovation as a

useful reminder that "judges are not God, and therefore some further enlighten-ment should be sought." John Francis, "Joseph Weintraub—A Judge for All Seasons," *Cornell Law Review* 59, no. 2 (January 1974): 186–196.

(97) "Paul Davidoff . . . 'the Ralph Nader of the movement' ": an example of Paul Davidoff's writing on the subject of affordable housing is Paul Davidoff, "De-cent Housing for All," in *America's Housing Crisis: What Is to Be Done?*, ed. Chester Hartman (New York: Routledge and Kegan Paul, 1983).

(99) "Charles Haar . . . four decades after his *Harvard Law Review* article condemn-ing . . . *Lionshead Lake*": Charles M. Haar, *Suburbs under Siege: Race, Space, and Audacious Judges* (Princeton, N.J.: Princeton University Press, 1996).

(99) " 'an extraordinary hiatus . . . during which the court's ability to handle the remedial problem came increasingly into question' ": Payne (1984), p. 902.

(100) "the chief justice, who often assigned himself headline-making cases": Wilentz authored major school-finance and capital-punishment opinions for the New Jersey Supreme Court.

(101) "what philosopher Isaiah Berlin calls 'negative liberty' ": Isaiah Berlin, *Four Essays on Liberty* (New York: Oxford University Press, 1969).

(102) "these sources of funds began drying up during Richard Nixon's truncated second term . . .": see Rachel Bratt, *Rebuilding a Low-Income Housing Policy* (Phila-delphia: Temple University Press, 1989).

(103) "The builder won not only the legal case but . . . the right to build": Peter Buchsbaum, "No Wrong without a Remedy: The New Jersey Supreme Court's Effort to Bar Exclusionary Zoning," *Urban Lawyer* 17, no. 1 (Winter 1985): 59–90.

(103) " 'a new judicial role in stimulating legislative responses. . . . [T]his is a most pleasing possibility' ": Payne (1984), p. 932.

6 The Politics of "No"

In addition to cited sources, this chapter draws on newspaper accounts and our own interviews for certain facts and quotations.

(112) "[the governor] . . . warned that the state courts would 'inevitably' step in if the politicians did not respond": Governor William Cahill's views on the statewide housing crisis were outlined in "A Blueprint for Housing," delivered to the New Jersey legislature late in 1970 and quoted in Richard Babcock and Fred Bosselman, *Exclusionary Zoning: Land Use Regulation and Housing in the 1970s* (New York: Praeger, 1973), p. 47; see also Michael Danielson, *The Politics of Exclusion* (New York: Columbia University Press, 1976), pp. 293–299.

(113) "the state's policy . . . amounted to no more than the sum of the exclusionary-zoning rules of its many municipalities": see Thomas Fleming, *New Jersey: A Bicentennial History* (New York: Norton, 1977), which describes the state's "paramount problem" as its "lack of identity, of community," and empha-sizes the "intense localism" of its politics (p. 193). See also Gerald Pomper, ed., *The Political State of New Jersey* (New Brunswick, N.J.: Rutgers University Press, 1986).

(113) "no statewide property tax or income tax . . . until the mid-1960s, when it imposed a modest sales tax": Fleming (1977) describes the "struggle for a statewide tax to reduce (not eliminate) the inequalities of New Jersey's localism" (pp. 203–204).

(113) " 'The Legislature is hardly equipped . . . in addressing itself to today's problems . . . ' a 1974 state bar association report concluded": the 1974 state bar report is cited in Alan Rosenthal, "The New Jersey Legislature: The Contemporary Shape of an Historical Institution; Not Yet Good But Better Than It Used to Be," in *The Development of the New Jersey Legislature from Colonial Times to the Present,* ed. William Wright (Trenton, N.J.: New Jersey Historical Commission, 1976), pp. 72–119.

(113) " 'Where do we often go for legislation? To the executive' ": Robert Wilentz is quoted in Rosenthal (1976), p. 107.

(113) "the Assembly is sometimes called the 'zoo' ": for a general discussion of the New Jersey legislature, see Alan Rosenthal, "The Legislature," in Pomper (1986), pp. 118–159.

(114) "Very much the urbanist, Ylvisaker believed it was 'dangerous' to give zoning powers to suburbs": our description of Paul Ylvisaker, his statements, and events in the later Cahill administration are drawn from Danielson (1976).

(115) "suburbanites saw plenty of reasons to resist. . . . Others began to raise environmental concerns": see generally Joseph Sax, "Some Thoughts on the Decline of Private Property," *Washington Law Review* 58, no. 3 (July 1983): 481–496.

(116) "the state became a national leader in protecting the environment . . . wetlands were saved from development": see Jerry English and John Sarno, "The Freshwater Wetlands Protection Act: Give and 'Take' in New Jersey," *Seton Hall Legislative Journal* 12, no. 2 (1989): 249–269.

(116) "*Robinson v. Cahill*": 62 N.J. 473, 303 A.2d 273 (1973).

(116) "a personal income tax . . . to pay the school bill": see Richard Lehne, *The Quest for Justice: The Politics of School Finance Reform* (New York: Longman, 1978); Gerald Pomper, "Conclusion," in Pomper (1986), pp. 254–255.

(118) "the Kean family is even more of a political dynasty than the Wilentzes": details on Governor Kean are from his autobiography, Thomas Kean, *The Politics of Inclusion* (New York: Free Press, 1988). His title is an obvious play on Danielson (1976).

(122) "Officials from Cranbury detailed the imminent demise of their history-rich town . . .": Lawrence Houstown, a Cranbury resident and development consultant, disputes the "grotesque" fears of the suburbs in his "The Road Not Taken to Mount Laurel," *New Jersey Reporter,* February 1985, pp. 32–37.

(131) "Governor Kean could use his conditional veto to dictate the result he wanted . . .": on the conditional veto see generally League of Women Voters of New Jersey Education Fund (Karen West, ed.), *New Jersey: Spotlight on Government,* 5th ed. (New Brunswick, N.J.: Rutgers University Press, 1985), p. 23; Donald Linky, "The Governor," in Pomper (1986), pp. 93–117. Ironically, the conditional veto was adopted as part of the 1947 reform of New Jersey's constitution—the same reform, some argue, that led historically to its Supreme Court's activism. See Peter Buchsbaum, "The Courts: The 1947 'Revolution,' " *New Jersey Reporter,* November 1982, p. 33; see also G. Alan Tarr and Mary Cornelia Aldis Porter, *State Supreme Courts in State and Nation* (New Haven: Yale University Press, 1988), pp. 184–196.

(135) "[Lipman] couldn't bring herself to support what she labeled a 'sham' ": Senators Lipman and Stockman both later reversed their position and offered

their grudging support to the Fair Housing Act. See Wynona Lipman, "The 'Fair' Housing Act," *Seton Hall Legislative Journal* 9, no. 3 (1986): 569–573; Gerald Stockman, "The Art of the Possible," *Seton Hall Legislative Journal* 9, no. 3 (1986): 581–584.

7 Can Bureaucrats Build Houses?

In addition to cited sources, this chapter draws on newspaper accounts and our own interviews for certain facts and quotations.

(137) "*Hills Development v. Bernards Township*, was the last of the *Mount Laurel* trilogy": *Hills Dev. Co. v. Township of Bernards*, 103 N.J. 1, 510 A.2d 621 (1986) ("*Mount Laurel III*").

(140) "the title of the article from which this observation was extracted": Alan Mallach, "Blueprint for Delay: From Mount Laurel to Molehill," *New Jersey Reporter*, October 1985, pp. 21–27.

(142) "Only a handful of judges had been removed . . . ; not once had a Supreme Court justice been rejected": see Thomas Fleming, *New Jersey: A Bicentennial History* (New York: Norton, 1977); League of Women Voters of New Jersey Education Fund (Karen West, ed.), *New Jersey: Spotlight on Government*, 5th ed. (New Brunswick, N.J.: Rutgers University Press, 1985).

(142) " 'social engineering on a scale never imagined by Marx or Engels' ": Governor Kean's version of the Wilentz renomination battle, on which we rely, is from Thomas Kean, *The Politics of Inclusion* (New York: Free Press, 1988), pp. 193–195.

(142) "the pull of personal history makes a difference in . . . a state that's almost as politically incestuous as the Hapsburg dynasty": John Kean, an ancestor of the governor's, represented South Carolina in the Continental Congress, "where he was the first member to propose the abolition of slavery." Ibid., p. 131. Kean notes his family's ties to Wilentz, ibid., p. 191.

(143) "Replacing Wilentz, [Kean] says, would have set a terrible standard": this was not the first time that Governor Kean made a judicial choice unpopular with conservatives in his party. In 1983 he reappointed Sylvia Pressler, a liberal judge originally placed on the bench by Democrat Brendan Byrne, to the appellate division of the state superior court, over the objection of the Republican senator from her district. That senator was exercising a privilege known as "senatorial courtesy," under which governors typically defer to the wishes of the local senator on such decisions. The state senate sided with Kean and confirmed Judge Pressler's renomination overwhelmingly. "[T]he episode demonstrates the triumph of a statewide principle—the independence of the judiciary—over a local principle—senatorial courtesy . . . the issue of Judge Pressler's renomination was not a partisan one. . . . The controversy galvanized a good government brigade in defense of Judge Pressler and the independence of the juduciary." John Pittenger, "The Courts," in *The Political State of New Jersey*, ed. Gerald Pomper (New Brunswick, N.J.: Rutgers University Press, 1986), p. 162.

(145) "a state that lacks a center—'So you live in New Jersey; which exit off the turnpike?' ": "New Jersey is a centrifugal state, with few forces holding it together. There is little sense of community, of belonging, except on the local level. The Turnpike, therefore, plays a unifying role." Angus Gillespie and Michael Rockland, *Looking for America on the New Jersey Turnpike* (New Brunswick, N.J.: Rutgers University Press, 1989), p. 9.

(145) " 'Practically every political decision winds up . . . as a legal decision' ": Alexis de Tocqueville, *Democracy in America*, rev. ed., vol. 1 (New York: Knopf, 1972).

(145) "The commonplace rationale for judicial activism . . . is that courts have a duty to enforce constitutional rights and provide fitting remedies": the literature on judicial activism is voluminous. For a sample, see Abram Chayes, "The Role of the Judge in Public Law Litigation," *Harvard Law Review* 89, no. 7 (May 1976): 1281–1316; Donald Horowitz, *The Courts and Social Policy* (Washington, D.C.: Brookings Institution, 1977); John Hart Ely, *Democracy and Distrust: A Theory of Judicial Review* (Cambridge: Harvard University Press, 1980); Alexander Bickel, *The Least Dangerous Branch: The Supreme Court at the Bar of Politics*, 2d ed. (New Haven: Yale University Press, 1981); Richard Gambitta, Marlynn L. May, and James C. Foster, eds., *Governing through Courts* (Beverly Hills, Calif.: Sage, 1981); Martin Shapiro, *Who Guards the Guardians? Judicial Control of Administration* (Athens: University of Georgia Press, 1988); Gerald Rosenberg, *The Hollow Hope: Can Courts Bring About Social Change?* (Chicago: University of Chicago Press, 1991).

(146) "a fear that . . . 'Leave it to the judges' will become the legislative refrain": for an analysis of this problem as it pertains specifically to New Jersey, see Pittenger (1986).

(146) "reformism has often been taken for granted": see Hans Linde, "Judges, Critics, and the Realist Tradition," *Yale Law Journal* 82, no. 2 (December 1972): 227–256; Morton Horowitz, *The Transformation of American Law, 1780–1860* (Cambridge: Harvard University Press, 1977).

(146) "pattern of interaction between justices and legislators": for a lucid exposition of this tendency in New Jersey, see G. Alan Tarr and Mary Cornelia Aldis Porter, *State Supreme Courts in State and Nation* (New Haven: Yale University Press, 1988), pp. 184–236.

(146) "The justices had to maintain a reputation for 'unpredictable assertiveness,' [Weintraub] said": quoted in Richard Lehne, *The Quest for Justice: The Politics of School Finance Reform* (New York: Longman, 1978), pp. 128–130.

(146) "the judges have fared best when they could enlist powerful allies to their cause": see Alan Rosenthal, "The Governor, the Legislature, and State Policy-Making," in *Politics in New Jersey*, ed. Richard Lehne and Alan Rosenthal, rev. ed. (New Brunswick, N.J.: Eagleton Institute of Politics, Rutgers University, 1979).

(147) "the legislation follows the court doctrine in form more than in fact": see Richard Briffault, "Our Localism: Part I—The Structure of Local Government Law," *Columbia Law Review* 90, no. 1 (January 1990): 1–115.

(147) "the Fair Housing Act . . . is a remarkable accomplishment": the quotation that follows is from Tarr and Porter (1988), p. 223.

(148) "[markets, politics, and rights] confound and collide with one another": see Charles Lindblom, *Politics and Markets* (New York: Basic, 1977).

(149) " 'partisan mutual adjustment,' bargaining through the vote": see Charles Lindblom, *The Intelligence of Democracy* (New York: Free Press, 1965).

(154) "The *Mount Laurel* judges, Serpentelli and his kind, were gone, replaced by seventeen judges": after the court upheld the Fair Housing Act in *Mount Laurel III*, Chief Justice Wilentz dissolved the special *Mount Laurel II* enforcement panel (Judges Serpentelli, Gibson, and Skillman) and designated one judge per

superior court district to hear the future exclusionary-zoning matters not disposed of by the Council on Affordable Housing.

(156) "The Hovnanian family story is an American classic": see Robert Goodman, *The Last Entrepreneurs: America's Regional Wars for Jobs and Dollars* (New York: Simon and Schuster, 1979).

(156) " 'He could understand the value of places that should be kept open for ballfields . . .' ": Joel Garreau, *Edge City: Life on the New Frontier* (New York: Doubleday, 1991), p. 337.

(160) "well-paid consultants, speaking with the imprimatur of the university, prepared to provide the road map": see, e.g., Robert Burchell et al., *Mount Laurel II: Challenge and Delivery of Low-Cost Housing* (Piscataway, N.J.: Center for Urban Policy Research, Rutgers University, 1983).

(162) " 'the Court was really more concerned with economic integration than with housing provision' ": John Selig, "Implementing Mount Laurel: An Assessment of Regional Contribution Agreements," Princeton Urban and Regional Affairs Research Center, Working Paper No. 14, June 1988, p. 9; and see Patricia Salkin and John Armentano, "The Fair Housing Act, Zoning, and Affordable Housing," *Urban Lawyer* 25, no. 4 (Fall 1993): 893–904.

(162) " 'taking a step back, it gets more complicated' ": for a critique of the economics underlying *Mount Laurel II* and the Fair Housing Act, see Mark Hughes and Peter Vandoren, "Social Policy through Land Reform: New Jersey's Mount Laurel Controversy," *Political Science Quarterly* 105, no. 1 (Spring 1990): 97–111.

(162) "what COAH was doing": for a discussion of COAH's efforts, see Colloquium, "Mount Laurel and the Fair Housing Act: Success or Failure?" *Fordham Urban Law Journal* 19, no. 1 (Fall 1991): 59–86.

(164) "Stephen Eisdorfer . . . who specialized in *Mount Laurel*–type matters for the Public Advocate": interestingly, after Governor Christine Todd Whitman abolished the Department of the Public Advocate in 1994, Eisdorfer joined Henry Hill's Princeton law firm.

8 Virtual Housing

(168) "social class, the prime culprit": William Julius Wilson, *The Declining Significance of Race: Blacks and Changing American Institutions* (Chicago: University of Chicago Press, 1978); compare Christopher Jencks and Paul Peterson, eds., *The Urban Underclass* (Washington, D.C.: Brookings Institution, 1991).

(168) " 'a word disappeared from the American vocabulary . . . segregation' ": Douglas Massey and Nancy Denton, *American Apartheid: Segregation and the Making of the Underclass* (Cambridge: Harvard University Press, 1993). See also Reynolds Farley et al., "Continued Racial Segregation in Detroit: 'Chocolate City, Vanilla Suburbs' Revisited," *Journal of Housing Research* 4, no. 1 (1993): 1–38.

(169) "not for a quarter of a century has Washington paid the slightest attention to integrating the suburbs": see Massey and Denton (1993); see also Nathan Glazer, "The Bias of American Housing Policy," in *Housing Urban America,* ed. Jon Pynoos, Robert Schafer, and Chester W. Hartman (New York: Aldine, 1980), pp. 428–430; Alan Mallach, *Inclusionary Housing Programs: Policies and Practices* (New Brunswick, N.J.: Center for Urban Policy Research, Rutgers University, 1984); George Metcalf, *Fair Housing Comes of Age* (New York: Greenwood, 1988).

(170) "Nixon 'draped the dreaded race-mixing shroud' ": the best treatment of race and federal housing policies through the Nixon presidency is Michael Danielson, *The Politics of Exclusion* (New York: Columbia University Press, 1976).

(170) "not one of [those bright ideas] has ever received adequate financial support": In late 1994, President Clinton announced that HUD's budget would be further cut back. Amid the austerity, however, one new enterprise-zone program awarded grants of one hundred million dollars to cities that had established public-private development partnerships. Philadelphia and Camden jointly received such a grant.

On housing policy during the past generation, see generally Anthony Downs, *Federal Housing Subsidies: How Are They Working?* (Lexington, Mass.: Lexington Books, 1973); Bernard Frieden and Marshall Kaplan, *The Politics of Neglect: Urban Aid from Model Cities to Revenue Sharing* (Cambridge: MIT Press, 1975); Katharine Bradbury, Anthony Downs, and Kenneth Small, *Urban Decline and the Future of American Cities* (Washington, D.C.: Brookings Institution, 1982); Rolf Goetze, *Rescuing the American Dream: Public Policies and the Crisis in Housing* (New York: Holmes and Meier, 1983); J. Paul Mitchell, ed., *Federal Housing Policy and Programs: Past and Present* (New Brunswick, N.J.: Center for Urban Policy Research, Rutgers University, 1985); Rachel Bratt, Chester Hartman, and Ann Meyerson, *Critical Perspectives on Housing* (Philadelphia: Temple University Press, 1986); Rachel Bratt, *Rebuilding a Low-Income Housing Policy* (Philadelphia: Temple University Press, 1989); Edward Lazere et al., *A Place to Call Home: The Low-Income Housing Crisis Continues* (Washington, D.C.: Center on Budget and Policy Priorities, 1991); Keith Aoki, "Race, Space, and Place: The Relation between Architectural Modernism, Post-Modernism, Urban Planning, and Gentrification," *Fordham Urban Law Journal* 20, no. 4 (1993): 699–829.

(171) "The answer is racism": Garry Wills, "A Tale of Three Cities," *New York Review of Books*, March 28, 1991, pp. 11–16.

(171) "Downs envisioned a coalition": Anthony Downs, *Opening Up the Suburbs* (New Haven: Yale University Press, 1973). For Downs's more recent reflections, see his *New Visions for Metropolitan America* (Washington, D.C.: Brookings Institution, 1994).

(172) "*children* . . . now ready to plant their own suburban roots": see Katherine Newman, *Declining Fortunes: The Withering of the American Dream* (New York: Basic, 1993); Anthony Downs, "The American Dream of an Affordable House: The Image Recedes," *Across the Board* 18 (December 1981): 58–63.

(172) " 'the everyday creates a sense of protective closure' ": Verlyn Klinkenborg, "Back to Love Canal: Recycled Homes, Rebuilt Dreams," *Harper's*, March 1991, p. 71.

(172) "a single metropolis": David Rusk's argument is from his *Cities without Suburbs* (Washington, D.C.: Woodrow Wilson Center Press, 1993); compare Peter Salins, "Cities, Suburbs, and the Urban Crisis," *Public Interest*, no. 113 (Fall 1993): 91–104.

(172) "Though this is interesting stuff for the policy maven, it's simply not going to happen": Downs (1994), ch. 9; compare George Sternlieb and James Hughes, "Structuring the Future," *Society* 21, no. 3 (March/April, 1984): 28–34.

(173) "lines between city and suburb . . . seem likely to sharpen": Thomas Edsall and Mary Edsall, *Chain Reaction: The Impact of Race, Rights, and Taxes on American*

Politics (New York: Norton, 1991); William Schneider, "The Suburban Century Begins," *Atlantic Monthly*, July 1992, p. 33.

(173) " 'Americans are priced out of buying or renting . . . were it not for a web of government regulations' ": Advisory Commission on Regulatory Barriers to Affordable Housing, *"Not in My Back Yard": Removing Barriers to Affordable Housing* (Washington, D.C.: Department of Housing and Urban Development, 1991).

(174) "When help was needed, [Americans] hardly ever failed to give each other trusty support": Alexis de Tocqueville, *Democracy in America*, rev. ed. (New York: Knopf, 1972), 1:191.

(175) "people who dream of sheetrock . . . are still at work": Melissa Greene, *Praying for Sheetrock* (Reading, Mass.: Addison-Wesley, 1991).

9 House of Dreams

(177) "The mayor, who began his career in the Tammany Hall tradition of boss politics, recreated himself as an ethnic John Lindsay": see generally Frank S. Levy, Arnold Meltsner, and Aaron Wildavsky, *Urban Outcomes: Schools, Streets, and Libraries* (Berkeley: University of California Press, 1974); Robert Lineberry, *Equality and Urban Policy: The Distribution of Municipal Services* (Beverly Hills, Calif.: Sage, 1977); Albert Karnig and Susan Welch, *Black Representation and Urban Policy* (Chicago: University of Chicago Press, 1980); Ira Katznelson, *City Trenches: Urban Politics and the Patterning of Class in the United States* (New York: Pantheon, 1981); Todd Swanstrom, *The Crisis of Growth Politics: Cleveland, Kucinich, and the Challenge of Urban Populism* (Philadelphia: Temple University Press, 1985).

(178) "Now [Camden's] chief industry is collecting scrap . . .": this account draws upon Daniel Lazare, "Collapse of a City: Growth and Decay of Camden, New Jersey," *Dissent* 38, no. 2 (Spring 1991): 267–275; Kevin Fedarko, "Who Could Live Here?" *Time*, January 20, 1992, pp. 21–23.

(179) "the sewer plant and the trash-burning plant and the two jails, were inflicted on Camden by cold calculation": see generally Richard C. Rich, ed., *The Politics of Urban Public Services* (Lexington, Mass.: Lexington Books, 1982).

(180) "The marina was not built because of any obvious need but because federal funds were available": see generally Jeffrey Pressman, *Federal Programs and City Politics: The Dynamics of the Aid Process in Oakland* (Berkeley: University of California Press, 1975).

(180) " 'gold fillings in a mouthful of decay' ": quoted in Tony Hiss, "Reinventing Baltimore," *New Yorker*, April 29, 1991, pp. 40–62.

(181) "*Savage Inequalities*, Jonathan Kozol's indictment of urban schools . . .": Jonathan Kozol, *Savage Inequalities: Children in America's Schools* (New York: Crown, 1991).

(182) " 'Either Camden does not raise taxes and faces long-term problems with the city's infrastructure or Camden raises taxes and faces loss of businesses and homeowners . . .' ": *Abbott v. Burke*, 100 N.J. 269, 495 A.2d 376 (1985). These dilemmas were pronounced in but not peculiar to Camden. See Thomas Murphy and John Rehfuss, *Urban Politics in the Suburban Era* (Homewood, Ill.: Dorsey, 1976); Katharine Bradbury, Anthony Downs, and Kenneth Small, *Urban Decline and the Future of American Cities* (Washington, D.C.: Brookings Institution, 1982); Michael Danielson and Jameson Doig, *New York: The Politics of Urban and*

Regional Development (Berkeley: University of California Press, 1982); Bryan Jones, *Governing Urban America: A Policy Focus* (Boston: Little, Brown, 1983); Michael MacDonald, *America's Cities: A Report on the Myth of Urban Renaissance* (New York: Simon and Schuster, 1984); Christopher Jencks and Paul Peterson, eds., *The Urban Underclass* (Washington, D.C.: Brookings Institution, 1991).

(182) "there are still those who remain hopeful of saving the city": Lynette Hazelton, "Laying the Foundation for Growth," *Black Enterprise* 16, no. 4 (November 1985): 44–52.

(182) "Each of these nonprofit operations . . . counts its successes only by the handful": see generally Neal R. Peirce and Carol Steinbach, *Corrective Capitalism: The Rise of America's Community Development Corporations* (New York: Ford Foundation, 1987); Michael Stegman and J. David Holden, *Nonfederal Housing Programs: How States and Localities Are Responding to Federal Cutbacks in Low-Income Housing* (Washington, D.C.: Urban Land Institute, 1987).

(184) " 'massive public-private effort to construct houses . . . ' ": see generally Dennis R. Judd, *The Politics of American Cities: Private Power and Public Policy* (Boston: Little, Brown, 1984); Paul Kantor with Stephen David, *The Dependent City: The Changing Political Economy of Urban America* (Glenview, Ill.: Scott, Foresman, 1988).

(184) " 'the slow suturing of something wounded, but very much alive' ": Kevin Riordan, "City Invincible: Camden's Long Road Back," *Camden Courier-Post,* July 6–10, 1986 (five-part series).

(184) "Michael Doyle, the priest at Sacred Heart Church . . . has been a great resource": Eils Lotozo, "Announcing the Impossible," *Applause* 17, no. 6 (June 1991): 17–19 (publication of WHYY, Philadelphia).

(187–188) " 'Suburbs appear . . . where happiness comes . . . from conformity to a generally accepted set of traditions and not from the pursuit of individual freedom' ": J. B. Jackson, *Landscapes: Selected Writings of J. B. Jackson,* ed. Ervin Zube (Amherst: University of Massachusetts Press, 1970).

(190) "O'Connor was wearing one hat too many": similar complaints were lodged against Peter O'Connor's dual roles, as lawyer and developer, in neighboring Cherry Hill.

(192) "The elderly, they complained, 'will attract gangs and dope' ": Gerald Marzorati, "From Tocqueville to Perotville: The Call-In Show Has Replaced the Town Square," *New York Times,* June 28, 1992, p. E17.

Sources

Selected Bibliography

Aaron, Henry. *Shelter and Subsidies: Who Benefits from Federal Housing Policies?* Washington, D.C.: Brookings Institution, 1972.

Abrams, Charles. *Forbidden Neighbors: A Study of Prejudice in Housing.* New York: Harper, 1955.

Advisory Commission on Regulatory Barriers to Affordable Housing. *"Not in My Back Yard": Removing Barriers to Affordable Housing.* Washington, D.C.: Department of Housing and Urban Development, 1991.

Altshuler, Alan, and José Gómez-Ibañez. *Regulation for Revenue: The Political Economy of Land Use Exactions.* Washington, D.C.: Brookings Institution, 1993.

Anderson, Martin. *The Federal Bulldozer.* Cambridge: MIT Press, 1964.

Aoki, Keith. "Race, Space, and Place: The Relation between Architectural Modernism, Post-Modernism, Urban Planning, and Gentrification." *Fordham Urban Law Journal* 20, no. 4 (1993): 699–829.

Baar, Kenneth. "Rent Control in the 1970s: The Case of the New Jersey Tenants' Movement." *Hastings Law Journal* 28, no. 3 (January 1977): 631–683.

Baltzell, E. Digby. *Puritan Boston and Quaker Philadelphia.* New York: Free Press, 1979.

Banfield, Edward. *The Unheavenly City Revisited.* Boston: Little, Brown, 1974.

Bellah, Robert, et al. *Habits of the Heart: Individualism and Commitment in American Life.* Berkeley: University of California Press, 1985.

Bellush, Jewel, and Stephen David, eds. *Race and Politics in New York City: Five Studies in Policy-Making.* New York: Praeger, 1971.

Bosselman, Fred, and David Callies. *The Quiet Revolution in Land Use Control.* Study prepared for U.S. Council on Environmental Quality. Washington, D.C.: U.S. Government Printing Office, 1972.

Bradbury, Katharine, Anthony Downs, and Kenneth Small. *Urban Decline and the Future of American Cities.* Washington, D.C.: Brookings Institution, 1982.

Bratt, Rachel. *Rebuilding a Low-Income Housing Policy.* Philadelphia: Temple University Press, 1989.

Bratt, Rachel, Chester Hartman, and Ann Meyerson. *Critical Perspectives on Housing.* Philadelphia: Temple University Press, 1986.

Briffault, Richard. "Our Localism: Part I—The Structure of Local Government Law." *Columbia Law Review* 90, no. 1 (January 1990): 1–115.

———. "Our Localism: Part II—Localism and Legal Theory." *Columbia Law Review* 90, no. 2 (March 1990): 346–454.

Browning, Rufus, Dale Marshall, and David Tabb. *Protest Is Not Enough: The Struggle of Blacks and Hispanics for Equality in Urban Politics.* Berkeley: University of California Press, 1984.

Calthorpe, Peter. *The Next American Metropolis: Ecology, Community, and the American Dream.* Princeton: Princeton Architectural Press, 1993.

Caplow, Theodore, Howard Bahr, et al., *Middletown Families: Fifty Years of Change and Continuity.* Minneapolis: University of Minnesota Press, 1982.

Cole, Richard. *Citizen Participation and the Urban Policy Process.* Lexington, Mass.: Lexington Books, 1974.

Crain, Robert. *The Politics of School Desegregation: Comparative Case Studies of Community Structure and Policy-Making.* Chicago: Aldine, 1968.

Dahl, Robert. *Who Governs? Democracy and Power in an American City.* New Haven: Yale University Press, 1961.

Danielson, Michael. *The Politics of Exclusion.* New York: Columbia University Press, 1976.

Danielson, Michael, and Jameson Doig. *New York: The Politics of Urban and Regional Development.* Berkeley: University of California Press, 1982.

Davidoff, Paul. "Decent Housing for All," in *America's Housing Crisis: What Is to Be Done?* ed. Chester Hartman. New York: Routledge and Kegan Paul, 1983.

Derthick, Martha. *New Towns-in-Town.* Washington, D.C.: Urban Institute, 1972.

Dobriner, William. *Class in Suburbia.* Englewood Cliffs, N.J.: Prentice-Hall, 1963.

Dolce, Philip, ed. *Suburbia: The American Dream and Dilemma.* Garden City, N.Y.: Doubleday, 1976.

Downs, Anthony. "The American Dream of an Affordable House: The Image Recedes." *Across the Board* 18 (December 1981): 58–63.

―――. *Federal Housing Subsidies: How Are They Working?* Lexington, Mass.: Lexington Books, 1973.

―――. *New Visions for Metropolitan America.* Washington, D.C.: Brookings Institution, 1994.

―――. *Opening Up the Suburbs.* New Haven: Yale University Press, 1973.

―――. *Rental Housing in the 1980's.* Washington, D.C.: Brookings Institution, 1983.

Ely, John Hart. *Democracy and Distrust: A Theory of Judicial Review.* Cambridge: Harvard University Press, 1980.

Fainstein, Susan, and Norman Fainstein. *Urban Political Movements: The Search for Power by Minority Groups in American Cities.* Englewood Cliffs, N.J.: Prentice-Hall, 1974.

Farley, Reynolds, et al. "Continued Racial Segregation in Detroit: 'Chocolate City, Vanilla Suburbs' Revisited." *Journal of Housing Research* 4, no. 1 (1993): 1–38.

Foley, Mary Mix. *The American House.* New York: Harper and Row, 1980.

Fried, Joseph. *Housing Crisis—U.S.A.* New York: Praeger, 1971.

Frug, Gerald. "The City as a Legal Concept." *Harvard Law Review* 93, no. 6 (April 1980): 1057–1154.

―――. "Empowering Cities in a Federal System." *Urban Lawyer* 19, no. 3 (Summer 1987): 553–568.

Gamson, William. *Power and Discontent.* Homewood, Ill.: Dorsey, 1968.

Gans, Herbert. *The Levittowners: Ways of Life and Politics in a New Suburban Community.* New York: Pantheon, 1967.

―――. *The Urban Villagers: Group and Class in the Life of Italian-Americans.* Rev. ed. New York: Free Press, 1982.

Garreau, Joel. *Edge City: Life on the New Frontier.* New York: Doubleday, 1991.

Gelfand, Mark. *A Nation of Cities: The Federal Government and Urban America, 1933–1965.* New York: Oxford University Press, 1975.

Gittell, Marilyn, et al. *Limits to City Participation: The Decline of Community Organizations*. Beverly Hills, Calif.: Sage, 1980.

Glazer, Nathan. "The Bias of American Housing Policy," in *Housing Urban America*, ed. Jon Pynoos, Robert Schafer, and Chester W. Hartman. New York: Aldine, 1980.

Goetze, Rolf. *Rescuing the American Dream: Public Policies and the Crisis in Housing*. New York: Holmes and Meier, 1983.

Goodman, Robert. *The Last Entrepreneurs: America's Regional Wars for Jobs and Dollars*. New York: Simon and Schuster, 1979.

Grieson, Ronald E., ed. *The Urban Economy and Housing*. Lexington, Mass.: Lexington Books, 1983.

Haar, Charles M. *Suburbs under Siege: Race, Space, and Audacious Judges*. Princeton, N.J.: Princeton University Press, 1996.

Halle, David. *America's Working Man: Work, Home, and Politics among Blue-Collar Property Owners*. Chicago: University of Chicago Press, 1984.

Hartman, Chester. *Housing and Social Policy*. Englewood Cliffs, N.J.: Prentice-Hall, 1975.

————, ed. *The Housing Crisis: What Is to Be Done?* New York: Routledge and Kegan Paul, 1983.

Hayden, Delores. *Redesigning the American Dream: The Future of Housing, Work, and Family Life*. New York: Norton, 1984.

Hays, R. Allen. *The Federal Government and Urban Housing: Ideology and Change in Public Policy*. Albany: State University of New York Press, 1985.

Hofstadter, Richard. *The Age of Reform*. New York: Vintage, 1955.

Hughes, James, and George Sternlieb. *The Dynamics of America's Housing*. New Brunswick, N.J.: Center for Urban Policy Research, Rutgers University, 1987.

Jackson, Kenneth. *Crabgrass Frontier: The Suburbanization of the United States*. New York: Oxford University Press, 1985.

Jencks, Christopher, and Paul Peterson, eds. *The Urban Underclass*. Washington, D.C.: Brookings Institution, 1991.

Jones, Bryan. *Governing Urban America: A Policy Focus*. Boston: Little, Brown, 1983.

Judd, Dennis R. *The Politics of American Cities: Private Power and Public Policy*. Boston: Little, Brown, 1983.

Kantor, Paul, with Stephen David. *The Dependent City: The Changing Political Economy of Urban America*. Glenview, Ill.: Scott, Foresman, 1988.

Karnig, Albert, and Susan Welch. *Black Representation and Urban Policy*. Chicago: University of Chicago Press, 1980.

Katz, Lawrence, and Kenneth Rosen. "The Interjurisdictional Effects of Growth Controls on Housing Prices." *Journal of Law and Economics* 30, no. 1 (April 1987): 149–160.

Katznelson, Ira. *City Trenches: Urban Politics and the Patterning of Class in the United States*. New York: Pantheon, 1981.

Kaus, Mickey. *The End of Equality*. New York: New Republic Books, 1992.

Keats, John. *The Crack in the Picture Window*. Boston: Houghton Mifflin, 1957.

Klinkenborg, Verlyn. "Back to Love Canal: Recycled Homes, Rebuilt Dreams." *Harper's*, March 1991, p. 71.

Kozol, Jonathan. *Savage Inequalities: Children in America's Schools*. New York: Crown, 1991.

Lasch, Christopher. *Haven in a Heartless World: The Family Besieged.* New York: Basic, 1977.

Lazare, Daniel. "Collapse of a City: Growth and Decay of Camden, New Jersey." *Dissent* 38, no. 2 (Spring 1991): 267–275.

Lazere, Edward, et al. *A Place to Call Home: The Low-Income Housing Crisis Continues.* Washington, D.C.: Center on Budget and Policy Priorities, 1991.

Lee, Eugene. *The Politics of Nonpartisanship.* Berkeley: University of California Press, 1960.

Levitan, Sar. *Programs in Aid of the Poor.* Baltimore: Johns Hopkins University Press, 1985.

Levy, Frank S., Arnold Meltsner, and Aaron Wildavsky. *Urban Outcomes: Schools, Streets, and Libraries.* Berkeley: University of California Press, 1974.

Lewis, David L. *The Public Image of Henry Ford: An American Folk Hero and His Company.* Detroit: Wayne State University Press, 1976.

Lindblom, Charles E. *The Intelligence of Democracy.* New York: Free Press, 1965.

———. *Politics and Markets.* New York: Basic, 1977.

Lineberry, Robert. *Equality and Urban Policy: The Distribution of Municipal Services.* Beverly Hills, Calif.: Sage, 1977.

Lipsky, Michael. *Protest in City Politics: Rent Strikes, Housing, and the Power of the Poor.* Chicago: Rand McNally, 1970.

Little, James, et al. *The Contemporary Neighborhood Succession Process: Lessons in the Dynamic of Decay from the St. Louis Experience.* St Louis: Washington University Institute for Urban and Regional Studies, 1975.

Logan, John R., and Harvey Molotch. *Urban Fortunes: The Political Economy of Place.* Berkeley: University of California Press, 1987.

MacDonald, Michael. *America's Cities: A Report on the Myth of Urban Renaissance.* New York: Simon and Schuster, 1984.

McKelvey, Blake. *The Emergence of Metropolitan America, 1915–1966.* New Brunswick, N.J.: Rutgers University Press, 1968.

MacLean, Nancy. *Behind the Mask of Chivalry: The Making of the Second Ku Klux Klan.* New York: Oxford University Press, 1994.

Mallach, Alan. *Inclusionary Housing Programs: Policies and Practices.* New Brunswick, N.J.: Center for Urban Policy Research, Rutgers University, 1984.

Martin, Duane. "The President and the Cities: Clinton's Urban Aid Agenda." *Urban Lawyer* 26, no. 1 (Winter 1994): 99–142.

Massey, Douglas, and Nancy Denton. *American Apartheid: Segregation and the Making of the Underclass.* Cambridge: Harvard University Press, 1993.

Metcalf, George. *Fair Housing Comes of Age.* New York: Greenwood, 1988.

Meyerson, Martin, and Edward Banfield. *Politics, Planning, and the Public Interest: The Case of Public Housing in Chicago.* Glencoe, Ill.: Free Press, 1955.

Mitchell, J. Paul, ed. *Federal Housing Policy and Programs: Past and Present.* New Brunswick, N.J.: Center for Urban Policy Research, Rutgers University, 1985.

Montgomery, Roger, and Dale Rogers Marshall, eds. *Housing Policy for the 1980s.* Lexington, Mass.: Lexington Books, 1980.

Mumford, Lewis. *The City in History: Its Origins, Its Transformations, and Its Prospects.* New York: Harcourt Brace and World, 1961.

———. *The Urban Prospect.* New York: Harcourt Brace Jovanovich, 1968.

Murphy, Thomas, and John Rehfuss. *Urban Politics in the Suburban Era.* Homewood, Ill.: Dorsey, 1976.

Myrdal, Gunnar. *An American Dilemma: The Negro Problem and Modern Democracy.* New York: Harper, 1944.

National Assessment of Educational Progress. *The Reading Report Card: Progress toward Excellence in Our Schools.* Princeton: Educational Testing Service, 1985.

Newman, Katherine. *Declining Fortunes: The Withering of the American Dream.* New York: Basic, 1993.

Orfield, Gary, and Carol Ashkinaze. *The Closing Door: Conservative Policy and Black Opportunity.* Chicago: University of Chicago Press, 1991.

Peirce, Neal R., and Carol Steinbach. *Corrective Capitalism: The Rise of America's Community Development Corporations.* New York: Ford Foundation, 1987.

Peirce, Neal R., with Curtis Johnson and John Hall. *Citistates: How Urban America Can Prosper in a Competitive World.* Washington, D.C.: Seven Locks, 1993.

Peterson, Paul. *City Limits.* Chicago: University of Chicago Press, 1981.

Porter, Douglas, ed. *Growth Management: Keeping on Target?* Washington, D.C.: Urban Land Institute, 1986.

Pressman, Jeffrey. *Federal Programs and City Politics: The Dynamics of the Aid Process in Oakland.* Berkeley: University of California Press, 1975.

Rainwater, Lee. *Behind Ghetto Walls: Black Families in a Federal Slum.* Chicago: Aldine, 1970.

Rich, Richard C., ed. *The Politics of Urban Public Services.* Lexington, Mass.: Lexington Books, 1982.

Rieder, Jonathan. *Canarsie: The Jews and Italians of Brooklyn against Liberalism.* Cambridge: Harvard University Press, 1985.

Riesman, David, with Reuel Denney and Nathan Glazer. *The Lonely Crowd: A Study of the Changing American Character.* New Haven: Yale University Press, 1950.

Rose, Carol. "Planning and Dealing: Piecemeal Land Controls as a Problem of Local Legitimacy." *California Law Review* 71, no. 3 (May 1983): 837–912.

Rosenman, Dorothy. *A Million Homes a Year.* New York: Harcourt Brace, 1945.

Rossi, Peter, and Robert Dentler. *The Politics of Urban Renewal: The Chicago Findings.* New York: Free Press, 1961.

Rusk, David. *Cities without Suburbs.* Washington, D.C.: Woodrow Wilson Center Press, 1993.

Salins, Peter. "Cities, Suburbs, and the Urban Crisis." *Public Interest*, no. 113 (Fall 1993): 91–104.

Schafer, Robert. *The Suburbanization of Multifamily Housing.* Lexington, Mass.: Lexington Books, 1974.

Schwartz, Barry, ed. *The Changing Face of the Suburbs.* Chicago: University of Chicago Press, 1976.

Solomon, Arthur. *Housing the Urban Poor: A Critical Evaluation of Federal Housing Policy.* Cambridge: MIT Press, 1974.

Stegman, Michael. *Housing Finance and Public Policy.* New York: Van Nostrand Reinhold, 1986.

Stegman, Michael, and J. David Holden. *Nonfederal Housing Programs: How States and Localities Are Responding to Federal Cutbacks in Low-Income Housing.* Washington, D.C.: Urban Land Institute, 1987.

Sternlieb, George, et al., eds. *America's Housing: Prospects and Problems*. New Brunswick, N.J.: Center for Urban Policy Research, Rutgers University, 1980.

Sternlieb, George, and James Hughes. "Structuring the Future." *Society* 21, no. 3 (March/April 1984): 28–34.

Swanstrom, Todd. *The Crisis of Growth Politics: Cleveland, Kucinich, and the Challenge of Urban Populism*. Philadelphia: Temple University Press, 1985.

Teaford, Jon. *City and Suburb: The Political Fragmentation of Metropolitan America, 1850–1970*. Baltimore: Johns Hopkins University Press, 1979.

Tiebout, Charles. "A Pure Theory of Local Expenditures." *Journal of Political Economy* 64 (October 1956): 416–424.

Tocqueville, Alexis de. *Democracy in America*. Rev. ed. New York: Knopf, 1972.

Verba, Sidney, and Norman Nie. *Participation in America: Political Democracy and Social Equality*. New York: Harper and Row, 1972.

Vernon, Raymond. *Metropolis 1985: An Interpretation of the Findings of the New York Metropolitan Region Study*. Garden City, N.Y.: Doubleday, 1960.

Wakstein, Allen, ed. *The Urbanization of America: An Historic Anthology*. Boston: Houghton-Mifflin, 1970.

Warner, Sam Bass, Jr. *The Private City: Philadelphia in Three Periods of Its Growth*. Philadelphia: University of Pennsylvania Press, 1968.

———. *Streetcar Suburbs: The Process of Growth in Boston, 1870–1900*. 2d ed. Cambridge: Harvard University Press, 1978.

———. *The Urban Wilderness: A History of the American City*. New York: Harper and Row, 1972.

Weiss, Shirley. *Residential Developer Decisions: A Focused View of the Urban Growth Process*. Chapel Hill: Center for Urban and Regional Studies, University of North Carolina, 1966.

White, Michael. *American Neighborhoods and Residential Differentiation*. New York: Russell Sage Foundation, 1987.

Wiebe, Robert. *The Search for Order, 1877–1920*. New York: Hill and Wang, 1967.

Williams, Norman, Jr., Edmund H. Kellogg, and Peter Lavigne. *Vermont Townscape*. New Brunswick, N.J.: Center for Urban Policy Research, 1987.

Wilson, James Q., ed. *Urban Renewal: The Record and the Controversy*. Cambridge: MIT Press, 1966.

Wilson, William Julius. *The Truly Disadvantaged: The Inner City, the Underclass, and Public Policy*. Chicago: University of Chicago Press, 1987.

———. "Race-Neutral Programs and the Democratic Coalition." *American Prospect*, no. 1 (Spring 1990): 74–81.

Wolfinger, Raymond. *The Politics of Progress*. Englewood Cliffs, N.J.: Prentice-Hall, 1974.

Wright, Gwendolyn. *Building the Dream: A Social History of Housing in America*. New York: Pantheon, 1981.

Interviews

We have identified those interviewed by their affiliation(s) most relevant to the narrative.

José Alvarez	Ex-mayor, Mount Laurel
Samuel Appel	Minister and social activist, Camden

Richard Bellman	Fair housing attorney
Art Bernard	Deputy and executive director, Council on Affordable Housing
Carl Bisgaier	Lead trial attorney in *Mount Laurel* cases
Shirley Bishop	Assistant director, Council on Affordable Housing
Wayne Bryant	State assemblyman, Camden
Marian Still Buck	Resident, Mount Laurel; member, Jacob's Chapel African Methodist Episcopal Church
Phillip Caton	Land use planner; *Mount Laurel* special master
Thomas Corcoran	Redevelopment official, Camden
Duane Davison	Township attorney, Freehold
José Delgado	Reform mayoral candidate, Camden
Michael Doyle	Pastor, Sacred Heart Roman Catholic Church, Camden
Alan Drake	Public relations officer, New Jersey Department of Public Advocate
W. Cary Edwards	Counsel and attorney general, administration of Governor Thomas Kean
Stephen Eisdorfer	Deputy public advocate, New Jersey Department of Public Advocate
C. Roy Epps	Executive director, Civic League of Greater New Brunswick (formerly the Urban League of Greater New Brunswick)
Angelo Errichetti	Mayor and state assemblyman, Camden
José Fernandez	Law clerk to Chief Justice Robert Wilentz
Robert Friant	Public relations officer, New Jersey Department of Community Affairs
Luis Galindez	Member, Concerned Citizens of North Camden
Sherie Galloway	Editor, *Honey of Camden*
John Gerry	Township attorney, Mount Laurel Township
Richard Goodwin	Developer, Mount Laurel
Robert Greenbaum	Developer's attorney
William Haines, Jr.	Mayor and state senator, Mount Laurel
Michael Hartsaugh	Township attorney, West Windsor
Henry Hill	Developer's attorney
Ara Hovnanian	Housing developer; member, Council on Affordable Housing
Cheryl Jenkins	Deputy to Governor James Florio
Harvey Johnson	Black People's Unity Movement, Camden
Thomas Kean	Governor, New Jersey

Robert King	Mayor, Mount Laurel
Thomas Knoche	Member, Concerned Citizens of North Camden
Martha Lamar	Planner
Ethel Lawrence	Community organizer and plaintiff, *Mount Laurel* litigation
Wynona Lipman	State senator, Newark
Jay Lynch	Special master, exclusionary zoning cases
John Lynch	Mayor and state senator, New Brunswick
Alan Mallach	Planner-activist, *Mount Laurel* litigation; director of housing and development, Trenton
Lerenda Matthews	Member, Concerned Citizens of North Camden
Kenneth Meiser	Trial attorney, *Mount Laurel* cases
Sidna Mitchell	Public relations officer, Council on Affordable Housing
Glenn Moore	Director, Central Staff, New Jersey Office of Legislative Services
William Moran	Township attorney, Cranbury
Michael Mouber	Township attorney, Mount Laurel
Frank Mull	Councilman, Mount Laurel Township
Joseph Nardi	Mayor, Camden
Thomas Ober	Representative, Carpenter's Union
Daniel O'Connor	Attorney and project manager, Fair Share Housing Development, Inc.
Peter O'Connor	Law reform director, Camden Regional Legal Services; attorney, *Mount Laurel* cases; founder and executive director, Fair Share Housing Development, Inc.
Douglas Opalski	Executive director, Council on Affordable Housing
Philip Paley	Developer's attorney
John Payne	Professor, Rutgers Law School; fair housing attorney
Stewart Pollock	Associate justice, New Jersey Supreme Court
Randall Primas	Mayor, Camden; commissioner, New Jersey Department of Community Affairs
Elizabeth Ransom	Land owner, Mount Laurel
Peter Reinhart	General counsel, K. Hovnanian & Sons; member, Council on Affordable Housing
Richard Remington	Reporter, *Newark Star-Ledger*
Kevin Riordan	Reporter, *Camden Courier-Post*
Mary Robinson	Community activist, Mount Laurel
José Rodriguez	Executive director, New Jersey Department of Public Advocate; member, board of directors, Camden Regional Legal Services

Richard Roper	Professor, Woodrow Wilson School of Public and International Affairs, Princeton University
Alice Rudderow	Land owner, Mount Laurel
Maurice Rudderow	Land owner, Mount Laurel
Paul Schopp	Economic historian
Sidney Schreiber	Associate justice, New Jersey Supreme Court
David Schwartz	State assemblyman; professor, Rutgers University
Eugene Serpentelli	New Jersey Superior Court judge; one of three *Mount Laurel* judges
Mary Smith	Plaintiff, *Mount Laurel* case
Gerald Stockman	State senator, Trenton-Princeton
Jeffrey Surenian	Author of *Mount Laurel* attorney practice guide
Jacqueline Sykes	Manager, Northgate Apartments, Camden
Warren Sykes	Manager, Northgate Apartments, Camden
Aaron Thompson	Mayor, Camden
Michael Traino	Mayor, Mount Laurel Township
Arnold Webster	Superintendent of schools, Camden
Guy Williams	Member, Civic League of Greater New Brunswick (formerly the Urban League of Greater New Brunswick)
Stuart Wood	Minister and housing activist, Mount Laurel

Index

About the Authors

DAVID L. KIRP, a professor of public policy at the University of California, Berkeley, is the author of *Just Schools: Race and Schooling in America*, *Gender Justice*, and *Learning by Heart: AIDS and Schoolchildren in America's Communities* (Rutgers University Press). JOHN P. DWYER, a professor of law at the University of California, Berkeley, is a nationally recognized authority on environmental and housing policy and law. LARRY A. ROSENTHAL is a lecturer in the Graduate School of Public Policy at the University of California, Berkeley, and has served as assistant editor of the *Journal of Policy Analysis and Management*.